Praise for *The Shanghai Free Taxi*

"Frank Langfitt achieved what generations of visitors to China only dreamed of doing: He devised an ingenious way to burrow into everyday life, and he came back with stories that are humane, candid, fast-paced, and compulsively readable. *The Shanghai Free Taxi* gives you the marrow of to-day's China in all its kindnesses and cruelties and wonders and absurdities."

—EVAN OSNOS, author of *Age of Ambition:*
Chasing Fortune, Truth, and Faith in the New China and
National Book Award Winner

"Driving in China is hard. Getting average Chinese people to open up about their feelings and opinions is even harder. In *The Shanghai Free Taxi* Frank Langfitt does both at the same time, driving a cab in the flagship city of a country in transition. Challenging to report but easy to read, this book reveals China's true transition: a profound search for identity in the world at large."

—PETER HESSLER, *New York Times* bestselling author of
Country Driving, Oracles Bones and *River Town*

"Frank Langfitt's stint as a taxi driver collecting tales of modern China has created a rollicking, delightful read. Enchanting."

—MEI FONG, author of *One Child*

"*The Shanghai Free Taxi* is a delightful, poignant, and revealing book. In his role as impromptu, volunteer chauffeur in Shanghai, Frank Langfitt got to see inside the lives of Chinese families of all backgrounds and social classes, and from many parts of the country. The result is a vivid look at the contradictory dreams, achievements, heartbreaks, and possi-bilities of modern China."

—JAMES FALLOWS, author of *Our Towns* and *China Airborne*

"A cleverly conceived, well-executed book by an engaging and empathetic storyteller. Langfitt offers up an appealing mix of humorous and poignant tales featuring individuals from different backgrounds who share just one common trait: all are struggling to find their places in and make sense of an era when their city, their country, and the world at large have been undergoing complex and often confounding transformations."

—JEFFREY WASSERSTROM, coauthor of
China in the 21st Century: What Everyone Needs to Know

"By creating a free taxi and offering free rides, veteran NPR reporter Frank Langfitt takes us on a journey across China and into the soul of today's Chinese civilization. We learn how a wide cross section of Chinese people live and think as the author provides an up-close view of their fears and aspirations and the forces that shape their lives in ways good and bad. I have lived in China for thirty years, and this book gave me new insights and brought me to places I have never been. Truly unique and compelling."

—JAMES L. McGREGOR, chairman of APCO Worldwide's
greater China region and author of *No Ancient Wisdom,
No Followers* and *One Billion Customers*

"*The Shanghai Free Taxi* presents a unique, kaleidoscopic view of Chinese society. Characters in this book open up, talking freely and truthfully in a way unimaginable elsewhere under the oppressive regime. It is a must read for anyone trying to gain rare and insightful glimpses into that complicated country."

—QIU XIAOLONG, author of *Shanghai Redemption*
and nine other *Inspector Chen* novels

"Frank Langfitt writes with the streetwise eye of a cabbie and the analytical mind of a foreign correspondent. This is today's China as it gossips, gripes and moans; strives, struggles and overcomes."

—PAUL FRENCH, author of *City of Devils* and *Midnight in Peking*

THE
SHANGHAI
FREE TAXI

THE
SHANGHAI
FREE TAXI

Journeys with the Hustlers and
Rebels of the New China

FRANK LANGFITT

WEIDENFELD & NICOLSON

First published in Great Britain in 2019 by Weidenfeld & Nicolson
an imprint of The Orion Publishing Group Ltd
Carmelite House, 50 Victoria Embankment
London EC4Y 0DZ

An Hachette UK Company

1 3 5 7 9 10 8 6 4 2

A CIP catalogue record for this book is available from the British Library.

ISBN (hardback) 978 1 4746 1231 9
ISBN (export-trade paperback) 978 1 4746 1232 6
ISBN (audio download) 978 1 4746 1253 1
ISBN (ebook) 978 1 4746 1234 0

Printed and bound in Great Britain by Clays Ltd, Elcograf, S.p.A

www.orionbooks.co.uk

For Julie, Katherine, and Chris

Contents

Cast of Characters, xi

Maps of Events That Occur in China and Shanghai, xv

CHAPTER 1.
Beginnings: Chen   1

CHAPTER 2.
Chinese New Year Road Trip: Rocky and Charles   11

CHAPTER 3.
Two Country Weddings: Charles, Rocky, Guo, and Ray   27

CHAPTER 4.
"Morality Is Relative": Beer, Amanda, and Fifi   45

CHAPTER 5.
"A Virtuous Circle Needs to Have a Beginning": Johanna, Max, and Fifi   71

CHAPTER 6.
A Woman Missing in the Mountains: Crystal and Winnie   101

CHAPTER 7.
Disillusioned with the New China: Chen, Sarah, Charles, and Ashley   117

CHAPTER 8.
The Dark Side of the Chinese Dream: Crystal and Winnie   143

CHAPTER 9.
Making China Great Again: Ray, Charles, and Fifi   157

CHAPTER 10.
President Donald J. Trump: Ashley, Ray, Chen, and Gong   175

CHAPTER 11.
Losing Hearts and Minds: Charles and Ashley   187

CHAPTER 12.
Rethinking the West: Charles and Ashley   205

CHAPTER 13.
Ashley's Dilemma: Ashley   223

CHAPTER 14.
President for Life?: Fifi, Ray, Sarah, Max, and Ashley   237

Epilogue   251

Acknowledgments, 273
Sources, 279
Index, 289

Cast of Characters
(in order of appearance)

Chapter 1

Yang: Frank's news assistant, a young man who helps him scheme up the Shanghai Free Taxi and accompanies him on road trips

Chen: a Shanghai pajama salesman who runs an underground church and moves his family to America to give his daughter a less stressful education

Chapters 2 and 3

Rocky: a farm boy turned Shanghai lawyer from Hubei province, whom Frank drives home for Chinese New Year

Charles: another passenger on the Chinese New Year road trip who works as a salesman in a Shanghai shipping-parts factory and later becomes a news assistant for a European newspaper

Guo: Rocky's mother, who overcame political persecution during the Cultural Revolution

Ray: Rocky's older brother and a fellow Shanghai lawyer who studied in America

Chapter 4

Beer: a slippery salesman who tries to sell Frank a used car to serve as his free taxi

Amanda: a former finance worker who has lost her family fortune in a pyramid scheme

Fifi: a former schoolteacher and psychologist who is married to a Frenchman who lives in Paris

Chapter 5

Johanna: a human rights lawyer who engages a Shanghai cabbie in a democracy debate

Max: a hairstylist from the countryside, who gives back by cutting the hair of elderly shut-ins for free

Chapter 6

Crystal: a Chinese American NPR listener, who enlists Frank's and Yang's help to search for her little sister, who has gone missing in the mountains of southwestern China

Winnie: Crystal's little sister, a former prostitute who tries to reinvent herself as an independent businesswoman and then vanishes

Chapter 7

Sarah: a young woman from the provinces, whom Frank helps move and who is trying to find her place amid the bright lights of Shanghai

Ashley: an investment banker and daughter of Communist Party officials, who moves to America in search of political freedom months before the election of Donald Trump

Chapter 10

Gong: the wife of pajama salesman Chen, who sets up a home for the family in greater Los Angeles

Jiali: Gong and Chen's teenage daughter, who was born in China

Yingying: the couple's younger daughter, who was born in America

SHANGHAI

Charles's Apartment

"Black Jail" where Li was held

North-South

Middle Ring

Inner Ring

Apricot Plum Garden

Nanjing East Road

The Bund

Pudong

People's Park
Tomorrow Square

Shanghai Tower

Ritz
Carlton
Pudong

Netmen work here

Jing 'an Temple

Yan'an

Fuxing Rd Ferry

Frank's Apartment

Maglev to Airport

Chen's Apartment

Xietu

Inner Ring

Longyang Road Station

Ray's & Rocky's Apartments, ~15km

S202

Huangpu River

Pudong

Humin

Middle Ring

Fifi's Apartment

S20

RUSSIA

KAZAKHSTAN

Farm where
Charles worked

KYRGYZSTAN

Urumqi

Tian Shan

Xinjiang

CHINA

Tibet

NEPAL

INDIA

BHUTAN

INDIA

The Nine-Dash Line

CHINA

VIETNAM

Spratly
Islands

PHILIPPINES

MALAYSIA

Winnie disappeared
Jinghong

BURMA

THAILAND

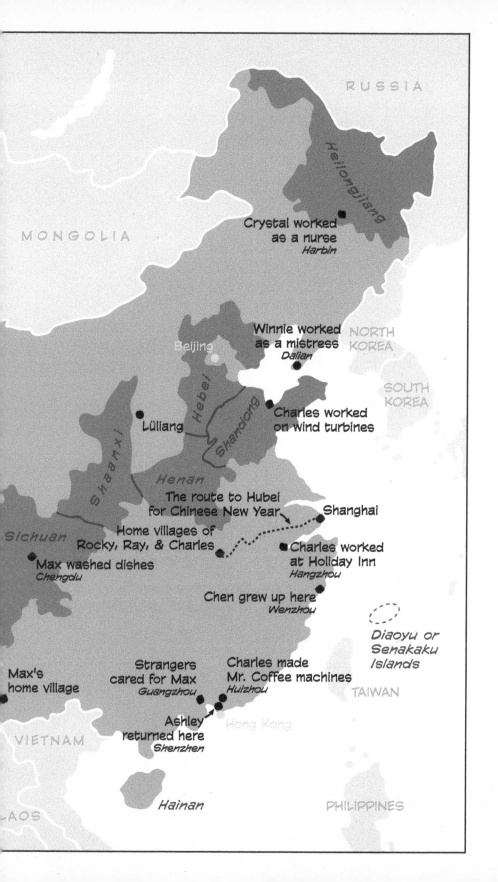

CHAPTER 1

Beginnings

Chen

———————————

IN THE SUMMER of 1982, between my graduation from high school and the beginning of college, I began driving a taxi in and around Philadelphia. I started at a suburban company called Narberth Cab, which had a dispatch office in a basement grotto beneath an Italian restaurant. Because I was the newest and youngest driver, the dispatchers often stuck me with the worst cab in the fleet, a 1970s Dodge Dart. When I pulled up to apartment buildings, the tailpipe spewed clouds of gray exhaust that sent crowds scurrying. We called it "the crop duster." Once the passengers stepped inside, though, the taxi became like a cozy corner bar. For a few miles or a long ride, customers talked about whatever was on their minds and what they really cared about: work, children, marriage, and their futures. For an aspiring journalist like me, it was ideal on-the-job training. My passengers often shared personal thoughts and feelings without fear of judgement and, occasionally, I saw them at their most vulnerable. I drove an elderly woman to a liquor store every few days to buy a bottle of vodka and hauled a middle-aged man home from a bar one afternoon and helped him up the stairs. One summer night, the dispatcher sent me to a house out on the Main Line. A young woman stood waiting in the doorway with two suitcases, but she wasn't heading to the airport. As I drove her to the home of a friend, she explained how her boyfriend had been so kind in the beginning.

"I got sucked into this," she said, gesturing as we passed the spacious stone houses with white columns and freshly cut lawns. The relationship had soured and she was determined to escape. As I pulled up to her friend's home, she wiped away her tears and thanked me for listening.

Nearly three decades later, I prepared to head to Shanghai for my new job as one of National Public Radio's correspondents covering China. It was a challenging assignment. Because of the authoritarian political system and circumspect culture, it wasn't always easy to get Chinese people to speak openly. I flew into Shanghai one summer day in 2011 and boarded the city's magnetic levitation train, one of the world's fastest with a top speed of 267 miles per hour. Gliding above magnetic rails, Maglev, as it's called, rocketed toward town at nearly 190 miles an hour, leaving the apartment blocks, cranes, canals, and farm fields outside little more than a blur. When we passed another train heading in the opposite direction, our carriage shook as if it had been struck by an earthquake. This was the impression the Communist Party wanted to leave with visitors: China was changing so fast, it felt like the tectonic plates were shifting beneath your feet. Maglev covered eighteen miles in less than eight minutes, but that was long enough to begin to see weaknesses beneath the impressive facade. Maglev, which had cost $1.2 billion, was already seven years old and a white elephant. The seats were worn and most sat empty because the $6 ticket was too expensive, and the train's route was inconvenient. Maglev dropped passengers nearly ten miles away from the city center. China had become the world's number two economy in record time, but only a small percentage of people had become genuinely wealthy. The quick train trip provided a revealing snapshot of China at that moment: a striking veneer with cracks just beneath the surface. The perception back in the West was different. Most Americans still thought China was on a tear—"our overlords" is how comedian Jon Stewart referred to the country's leaders on the *Daily Show.* The reality, though, was more worrisome and complicated. China's staggering economic growth rates had slowed to a still-enviable level above 6 percent, but the country's boom was over. Government corruption had metastasized. The Chinese now routinely referred to the last ten years as a "lost decade," because the government had done so little to address major problems such as air pollution and China's business model, which even party leaders acknowledged had run its course.

This was my second tour of China. I'd worked as a newspaper correspondent in Beijing from 1997 to 2002. Upon my return to the country, I also noticed many encouraging changes in my years away. Though not yet rich, many Chinese were much more prosperous and sophisticated, and online speech was flourishing. I was surprised to find the party allowed a whirlwind of criticism, often targeting the government, to swirl around massive digital platforms such as Sina Weibo, a microblog service considered the Twitter of China. In my first months in Shanghai, it became clear the Communist Party was losing the faith of its people and losing its way. After more than three decades of economic reform, rising living standards, and opening to the world, the globe's most populous country was at a crossroads and something had to give. How would the party respond to the tremendous changes and rising expectations of its own people? Would it adapt and become more open or revert to its authoritarian instincts? In 2011, it was anyone's guess.

Shanghai, China's showcase city, seemed a good place to begin to search for answers. A mix of East and West, it was one of the world's largest cities, with twenty-four million people ranging from rice farmers to billionaires, and covered an area the size of the US state of Delaware. It was also a study in contrasts: urban and rural, glittering and gritty, rich and poor, idiosyncratic, grandiose, outwardly confident but inwardly insecure. I wanted to know what ordinary Chinese were thinking at this crucial moment and what mattered to them, but finding out would require a new strategy. Despite the relative freedom on the Internet, many Chinese were still cautious about speaking their minds and would become even more so in the years to come. To try to understand Shanghai from the ground up, I settled on what had worked so many years earlier in my hometown of Philadelphia: a taxicab. The idea seemed ludicrous, but logical. In a cab, no one else can hear what you say. What better way to encourage people who are naturally shy with reporters to speak candidly? I tried to replicate my experience in Philadelphia and went to local taxi companies asking for jobs. The bosses shook their heads and laughed. They told me that, unlike in America, foreigners weren't allowed to drive cabs in China. So, in a city where people were constantly reinventing themselves and hatching new schemes, I came up with a novel business model: free cab rides in exchange for conversation.

Roof lamps are banned on private cars in Shanghai, so my news assistant, Yang, had white magnetic signs made. One set of signs read 免费爱♥车, or literally "Free Loving Heart Taxi," which sounds better in Mandarin than it does in English. Another pair said, 交上海朋友，聊上海生活，or "Make Shanghai Friends, Chat about Shanghai Life." The biggest sign, draped over the hood, read: 我♥上海, or "I ♥ Shanghai."

Though my feelings about Shanghai were a bit more complicated, there was much I came to love about China's second city and its people. Shanghai was a visually astonishing mix of modern buildings that evoked Las Vegas and Tokyo and colonial architecture reminiscent of London and France. Brimming with energy and drive, it operated on a scale that dwarfed Manhattan. Within blocks of where my family and I would settle stood two skyscrapers taller than the Empire State Building and a third, Shanghai Tower, that would exceed two thousand feet when finished. I'd never lived in a more dynamic city, with so much ambition and potential. As I pursued my taxi experiment, I worried nobody would actually accept a ride, so I began cautiously and rented a Toyota Camry. I spent days getting up the nerve to go out driving, while the signs sat rolled up in a duffle under my desk. One rainy Sunday night in June 2014, I headed out on the town, still worried that people might laugh when they saw my car. But like so much that was to follow, the reactions to the cab were as surprising as they were illuminating. After fifteen minutes, I picked up a Chinese man in front of the Peace Cinema across from People's Park in the heart of the city and promptly got lost. My passenger had spent the past two decades in Tokyo and was visiting Shanghai as a tourist, so he was even more disoriented than I was. He gave me the address of his hotel, which I struggled to find using my GPS. After a series of wrong turns, I finally dropped him off within walking distance of where he was staying. I felt embarrassed by my incompetence, but my poor service didn't faze my passenger; he was just happy to chat with a foreigner and get a lift home. I found when you offer something for free, people don't expect too much. When pedestrians saw my free taxi, they didn't laugh or scowl but smiled, nodded knowingly, and gave me a thumbs-up. They liked the idea that someone was helping strangers and asking for no more in return than a chance to talk and learn. Bargain hunters by nature, Shanghainese also recognized a good deal when they saw one. As for the state security agents who kept an eye on me because I was a foreign reporter, they knew about the free taxi but never bothered me. I later heard that one of the agents liked the radio stories the free taxi generated.

Not everyone immediately grasped what I was doing. After filling up the tank one morning, I spotted an elderly couple standing in the rain and offered them a ride. They hopped in and sat silently in the back. Usually my passengers were intensely curious and inter-viewed me in a wonderful reversal of the usual journalistic process.

"Where are you from?" they'd ask. "Why are you doing this? Is this your full-time job?"

I always explained I was a reporter.

"Oh, do you need an assistant?" some would respond.

And nearly every passenger asked this: "Is your wife Chinese?"

The elderly couple, though, said almost nothing and directed me to a nearby hospital, where they planned to pick up medicine. I pulled up to the crowded hospital gate about ten minutes later. The lady fumbled with her change purse, pulled out a 10 yuan note—about $1.60—and prepared to hand it to me. I explained that I couldn't accept her money.

"I'm not a black [illegal] cab," I said in Mandarin. "I'm a free loving heart taxi."

The couple, who had apparently not read the signs on my car, beamed with surprise at their good fortune and headed into the hospital.

On the way to the office one morning, I drove to the city's Fuxing Road Ferry stop to search for customers. The ferry is one of the best deals in town: a cheap ticket with a spectacular view. For about 30 cents, you can ride across the Huangpu river gazing at futuristic glass-and-steel towers on one side and, on the other, the Bund, the city's British colonial waterfront with neo-Gothic, beaux arts, and art deco buildings dating to the early twentieth century. The ferry pulled into the dock with a shudder and scores of electric scooters poured out, roaring up the metal ramp and scattering into the streets. A migrant laborer who worked on a nearby construction site strolled over to admire my signs.

"I've lived in Shanghai for six years," said the man, who wore a yellow hard hat. "I've never seen a car like this, ever."

Ferry workers in blue uniforms crowded around, taking photos with their phones. Behind them, on the back of a grimy Vespa-style scooter, sat a man with a buzz cut who wore shorts and a clean, white T-shirt. When he asked where I was from, I told him the United States.

"Oh," he said, "my wife and two daughters live outside Los Angeles."

Eyeing the signs on my car, Chen asked another question: "Are you a Christian?"

I said I was and attended an international church on the other side of the river.

"I'm a Christian, too," Chen said.

Chen was thirty-seven years old with graying temples, alert eyes, and an air of self-possession that set him apart from the millions of people who raced around Shanghai each day chasing the next opportunity. He hadn't seen his family in months and was looking forward to joining them in America, which is known in Chinese as *Meiguo*, "the beautiful country."

"My wife just got a green card!" said Chen, who added that he had a young daughter who'd been born in the United States. He told me he had sent his family to America because the academic pressure in Chinese public schools was crushing his elder daughter. She had worked until ten or eleven every night on homework, and the strain had damaged her eyesight. Teachers also hit the girl, slapping her face so hard it sometimes made her dizzy. Like millions of migrants, Chen had come to Shanghai from a nearby province for higher wages and a better life. He worked as a pajama salesman at a clothing market where my wife, Julie, often had dresses made. Chen had his own apartment here but was trying to leave Shanghai and buy a house in Los Angeles. People had left China for centuries for better opportunities overseas, but over the past several decades the country had been the world's greatest economic success story. Whether you were a hustler from the provinces or a Harvard MBA, Shanghai was a magnet for talent and ambition. Chen, though, didn't like what the system was doing to his daughter and he didn't like the Communist Party. He wanted something more civilized, more sustainable, and he wanted out.

Rich Chinese were already scooping up green cards and foreign passports so they could provide their children cleaner air and
a more engaging education while sheltering their fortunes from
an authoritarian regime that could detain people and seize assets
at will. If China was going to take over the world, as so many in
America seemed to believe, why were so many Chinese hedging
their bets? Even a pajama salesman had an exit strategy. Getting to
know Chen helped me begin to appreciate some of the complexi-
ties of China at this moment and some of the challenges its people
faced. Decades of breakneck growth had transformed hundreds
of millions of lives, but it had also taken a toll and, for some, the
path forward was getting harder. In Shanghai and other top cities,
real estate prices grew 13 percent annually just from 2003 to 2013.
Clouds of pollution became so dense at times, my family and I
could barely make out the balcony of the apartment next door.
Now that many Chinese people had at least some wealth, they
wanted more, not just materially but spiritually and psychologi-
cally. Many longed for a more humane society, one that instilled
a pride that went beyond towering skyscrapers and lightning-fast
trains. For people such as Chen, that meant moving to the United
States, which offered a level of freedom that leaders in Beijing
thought was dangerous.

I set out to drive my free taxi to learn what ordinary people
wanted, how they saw themselves, their country, and the wider
world. Over the next few years, I drove scores of passengers, everyone from factory workers and farmers to retirees, bankers, lawyers,
and even a psychologist. Many returned the kindness, inviting me
into their homes and lives and sharing their hopes and fears. What
began on the streets of Shanghai turned into an odyssey that led
me to villages in central China, into the mountains along the Lao
border, and beyond, to Paris, Los Angeles, Chicago, and Kalamazoo.
Over the years, I got to know an increasingly sophisticated generation of Chinese as they pursued their dreams and tried to make
their homeland a better place. I drove Rocky, a poor farm boy

turned Shanghai lawyer, back home to his village for his wedding, serving as his chauffeur for the festivities. I shuttled a hairstylist named Max to appointments where he gave free haircuts to elderly shut-ins in hopes of making China a kinder place. I even made it to Los Angeles to visit Chen as he struggled to build a new life for his immigrant family in Donald Trump's America. In my experiment, I did not adhere to strict rules. On long journeys with multiple passengers in the countryside, I didn't drive my Shanghai Free Taxi, but rented larger vans and an SUV, accompanied by my assistant, Yang, who recorded conversations as I drove. Meeting my passengers outside of China, I spent hours chatting and strolling with them through the streets of Western cities. In case the Chinese government wants to punish them for anything they've said in the following pages, I've used their English names, Chinese surnames, and, in one case, a pseudonym, Ashley, to protect their identities.

When I first got to know these people, they offered hope to a country that was mired in corruption and stuck in an authoritarian system that seemed like it couldn't last. In the ensuing years, though, the political landscape in China and the West changed dramatically in ways few had anticipated. Xi Jinping became China's president and championed a vision he called the Chinese Dream. But was it a dream for individual Chinese or the dream of the Communist Party? Later, Xi (pronounced "she") declared that China had entered a New Era, a new period in modern Chinese history when the country would assert itself as a global power. The New Era would also mark the end of China's nearly four decades of economic reform and slowly increasing freedoms. As Xi took China in a more sharply authoritarian direction, American voters would stun the world and elect a leader who had little regard for democratic norms or a free press. The United States had once been a beacon of freedom for so many Chinese, including the hundreds of thousands who demonstrated for democracy in Tiananmen Square in 1989. The election of Donald Trump left some liberal Chinese to question what system, if any, to believe in.

Given its size, complexity, and speed of change, China is extra-ordinarily difficult to capture. What follows is not a scholarly thesis on the future of the world's other superpower, but simply the story of the people I met through the Shanghai Free Taxi as they grappled with personal challenges and tried to navigate this uncertain and pivotal moment in the history of modern China and the Western world.

CHAPTER 2

Chinese New Year Road Trip

Rocky and Charles

════════════════════

I N THE WINTER of 1998, while working as a correspondent for the *Baltimore Sun,* I traveled with a Chinese couple during the world's largest annual mass migration, when hundreds of millions of workers leave the cities and return home to the countryside for Chinese New Year. I met the couple, Chen and Li, in Beijing's cavernous West Railway Station. Along with two thousand other passengers, this construction worker, housemaid, and I pushed and shoved our way onto an aging train and spent more than a dozen hours rocking down the tracks south toward Hefei, the capital of Anhui province. The trip was grueling. Men battled for space on the overhead racks, jamming luggage in so tight that a suitcase crashed down on a passenger's forehead, leaving a bloody gash. By evening, the train's metal squat toilets were clogged and the air was thick with cigarette smoke. Passengers tossed the shells of sunflower seeds, orange rinds, beer bottle caps, and even cooked rice into the aisle as though they were composting. Bleary-eyed and rumpled, we left the train in Hefei and took two buses to get to Chen's farming village.

When we arrived, five hours later, Chen walked across his family's muddy yard toward Honghong, their three-year-old daughter whom they hadn't seen in eleven months. The little girl dashed off, scattering chickens and roosters. Honghong didn't recognize her father. I learned a lot on that trip about the hardship that Chinese migrant workers endure, but after a couple of nights shivering inside an unheated farmhouse in subzero temperatures, I couldn't take the cold anymore. I thanked my hosts, flew back to Beijing, filed my story, and thought I'd never take that brutal annual journey to the countryside ever again.

I was mistaken.

In 2015, seventeen years later, I decided to travel with migrants back to Hubei province in central China to see how the annual holiday trek had evolved. How difficult would it be to travel back to China's heartland now? What were the people and the conditions like? I'd spent the previous six months picking up passengers in my free taxi on my commute to and from work. It seemed a good time for a road trip. So much had changed in China since the first time I'd traveled to the countryside for the new year. Instead of packing into a crowded train, I would rent a seven-seat Buick van and take the interstate—China's equivalent of I-70—which had only been completed just a few years earlier. Had I retraced the old route by rail from Beijing to Hefei, the trip would have taken just under five hours by bullet train. Not only had China's infrastructure modernized, so had its people. My fellow travelers this time weren't poor peasants living on the margins of society, but the next, upwardly mobile, generation: a lawyer, his fiancée, and a salesman for a Shanghai shipping-parts factory, all college educated.

We found them after Yang, my assistant, posted an advertisement to NPR's forty thousand followers on Weibo. In the spirit of the free taxi, we offered a ride home for Chinese New Year and selected two men from among the respondents, Charles and

Rocky, who didn't know each other but were fortuitously from the same part of Hubei. Both were heading home to prepare for their weddings. Like many educated young Chinese, the men had chosen English names. Rocky took his from the fictional, million-to-one-shot boxer from my hometown, Philadelphia. Both were eager for a free ride that would save them time and money. During a preliminary conversation at my office, Rocky encouraged me to choose him, promising that his older brother, Ray, would make a great interview because his story epitomized President Xi's Chinese Dream. (China introduced its one-child population policy in 1979, but Ray was born before that and lived in the countryside, where couples were permitted to have two children.)

After Xi became head of the Communist Party in 2012, he went to an exhibit at the National Museum of China on Tiananmen Square called "The Road to Rejuvenation," which traced China's trajectory from the dark days of defeat in the Opium War (1839–1842) to the age of prosperity under party rule. Here President Xi began to lay out his vision for the Chinese Dream, a play on the American Dream that appealed at least in part to personal aspiration. But Xi also inextricably tied the Chinese Dream to the continued political dominance of the Communist Party and a restoration of China to a central place on the world stage.

"We must continue to strive to achieve the Chinese Dream and the nation's great revival," Xi told the National People's Congress, China's rubber-stamp parliament.

I didn't want to spend Chinese New Year listening to someone bore me with Communist Party talking points, but I always learned something new on every journey, so I decided to give Rocky a ride. I picked up Rocky and his fiancée, Piao, early one morning outside the walls of my apartment compound. Physically, Rocky seemed almost a different species from the migrant workers I'd accompanied home in the 1990s. In one of the fashion quirks of that era, Chinese migrant men, who were often unshaven, wore wrinkled suit coats with the label still stitched to the sleeve.

Impoverished and unsophisticated, they dwelled at the bottom of the urban socioeconomic ladder and mistakenly thought that leaving a label on a sleeve conferred at least some meager status. Rocky, on the other hand, wore rimless glasses, a stylish, black, collarless jacket, a gray and white sweater, and pressed jeans. He would've easily blended in on the streets of any American city. I wondered how different these city dwellers would be from the family members they were returning to see in the countryside.

We entered the People's Road Tunnel and dipped under the Huangpu river. We met my other passenger, Charles, in front of the Jing'an Temple, a Buddhist shrine made of Burmese teak with gold-colored spires that sat along Nanjing West Road, the city's traditional shopping street. Charles, who wore a gray tweed jacket with a collar and epaulets, insisted on putting his roll bag in the back of the van himself. From there, I drove up onto the Yan'an elevated highway and headed west through the city's glass-and-steel canyons.

At first, the conversation was awkward. Yang sat in the front seat and pointed a shotgun microphone, which resembles a long pistol, toward the passengers in the back. Most people are wary of microphones, but Chinese are especially so because they're afraid they'll say something critical that will somehow get back to the authorities. At this point—it was early 2015—that kind of thing almost never actually happened, but I understood the concern. To warm up my passengers, I asked them to recall earlier journeys to the countryside over Chinese New Year, the biggest holiday on the country's calendar. Charles, who sold ship heating-system parts from a Shanghai factory, said in the old days the trains were so crowded, some people rode inside the putrid, cramped bathrooms.

"You feel people are living with absolutely no dignity," Charles said. "If you want to get in the toilet and use it, you have to ask someone in there to get out. You beg them, because most of the time, they're sleeping."

Now that China has better roads and car rental companies, Charles said more people were doing what we were: carpooling. I had more than five hundred miles of driving ahead and beyond getting my passengers to open up, my goal was simple: don't crash the van. Driving in China is unpredictable, and many drivers in the countryside pay even less attention to traffic rules than city drivers. As I continued west, BMWs and Mercedeses blew past us doing one hundred on the right shoulder. I was accustomed to creative driving in the provinces. One afternoon, when I was driving down a highway in the central Chinese city of Wuhan, I saw a car on my side of the road heading straight toward me. Simultaneously horrified and amused, I eased my car to the shoulder and let him pass. He was probably a first-time driver who had missed his exit and thought it was easier to do a U-turn and dodge oncoming traffic than keep heading in the wrong direction.

About two hours into our trip, we came to a tollbooth. The toll taker, a young woman, swiveled in her chair at an exact ninety-degree angle and reached out her hand like a robot to take my four bucks. Her smile was plastered on and the effect was creepy. I tried to smile back but couldn't hide my discomfort.

"This is a work requirement," said Charles. He figured the toll taker was under instructions to smile to improve public service, which is often wretched.

"If you go to government agencies and you see an official, they give you a stinky face," Charles said. "This fake smile is a lot better."

As we pulled away, the toll taker broke character, smiled naturally, and blushed.

"She's shy," said Rocky, pointing out that she seemed surprised to see a foreigner out here beyond the big cities.

As we continued west, we left China's crowded, wealthy coast and entered the country's sprawling interior. Rows of cookie-cutter apartment blocks gave way to fields of sorghum and rice. We passed trucks with giant cages filled with pigs and dodged farm families as they putt-putted down the highway in three-wheeled, flatbed scooters. When we hit Anhui, the poor province where I'd spent Chinese New Year in the 1990s, the plains rose, forming an accordion-like landscape of small mountains. We passed through a series of tunnels and, except for the Chinese characters on the green highway signs, it looked like stretches of the Pennsylvania Turnpike. Rocky cued up a song on his iPhone he thought I'd recognize.

Almost heaven, West Virginia
Blue Ridge Mountains, Shenandoah River

Driving through the mountains of central China listening to John Denver's "Take Me Home, Country Roads" seemed oddly appropriate as Charles and Rocky headed home to their rural roots for the holidays. It's a song of longing for a rural world that—in the case of China—had fallen behind the country's big cities and was beginning to disappear. John Denver first entered China's consciousness in 1979 when he played at the Kennedy Center for Chinese leader Deng Xiaoping. Deng was visiting Washington, DC, to lay the groundwork for establishing diplomatic relations with the United States. As China slowly opened to the world, Denver and other unthreatening pop acts such as Wham! performed here. Most young Chinese had little access to English-language textbooks, so they learned by listening to "Country Roads," the Carpenters' "Yesterday Once More," and George Michael's "Careless Whisper."

We were now about four hundred miles into the trip. Traffic was thinning out and the road was still as good as anything you'd find in the United States—such a change from my first years in the country. Zipping down the highway at eighty, I raved about the road improvements. Charles responded with a story about how his home village got its first paved road a few years ago. Citizens contributed anywhere from $160 to about $300 each to build it. But—as was often the case in China—the construction process was opaque and the road was already beginning to crumble in places. Charles blamed the usual suspect for faulty construction: skimming.

"My uncle was a village chief nearby," said Charles. "My mother said that my uncle siphoned off some money from an engineering project. When I heard about it, I wasn't very happy."

Later, away from the other passengers, Charles told me how he too had benefited from the corruption that was woven into the Chinese system. He'd been a lazy student and, when preparing for high school, had scored poorly on the entrance exam. His family found some relatives' friends with connections at the county's best high school and paid a bribe of more than $3,000 to get him admitted. It was a huge amount of money at the time, more than a third of the price Charles's family had paid for their apartment.

"It's a big burden for the family," Charles told me later. "I feel very guilty."

Unchallenged rule allowed the Communist Party to make quick, disruptive changes, such as taking land from farmers to build factories, that boosted economic growth. But with no external check on the power of the party—which controls the police and the courts—corruption became a natural, accepted part of life here.

Up until now, Rocky had been a relaxed presence in our rolling conversation, but the story about Charles's uncle got him thinking. Like Charles, Rocky also grew up in a poor farming village where he said many people just accepted corruption as a way of life. After decades of poverty and isolation, they were happy for any scraps the government tossed their way.

"Chinese farmers are the simplest farmers in the world with very, very low demands," said Rocky, uncharacteristic contempt creeping into his voice. "When the government does just a little bit for them, they feel it's a huge blessing. They thank the government and the Communist Party. Actually, it's nonsense."

When conversations focus on these sorts of systemic problems, many Chinese either throw up their hands and say *mei banfa*— "there's nothing you can do about it"—or they talk about the need for checks and balances, perhaps even some kind of representative government, which the party knows is a direct threat. Sensing the conversation might drift into politics, Charles intervened.

"This interview has become too sensitive. Change the topic," he said. "It's common in China," Charles continued, switching to English: "Self-censorship."

This aborted exchange lasted just a couple of minutes, a tiny fraction of the several days we would spend together on this trip, but it was profound and a sign of things to come. The Communist Party knows that if people can't talk about politics, they can't begin to work through how they might change the system. Every curtailed conversation, every hesitation, is one more tiny victory for authoritarianism and the political status quo. What none of us in the van knew at the time was how much the Communist Party would drive self-censorship and fear in the years ahead.

As the sun set over the mountains, we closed in on their hometowns, and the local pride of these urban transplants began to swell. Charles said his county was known for professors; Rocky said his was known for journalists. Charles had heard of one, Yang Jisheng, a former reporter at the Chinese government's New China News Service. Yang wrote a book called *Tombstone: The Great Chinese Famine, 1958–1962*, about the catastrophic, man-made famine during Mao Zedong's Great Leap Forward. Trying to transform China's economy, the party shifted labor away from food production and toward backyard blast furnaces, while pushing flawed agricultural policies that actually reduced harvests. When local officials exaggerated crop yields to please higher-ups, the government seized more and more grain from farmers, leaving people to starve. Based on an exhaustive study of local archives, Yang estimated more than thirty-six million people died from famine and famine-related illness in China at the time. Naturally, the Communist Party banned the book. Yang explained the party's thinking in an essay in the *New York Times,* which is also blocked by the government but for broader reasons.

"A full exposure of the Great Famine could undermine the legitimacy of a ruling party that clings to the political legacy of Mao," Yang wrote, "even though that legacy, a totalitarian Communist system, was the root cause of the famine."

Mao is a complex figure in China. People admire him for uniting the country after a chaotic era that included Japanese occupation and a civil war, but he stayed in power far too long. Had he stepped down much earlier, he wouldn't have had the opportunity to devastate the country with the Great Leap Forward and later the Cultural Revolution. Though Mao caused most of his damage through flawed policies, he, Hitler, and Stalin are the three political leaders responsible for the most deaths in the twentieth century. Some Chinese know the real history behind the man-made famine of the Great Leap Forward, but Charles said many don't seem interested. He switched to Mandarin to tell Rocky about the famine and the death toll.

"I haven't read this book," said Rocky, who asked no questions.

Around 7 p.m., I dropped Charles off at his family's apartment. I'd been driving for nearly thirteen hours; my eyes were stinging and my shoulder muscles ached. Rocky pressed me to drive one more hour through the dark to his village, where his mother had prepared dinner and was adamant about hosting us. Ordinarily, I would have agreed, but I was worried about navigating a country road at night with no lights or guardrails. I also didn't have the energy for the hospitality that might await. Chinese are extremely hospitable to foreign guests, which can sometimes take the form of pressuring them to eat dish after dish, smoke cigarettes, and drink baijiu, a white liquor often made with sorghum, wheat, or barley. As I listened to Rocky's mom, Guo, imploring him over the phone to bring me to the village, I apologized and told Rocky I was too tired. Rocky gave his mother the bad news.

"Hey, Ma, Americans don't like to stay in other people's homes," said Rocky, speaking in rapid-fire Mandarin that he hoped I wouldn't understand.

After a much-needed night's sleep, I drove Rocky and Piao the next morning to pick up their marriage license at a government office in the county seat. Piao, who wore a puffy beige overcoat and a red scarf, stood in line with Rocky as they handed over their forms to a clerk. Other brides-to-be wore red coats and carried red handbags, as red is an auspicious color in China for weddings and the coming new year.

"This marriage certificate costs just nine yuan"—about $1.50—"very cheap," Rocky noted happily.

"Why so cheap?" I asked.

The price was a gesture of goodwill on behalf of the government, as well as a play on words, which is common in Mandarin. The character for "nine" in Mandarin is pronounced "joe," which sounds just like another character that means "permanence." The clerk handed the couple their license and we stepped out into the sunlight. There were no family members to witness the moment, so I pulled out my camera, took off the lens cap, and turned wedding photographer to capture the milestone. Before I snapped the photo, though, I noticed a woman standing in front of the entrance to the marriage office with her two-year-old son, who had a buzz cut and wore a green-and-white-checked jacket. As I tried to focus on the happy couple, the mother pulled down her son's blue corduroys and held his penis as he sprayed the steps that led up to the office. If you think this might have shocked any of the couples here on their special day, you would be mistaken. I seemed to be the only person who even noticed. There aren't many public bathrooms in rural China, so parents dress their children in split pants so they can relieve themselves in public, largely out of necessity. But this moment also spoke to the chasm that remained between much of China's countryside and its increasingly cosmopolitan cities such as Shanghai. When I'd first returned to China in 2011, I was so struck by the bright lights and affluence that I thought the country would inevitably become more liberal and sophisticated. But a peeing kid outside a government marriage office was one tiny reminder of how much further the country had to go.

We headed off toward Rocky's village, down a road that ran along the edge of a river that was filled with mounds of gravel. Heavy machinery had gouged out the waterway, turning it into a gravel pit to feed an endless expansion of new roads and apartment buildings. What I thought might be a nostalgic drive with Rocky back to the old homestead soon turned melancholy. In China, even more so than in much of the rest of the world, you can't go home again.

"In the past, the ecosystem of the river was really great," said Rocky glumly. "Finless porpoise from the Yangtze river would swim back up this river. Now, there are none. Some sections were dammed, so the fish can no longer swim out to the Yangtze. The entire ecosystem, including the riverbed and water plants, is gone."

As we approached his village, I asked Rocky how he went from being a farm boy in central China to working as a lawyer hundreds of miles away in a megacity like Shanghai. The way people like Rocky have leaped up the socioeconomic ladder has been among the most exciting and encouraging aspects of the China boom. Piao offered her own explanation for Rocky's success.

"The entire village thinks his family sits on good land," she said. "It has good feng shui, so both sons can go to college and find good jobs."

Feng shui, which literally means "wind and water" in Mandarin, is used to orient buildings and interiors so that they are in harmony with natural and invisible forces that many Chinese believe produce good fortune. It's vaguely related to the type of thinking that leads to a marriage license costing 9 yuan. But like many Chinese today, Rocky didn't buy it.

"Everyone's fate, career, and job are the results of one's struggle," he said firmly. "They don't fall from the sky. It has nothing to do with feng shui. If I didn't take the bar and sat around at home, what use would good feng shui have been? Would a job have fallen from the sky?"

We pulled into the village, which was a series of two- and three-story farmhouses surrounded by parched fields. Some of the homes were gray and unpainted, while others had crosshatched exteriors in argyle patterns. As we stepped out of the van, a rooster crowed and Rocky's father darted across the ridge above, lighting strings of firecrackers and rockets to welcome us. After introducing me to his father, Rocky led me up to the roof of his family's two-storey house, which was pastel yellow and had red Chinese lanterns hanging from the balcony. He pointed to a camphor tree in the yard.

"When I was little, my grandma planted a little sapling here," Rocky said. "When I grew up, it grew up, too. Because its trunk has split into two branches, they represent us, the two brothers."

We looked out over the brown hillsides, some of which had been stripped of timber.

"Many trees here have been felled," said Rocky. "This tree will always be kept. We hope this tree will still be standing here, hundreds of years from now, even if we would not live here in the future."

Rocky's village could not be more different from Shanghai. There are no honking horns, crowds, or flashing LED lights, just the sound of the wind and the clucking of chickens amid one of the country's scarcest commodities: fresh air. The village is a throwback to an earlier era before China's economy exploded. Rocky loves the countryside, but both he and his village have changed forever, and there's no going back.

"Our parents had long-term plans to get us a good education so we could walk away from this impoverished land," Rocky said. "I like the quietness of the countryside—the chicks, ducks, fish, and birds—but if you ask me to come back now, after a short while, I would feel really uncomfortable."

Rocky's mom, Guo, who had pressed relentlessly for me to visit the night before, approached, and I braced myself for what I feared might be overbearing hospitality. Instead, she turned out to be a warm, refreshingly unself-conscious woman with copper-tinted hair and—I would later learn—an indomitable spirit.

"My and my husband's tombs are all completed," she said cheerily by way of introduction. "Wanna take a look?"

Seeing a tomb is not the first thing that comes to mind when I meet someone, but Guo, fifty-nine, was so enthusiastic about her final resting place, I couldn't resist. She led me down a dirt path to a small clearing where three sets of tombs were tucked into a hillside overlooking a valley. Two of the tombs, which contain the remains of her and her husband's parents, had elaborately carved facades with images of fish, which is a homophone for the Chinese word that means abundance, and cranes, which symbolize longevity. Guo and her husband's tomb still needed work; it was just a rough wall of gray bricks. By tradition, Rocky and Ray should have built the burial chamber.

"If you don't prepare this when you are growing old, people would say your sons aren't showing enough filial piety," Guo said. But Guo, who had succeeded in life by ignoring what others thought, pointed out that her boys were too busy with their law practices in Shanghai, so she hired workers to build the tomb for her.

"How can they have time to come back for this stuff?" said Guo, who embodied some of the best traits of many successful Chinese: flexibility and pragmatism.

Guo and her husband are subsistence farmers, growing rice, carrots, cabbage, and turnips in a small garden near the edge of a pond. After Deng Xiaoping began to turn away from a command economy and push China forward with market incentives in the 1980s, Guo opened a series of businesses to raise money for her boys' education. She ran a fruit stand in a nearby town and a small shop that sold special funeral clothes for the dead, a Chinese tradition. Guo borrowed money from relatives and used her savings to put the boys through college.

"Let me tell you, there are almost no other kids like ours in this village," she told me proudly.

When her son Ray had a daughter, Guo moved to Shanghai to help care for her, as many Chinese grandparents do. At first, she was lonely and miserable because she couldn't communicate. As a child, Guo had never learned Mandarin, the national language that binds the country together, because she was forced to leave school after the second grade. With so little formal education, she could only speak her village dialect, which is incomprehensible outside of Hubei province.

"When I first got to Shanghai, I cried often," Guo told me. "Back then, my granddaughter was still little. I had no one to talk to. Every day when the door was shut, it was like sitting in a prison."

But Chinese of Guo's era are accustomed to *chi ku,* which literally means "eat bitter," or bear hardships and adapt to whatever challenges life throws their way. Ray's wife and her mother taught Guo Mandarin, including how to read and write the characters, and Guo eventually settled into life in the big city. As I stood admiring the family tombs, Guo's phone rang. She answered in the village dialect with a few words of Mandarin and then hung up. All I could understand was, "There's a journalist interviewing me."

"They're all coming to see you!" announced Guo, who told me I was the first foreigner ever to set foot in the village. I trudged back down the path through fallen leaves to the house, while Rocky's various aunties made their way up the ridge in their winter coats and high-heeled boots. I shook each one by the hand while they used their free hand to cover their mouths, laughing nervously at the gray-haired white man towering over them. I was surprised that in 2015 there were still villages in China, probably many, where most residents had never encountered a foreigner. These villagers, just five hundred miles from Shanghai, were a decade or more behind the country's coastal urbanites in terms of outlook, experience, and thinking. The aunties cued up a boom box and prepared to show us a dress rehearsal of the show they planned to perform at Rocky's wedding in a couple of days. They'd been working on their dance moves for months. Guo changed into a purple velvet jacket and raspberry-colored leopard-print blouse—a sort of fashion mash-up popular in rural China. Before the music began, the boom box played a few snippets of completely out-of-context English.

"Chicken or fish? Fish comes with rice," said a British-accented voice.

"What looks good to you?"

"I had chicken last night."

It turned out someone had recycled an English-language conversation cassette and taped over it with dance music. A thumping beat then roared out of the speakers and the aunties, who'd formed a line in the courtyard, snapped to attention. Guo and her relatives began swinging their arms from side to side, pivoting on the balls of their feet, and raising their hands over their heads as if performing pirouettes. To the untrained Western eye, it looked a lot like country line dancing. In fact, it was a popular form of exercise that retired women engage in in public spaces across the country, including outside my Shanghai apartment complex. Guo said it was also a big improvement over the aunties' earlier pastime, playing mah-jongg, which involves gambling and can often end with arguments.

After the dress rehearsal, Rocky led us down the hillside to the fields where he used to water crops and harvest peanuts as a kid. The terraced rice fields where he once played now lay fallow. A mangy-looking water buffalo stood tethered to a tree.

"Now, nobody takes care of this place," Rocky said. "We had thought about coming back to the village after we get old, but I think this may not come true. By then, our family members and children will be in the cities and the people who we shared our life with and family elders may have passed away. There will be fewer and fewer things to feel nostalgic about."

Chinese villages like Rocky's were disappearing all the time as people moved to the cities for jobs. Weeds grew up in abandoned homes and the roofs caved in. Since the early 2000s, an estimated 920,000 villages have vanished across rural China. Guo spends most of the year in Shanghai, leaving her husband alone in their farmhouse.

Bam! Bam! Bam! Rocky's father lit off more fireworks to signal the arrival of more visitors. We rushed down the hill to a black BMW that had just rolled up.

"Frank, this is my big brother, Ray," said Rocky, speaking English for practically the first time in two days. Rocky seemed to be trying to impress his older brother, who'd spent two years studying for a master's of law in the United States. Ray was confident, handsome, and dressed nattily, like a downtown lawyer, in a crisply ironed shirt that had somehow remained unwrinkled on the five-hundred-mile drive from Shanghai.

"Nice to meet you," said Ray's daughter, Dora, who addressed me in English and seemed remarkably poised for six. She derived her English name from the *Dora the Explorer* cartoon, which Chinese watch on satellite TV and online. I thought back to my first Chinese New Year trip to the countryside in 1998, when I met Chen's three-year-old daughter, Honghong, who didn't recognize her father because he'd been gone for nearly a year working construction in Beijing. With a lawyer's salary, Ray could afford to keep Dora in Shanghai along with his mother.

The family stood around admiring Ray's shiny BMW. Guo patted the roof of the car as if it were a prized beast. Then she reached into the trunk and pulled out new clothes Ray had brought from Shanghai as gifts for the New Year. Scooping them up in her arms, Guo trudged back up the dirt path to her farmhouse and continued to prepare for the wedding.

CHAPTER 3

Two Country Weddings

Charles, Rocky, Guo, and Ray

A COUPLE OF DAYS later, we gather in town to drive to Rocky's village for the ceremony. My blue van takes up the rear of the procession and it's hard to keep up because—even though pink ribbons are draped across all our vehicles—nobody in town cares that this is a wedding party. In fact, nobody in town cares about us at all, which is a typical experience in China. A taxicab cuts me off, then a Peugeot, then I'm trapped behind a dusty bus. Just as I'm about to catch up to the wedding party, a woman pushes her wooden cart in front of my van. Finally, I settle in behind the last car in the procession, a white SUV made by the Chinese company BYD, which stands for Build Your Dreams.

Since I'm driving the biggest vehicle, I stop along the way to pick up some of the family's friends and relatives. As each passenger climbs in, they do a double take when they see a white guy at the wheel, which not only surprises them but provides great face—or honor—for the groom. I explain I'm a friend of Rocky's from

Shanghai and—as unlikely as that seems—everyone quickly accepts it, because to live in China today is to expect the unexpected.

As we head toward the village, Ray leads the pack in his BMW. Rocky, who wears a three-piece suit and a red tie, stands up through the sunroof with Piao, who is ethnic Korean and dressed in a magnificent *hanbok,* a traditional Korean dress. As the couple smiles and waves, the BMW winds along the paved road, crossing terraced fields and passing an old woman walking with a bamboo pole balanced on her shoulders, a wicker basket hanging from either end.

The couple arrives to a hero's welcome. Members of a six-piece band wearing green People's Liberation Army uniforms with red epaulets blast out a tune on trombones, trumpets, a bass drum, and a tuba. Winter has drained the village of color, and the procession heads up the dirt path on foot beneath an overcast sky, passing barren trees and gray concrete houses. Ray's daughter, Dora, leads the way, carrying a bouquet of pink roses. Piao is a riot of color in her *hanbok,* with its bright red skirt and green jacket with flowers on the sleeves. The air fills with clouds of gray smoke and the sound of explosions as boxes of fireworks and strings of firecrackers ignite. Purple, red, pink, and green confetti rain down from the sky as Dora cowers with Piao, covering her eyes with her arm for protection. This feels less like a wedding celebration and more like an artillery barrage. For many Chinese, there is no such thing as too many fireworks. The explosions subside and the wedding party passes beneath an inflatable red-and-gold gate adorned with a dragon and phoenix, which symbolize good luck and a harmonious marriage. They then step along a red carpet through a walled courtyard beneath pink, blue, yellow, and green bunting like the kind you see fluttering in parking lots at American car dealerships.

After just a day's work, Guo has transformed her simple home. Red lanterns hang from the ceiling and the Chinese character for double happiness appears on each step of the staircase that leads to the second floor and the matrimonial suite. Two teddy bears representing the bride and groom sit on the bed that is stacked high with red quilts. Family and friends gather around the dining-room table, which is covered with sticks of incense and plates of fruit, nuts, and sunflower seeds. A framed poster of Mao wearing a flowing green robe billowing in the wind dominates the far wall. Mao died in 1976, but you see his picture in farmhouses across China's countryside. Ray, who wears a charcoal suit and a red scarf, takes the microphone and speaks in Mandarin, not the village dialect, so I can follow. He speaks proudly of watching his little brother, who is six years younger, transform from village kid to city lawyer. The local Communist Party secretary gives a short speech. I'm told later he was a little nervous to have me there—not because I'm a reporter, but because he felt pressure to make a good impression on a foreigner. Rocky drops down on one knee and puts a ring on Piao's finger, Piao does the same, and—after a ceremony that has taken less than fifteen minutes—they're married.

Members of the village dance troupe, many of them Rocky's aunts, change into their uniforms, which include short red dresses, matching red pants, embroidered green jackets, and purple pompoms. The music starts and they run through a series of dances, joined by Piao and a drunken guest who drags his laughing wife into the action. Toward the end of the celebration, a hit song that's taken over the Internet in recent months begins playing. It's called "Xi Dada Loves Peng Mama," and it's an ode to the love Xi Jinping is said to feel for the country's first lady, the famous People's Liberation Army singer Peng Liyuan. The rough translation goes like this:

> *China produced an Uncle Xi,*
> *He dares to fight the tigers.*

"Tigers" refers to the powerful officials Xi has already jailed for corruption.

Not afraid of heaven, not afraid of earth,
People want to see him even in their dreams!

This song was already such a staple that few at the wedding paid much attention to it. Nevertheless, it would prove a building block of the cult of personality that state propaganda organs would craft for Xi in the coming years. The food consumed, the white liquor drunk, friends and family drifted out of the courtyard and back down the hill. Soon, the house was nearly empty. I hadn't wanted to bother Guo on this important day, but I wanted to learn more about her past, so I invited her to sit with me on plastic stools along the ridge. A light rain began to fall.

"Today is a big day for my son," said Guo, who wore a burgundy sweater, a string of pearls, and a jade bracelet. "I really didn't expect this. I didn't dare to expect this. We were born in a different age."

Guo not only grew up in a different China, she might as well have grown up on another planet. Her family, which owned a few acres of farmland, had been mildly prosperous. They had hired a relative to help work it, which was enough for the communists to label Guo's family "rich peasants." In 1966, Mao launched the Cultural Revolution, which was an assault on his political enemies and the bourgeoisie designed to save a revolution he saw as under threat. As many as 1.5 million people were killed or committed suicide, while 36 million suffered political persecution, including President Xi and his father. Guo, who was then in second grade, was also targeted. Because she came from a "bad class," she was banned from attending school.

"I saw kids running to school and followed them," Guo recalled. "The kids said: 'Why are you here? You are not one of us. Your family is from the landlord class.'"

With no classes to attend, Guo spent her days tending crops and evenings making cloth shoes, producing about one pair a week.

"Many kids didn't play with me," she recalled. "All the kids bullied me. It was very pitiful when I was little."

Uneducated, Guo grew up illiterate with no marriage prospects: "Who had the guts to marry me?" said Guo, who is disarmingly matter-of-fact about her suffering and shows no self-pity. Guo's mother hunted for a suitable match, settling on a man whom Guo had never met. He happened to be available because his family had its own political problems. His uncle had been an officer in the Nationalist army and had fled to Taiwan after the Nationalists lost the Chinese civil war to Mao's army. Guo's marriage was one of political convenience, though not in the way we generally think of it.

After Mao's death, Deng Xiaoping began to reform the rural economy and let farmers sell some of their produce. Guo, as is her nature, leaped at the opportunity. She sold some of the vegetables she grew to workers at a nearby mining camp. She used her tiny profits to buy gloves and socks and then sold those to people in her own village.

"That's how I first learned to do business," Guo told me.

Ray likes to say that if his mother had been born a generation later, she'd be running a big company by now. I have no doubt. The fact that the Communist Party routinely takes credit for lifting people like Guo out of poverty is insulting. It was the Communist Party's disastrous policies that held Guo and hundreds of millions like her back, wasting untold human potential. Under Deng, the party made a series of shrewd, innovative, and risky policy choices that set the country on track for spectacular growth. But perhaps the government's most beneficial decision was to get out of the way of the Chinese people. Through it all, Guo says she bears Mao no ill will.

"I don't hate him," said Guo. "Everyone thinks he's a remarkable person and I agree. He liberated the entire country. What happened to me was restricted to this household. What Chairman Mao did was good for the entire country."

When Guo's boys were growing up, hardly anyone in the village went to college. Her husband opposed them attending; he wanted Ray and Rocky to leave the village to work, so they could send back hundreds of dollars a year in wages. Having been denied an education, Guo was determined her boys would get one.

"Everybody was against my idea," she recalled.

But she stood her ground and poured her savings into the boys' tuition. The more I drove people around Shanghai and China, the more I met women like Guo, who seemed to be the backbone of the country. Often unappreciated and fighting what was still a patriarchal system, they expressed strong opinions, defied authority, and refused to back down.

After Ray graduated from college, he spent three months studying for the bar, ten hours a day.

"The year when I passed the bar exam, the pass rate was around eight percent," he told me.

When I mentioned that Rocky had told me he represented the Chinese Dream, Ray smiled thoughtfully. Standing on the muddy ridge, next to the family's outhouse, he launched into a soliloquy, providing a balanced analysis of his homeland at this critical stage.

"Today, many may see China as a powerful and wealthy country, but compared with developed nations, there is still a big gap," said Ray, striking a modest tone that President Xi might have been wise to adopt. "Personally, I think the level of our education, our management skills, level of legislation, and law enforcement and soft power lag far behind the US."

As China grows wealthier, Ray said, people will expect better health care, better education, and better-quality products—and that will require more efficient, more honest government. People "will have higher and higher demands, particularly for the government. I think in today's China, the area that most needs change is the government. Their management capability and officials' *suzhi* need to be greatly elevated."

Suzhi, which is pronounced "sujer," is one of my favorite Chinese words. There is no exact translation in English, but it means a person's inner quality, character, basic essence. Ray sees many people today competing to buy luxury goods because they don't have more meaningful pursuits. He wants the government to pour more resources into public services and for more people to have the opportunity to serve society and reach areas the government can't. Ray was describing civil society, which the government would actually crack down on in the years to come, seeing independent organizations as a potential threat to its monopoly on power. Ray thought China's future success hinged less on the dazzling construction boom that had defined the country for the past two decades, and more on how people were treated.

"You don't necessarily need to build too many skyscrapers, but everyone needs to be respected," Ray said. "Everyone's creativity can be unleashed. When people's basic living is guaranteed, they will do things they like. Think about it. If 1.4 billion people's creativity is mobilized, everyone does things they like and lives with dignity. If this comes true, it will be a blessing for the country. It will also be a remarkable thing for the world."

I thought about Shanghai, a dynamic city full of ambition and energy. Local leaders dreamed that one day it would rival the world's two great financial capitals, London and New York. They even dotted a section along the Huangpu river with museums, mimicking London's south bank of the Thames. But Shanghai still operated within an authoritarian system that saw free expression and free thinking as a threat and that crushed even its weakest critics. How could Shanghai provide the creative environment necessary to become a great, global city—the kind of community Ray dreamed about? President Xi's dream was hundreds of millions of people working to restore China to its former glory on the world stage. Ray, on the other hand, was more focused on ordinary Chinese living with dignity and respect, having the freedom to pursue their own goals and make China a better country in their own way. This sounded less like Xi Jinping's Chinese Dream and a bit more like the American Dream. And the problem was, given the direction China was heading, it was hard to see how you could have both.

The sky, which had been overcast since dawn, was darkening. Yang, who'd spent the past two days helping to record conversations in the village, and I needed to get on the road. Guo, Ray, Rocky, and the rest of the family walked us down the path to the van. Guo insisted on giving us one hundred eggs—"They're organic!" she declared—which my family ate for breakfast over the next several weeks.

On the way back to Shanghai, Yang and I stopped at the same tollbooth where we'd had that odd encounter on the trip down. The toll taker, this time a man, moved with the same animatronic efficiency as the previous one. In the moment, this just seemed an eccentric example of life in provincial China, an anecdote to tell over beers back in Shanghai. But later, when I thought about it, it seemed more sinister, a sign of what lay ahead.

"Why do you move this way?" I asked, genuinely baffled. "It looks strange."

The toll taker stared at me.

"Our leader thinks it looks good," he said, speaking through clenched teeth and a rictus grin.

"Really?" I said in disbelief.

Yang followed up with a question.

"Is there a camera watching you?" he asked.

The man nodded slowly, casting his eyes toward the ceiling and the unseen gaze shaping his behavior.

BEFORE I LEFT Hubei province, I checked in on Charles, who was busy planning a wedding banquet of his own. One morning, we went to a sprawling outdoor market, where we had to navigate darting chickens and swerving motor scooters on the way to buy one hundred pounds of fish and pork for the grand meal. It was part of the dowry that Charles's future father-in-law required. He also insisted Charles's father, who worked as a security guard, buy nearly $1,300 worth of cigarettes—or the equivalent of four months' salary—to give away at the wedding.

"It's a big burden," said Charles, who added that when he was young and people were much poorer, they just gave gifts of cloth so families could make clothing.

"In Mao's time, they said, 'No gifts, just Mao's books.'" Charles recalled. "Now, they give hundred-yuan bills"—the equivalent of about $15—"with Mao's picture on them. Mao's the most loved man in China. Everybody loves Mao," Charles joked, "because he's on that bank note."

After we dropped off the meat, I drove Charles deep into the countryside. He wanted to show me his home village so I might better understand where he had come from and what he valued. We drove into town on a single-lane paved road—the same one from which Charles's uncle had siphoned off money. It was barely wide enough for my van, and I steered carefully to make sure the wheels didn't slip off and send us tumbling into the rice fields below. Farther down the road, Charles pointed to a small school-house on top of a hill where he'd once studied.

"It's abandoned," Charles said. "It's very common in Chinese rural areas, because there are fewer and fewer children." Like Rocky's village, Charles's was a victim of China's economic boom and rapid urbanization.

We pulled into the driveway of the house of one of Charles's uncles, where the family was preparing to slaughter a pig in advance of Chinese New Year. Charles wanted me to see the process to gain a deeper appreciation of how life really works on a Chinese farm. As relatives and villagers gathered around, butchers in purple smocks and knee-high rubber boots walked down to a crumbling pigsty carrying a length of rope and a big metal hook. The animal, a cross between a pig and a boar, had brown, bristly hair. It leaped up to bite one of the butchers, who drove the shiny hook through its mouth. The pig shrieked in a way that sounded almost human.

As the men pushed and pulled the pig, it locked its knees and tried to dig in its hooves, which scraped across the concrete driveway. It took seven men to lift the animal onto a giant wooden slab and hold it down as it rolled about, kicking. Blood trickled down the pig's throat and the squealing began to sound like steam escaping. A butcher drew a long knife and sliced the pig's throat, sending a crimson stream pouring into a plastic bucket, where it would be saved to make blood cakes. As death grew closer, blood seeped into the pig's lungs, turning the piercing shrieks into a gurgle.

"Can you bear this?" asked Charles.

"I can, but the pig can't," I said, trying to make light of something I found gruesome.

In truth, I could barely watch, but I didn't want Charles to see me as a pampered urbanite. As blood drained from the carcass, the squeals grew less frequent, then subsided. The pig's head dropped and its body went limp.

"I kind of enjoy this," said Charles, referring not to the violence, but to the slaughter's place in rural culture. "Every time there is a slaughter, I will come and take pictures."

Charles pointed out that as villages like his empty out and more people move to cities like Shanghai, fewer people have a connection to the roots of a nation that not long ago was mostly agricultural. "Many people," he said, "don't really appreciate where their food comes from."

"City people, many children, they don't even know how a potato or an apple grows," Charles said. "They think it comes out of a machine. But for me, I know how we get our daily meat."

In a country where hundreds of millions had moved from farm to city since the 1990s, what did roots really mean? Rocky and Ray didn't even have time to build their parents' tomb and would never return to their village for longer than a visit.

We went inside the house and sat in the dark at a wooden table while a squawking chicken flitted in and out of the room. Having shown me a little about where he'd come from, Charles described his journey from Hubei to Shanghai. It was not the fairly straight path that Rocky and Ray had taken. Instead, it had been an often painful and lonely trek across China in search of work to support his family back home. Charles wanted to work in international trade and improve his English so he could earn more money. But because he scored poorly on China's college entrance exam, he was unable to choose what he wanted to study. Instead, he was assigned to an animal science program, a subject in which he had no interest, at an engineering school in one of China's most polluted cities. Charles said nobody in the program wanted to study animal science, which might lead to a job as a large-animal veterinarian or a feed salesman, because it would just shackle a student to the countryside they were trying to escape.

"The department needed to enroll some students to keep running and truly nobody intended to go there," Charles said.

Charles graduated in 2008, which was the year of the Beijing Olympics but also the start of the global financial crisis, which began in the United States. He went to job fairs with classmates, but couldn't find work because he didn't have a suitable degree and companies weren't hiring as much because of the downturn.

"We were college graduates with normal intelligence, willing to work hard, but no one gave us a chance," he said.

Charles spent the next few years traveling more than ten thousand miles across the country, hopping from job to job. A cousin helped him find work in a factory in Huizhou in southern China working twelve-hour shifts making handles for Mr. Coffee machines for about $240 a month.

"I felt hopeless in the factory," said Charles, so he moved north to Hangzhou, not far from Shanghai, where he worked as a waiter in a Holiday Inn. Looking for better work and less competition, he traveled to Xinjiang in China's far northwest, where his father worked as a barber. Charles considered a job as a translator in Kabul working for a Chinese construction company. After that, he pursued an ad for an export salesman, which seemed to offer the opportunity for foreign travel. He took a bus and arrived at a remote farm just a few dozen miles from the Kazakh border. In the distance, he could see the snowcapped peaks of Tian Shan, the Heavenly Mountains. Charles soon learned that the farm did not yet have any fruit to export and that his job was to help grow it. He spent the night in a bungalow, where two fellow female workers shared a room. The farm had no animals or machinery, so the next morning the boss ordered Charles to put a rope over his shoulder and pull a steel plow through the fields while the two women planted watermelon seeds behind him. Instead of traveling abroad as a salesman, Charles had been hired to work as an ox. He felt stupid and humiliated.

"It's a modern world and I'm working like a primitive man from the Stone Age," Charles recalled. "Even in my hometown people don't do this."

The conditions at the farm were bad. One of the women, who had also been tricked into coming there, said she hadn't showered for ten days. When Charles got up the courage to tell the boss he was leaving, the boss became furious and threatened to beat him.

"We agreed, you are working here!" he said. "We paid your fare to get here."

"I was startled and terrified, and cried actually," Charles told me.

Charles eventually negotiated his exit. He grabbed his suitcase, which was full of books and weighed over thirty pounds, and began walking in search of the main road. Charles continued his journey working around China. He took a job building wind turbines on the coast, which meant hours working in the hot sun. He sometimes lived alone, surviving on noodles from snack shops. Eventually, he found a job in a machinery factory in eastern China, where he was able to practice his English on sales trips to Pakistan. Now, at the factory in Shanghai where he sells heat exchangers, he makes $1,200 a month, almost five times his starting salary at the Mr. Coffee factory seven years earlier. I asked Charles where he'd like to be in five or ten years and what kind of satisfying work he'd like to do. He stared at me blankly.

"I've never thought of this," he said. "Based on my previous experiences, these expectations have no impact at all. The only thing I should do is improve myself."

"Do you mean that it's not worth dreaming, because it's so hard?"

"Yes," he said. "I don't see any chance so far to get near that kind of dream."

Charles said in his travels from job to job, room to room, he'd suffered from depression. "Sorry," he said, as he broke down in tears, stood up, and walked away. He returned in a couple of minutes, tried to continue, but broke down again. Migrants like Charles had provided the muscle behind China's boom. They'd earned far more than they ever could have if they'd stayed back home on the farm, but they'd also paid a heavy price in loneliness, alienation, and often abuse.

Darkness was approaching. As I drove Charles out of the village on the single-lane road, we came upon a local cab driver in a small red car heading in the opposite direction. The road wasn't wide enough for both of us. Even though I had the bigger vehicle, the cabbie refused to back up. He waved his hands, gesturing for me to reverse. The road had no guardrails and was wedged between a hillside and a ten-foot drop-off. I put the van in reverse and began to back up. My tires were so close to the edge of the road I couldn't even see it. Then I felt a loud thump and the van lurched to one side. I slammed on the emergency brake and jumped out to see the left rear tire hanging over a rice field. A lump formed in my throat and my mind began to race. I would never find a tow truck this deep in the mountains. I couldn't leave the van here because it would soon be dark and a car was certain to plow into it. If the van slipped any more, it would roll into the rice paddy. What would I tell my editor back in Washington? I told Yang and Charles to get behind the van and, when I gave the signal, lift and push. I hopped back into the driver's seat, threw the car into gear, popped the emergency brake, and hit the gas. To my relief, there was enough power to drag the van back from the edge.

All this time, the cab driver stood next to his car watching, never offering help or saying a word. When I leaned out my window and motioned for him to back up, he again refused. He didn't care that I had almost rolled my van and that my vehicle was far more difficult to handle than his tiny sedan. The time for politeness and negotiation was over. I got out and began gesturing and cursing in English. He seemed surprised by my anger. Eventually, he climbed back in his car, backed up, and allowed me to pass.

Back on the road, Charles spoke up.

"The way you deal with these people is not . . ."

"Polite?" I said.

"I know it's not impolite on purpose, but not necessary, in my opinion."

"I was too hard on him?" I asked, incredulous. "He made me back up and I am in a big car, and it was dangerous and I almost drove off the road and he still wouldn't move. That doesn't seem to me appropriate in any culture."

"I understand," said Charles. "But sometimes shouting doesn't solve the problem."

Suddenly I was worried. I thought back to my midtwenties, when I worked as a reporter in a small city called Hazard in the coalfields of southeastern Kentucky. There were just five thousand people and everyone seemed to know each other.

"Is he a relative of yours?" I asked Charles, referring to the cabbie.

"No, but some taxi drivers are our relatives' relatives. In my opinion, the situation was not that bad that you needed to use that . . ."

"Tone of voice?"

"Yeah."

"Maybe I've been living in the city for a while."

"Do you do this in America? I don't think so."

"Yell at people?"

"Yeah. Strangers."

"Yes. If somebody won't give way—and they contribute, in this case, to me driving off the road."

"I think there should be some negotiation after that. Ask them to please drive back to somewhere else."

"But we tried to ask him to do that and then he . . ."

"You just asked once or twice. I think you should ask a few times more."

"Really? How many times?"

"Until you feel he's determined not to move."

This is a difference between a traditional Chinese approach and that of many Americans. In China, you should try to take more time, be patient, be oblique, keep your feelings hidden. In conversations, you touch on the main point, chat about other things, then circle back. Many Americans are more direct and less concerned with concealing anger. Charles said I should have given the cabbie time to save face instead of humiliating him.

"You were not happy because this cab driver isn't as civilized or doesn't have as much politeness education as you do," said Charles. "He's not that well educated. Usually in our culture we try to give them a step, so they can step down. This anger isn't worth it. You know why? You are focusing on who is right and who is wrong. And, actually, I totally agree with you. Even if you are stupid, you should know some basic rules. But my opinion is about the way we solve this problem, the way we deal with these stupid people. You cannot teach these people. You just have to live with them. So, you'd better play by their rules."

I knew Charles had a point. I'd lived in China for years and yet I still let these incidents frustrate me. Charles was also touching on one of China's biggest challenges. While there are more and more people like Charles, Rocky, and Ray—who have risen from humble beginnings and become thoughtful citizens—there are still hundreds of millions of people who are more like the cabbie, who have no experience of the wider world, little sense of civic responsibility, and not much concern for the rights of others. They are people more sophisticated Chinese might describe as having low *suzhi*. In fact, many Chinese argue their country needs tough leadership, not more freedom, to keep people with low *suzhi* in line. Chinese life is uncivil for many reasons, including a history of intense poverty, poor civic education, and political upheaval. The Cultural Revolution savaged Confucianism, which governed social behavior, and ripped up social bonds, encouraging children to snitch on their parents and students to torture and even kill their teachers. The more I drove, the more I began to think that the transition to a more civil, liberal society that Americans like me had thought inevitable might take a very long time.

CHARLES WAS A second-generation migrant. He had spent his childhood separated from his father, who had lived away from home for two decades, mostly working as a barber. The day before Charles's wedding, he asked his father to cut his hair in order to feel closer to him and give the old man face. Charles sat in a chair next to the washing machine in the family's enclosed balcony, which looked out over a muddy courtyard littered with broken bricks. His father, Shenhua, who wore his gray security guard's uniform, wrapped a yellow sheet around his son's neck and began to snip away. After a few minutes, the scissors fell from his hands and clattered across the tile floor.

"Since my hand was messed up, I can't really cut hair," said Shenhua, slurring his words slightly.

Shenhua explained why. A couple of years ago, he had been working in Xinjiang, in China's far northwest. One night, he cooked Chinese hot pot at a friend's place, using a coal stove. They never put out the coals, left the stove in the room, and drifted off to sleep. "You were probably drinking alcohol," Charles said.

"Yeah," said Shenhua, shaking his head in embarrassment.

"I didn't wake up," Shenhua continued, speaking slowly and pausing for seconds between sentences. "Other people rescued me. When they found me, I had been unconscious for more than twenty hours. The guy that was with me died."

Shenhua had slept on his chest, with his right hand—the one he holds his scissors with—underneath his body. It was severely damaged by the loss of blood flow. The hand swelled and turned black, and doctors thought it needed to be amputated. Shenhua was able to get it operating again but still didn't have much of a grip, which meant he could no longer cut hair professionally. Switching to English, Charles told me he had asked his dad to cut his hair to boost his confidence and encourage him to rehabilitate his hand. Before the accident, Shenhua, a former soldier, cut hair quickly and was known for his smarts and humor.

"But now, he doesn't speak a word," Charles said, "because the accident caused some damage to his brain."

Shenhua removed the sheet and blew the hair clippings off the back of his son's neck.

"Very good, very good," I said in Mandarin so Shenhua would understand the compliment. "And it's free."

"Free," said Charles, "and priceless."

The next day, I drove Charles to the farmhouse of his bride, who emerged wearing a red lace veil and walked with a posse of friends and family down a narrow country road, two attendants holding up her white dress to reveal burgundy stockings and matching hiking boots. At a restaurant, the couple exchanged rings as heart-shaped confetti showered down. Shenhua, who wore a gray suit and a blue-checked shirt buttoned at the top, stepped on the stage to speak, but after delivering a brief greeting, he paused and stared blankly out at the tables of guests, then looked at the floor, his eyes turning red and moist. Charles's mother quickly stepped onstage and took the microphone, rescuing her husband. Like so many Chinese men, Shenhua had left the countryside for China's booming cities to improve the life of his family. But along the way, he traded better wages for his children's childhood. Separated from family and home, he paid for his long absence with the use of his right arm and some of his brain, leaving him unable to honor his son with a speech on his wedding day. But Charles, as always, took it in stride. This had been the price of progress in China, an inescapable truth. Once worried that he might never marry, Charles was delighted today to be settling down with a woman who spoke the same dialect and would raise their children with a respect for China's rural ways. And from now on, he told me, he would let his hair grow long before coming home so his father could cut it.

CHAPTER 4

"Morality Is Relative"
Beer, Amanda, and Fifi

=========================

W HEN I FIRST started the free taxi service, I drove a rented car
just in case my venture failed. Once I found people were
willing to take a chance on a free lift, I decided to buy a car
to try to save money. New car prices in China are ridiculously high,
so I headed to a used-car dealership about half an hour from my
apartment. I walked into the unheated showroom one January and
glanced at the company logo, which resembled CarMax, the US
used-car giant. A young salesman in a blue company-issued blazer
with flecks of dandruff sprinkled across the shoulders greeted me.
Were CarMax and his employer connected? I asked hopefully.

"We have no relation with CarMax, but we copy their model,"
the salesman said with unusual candor.

I remarked at how similar the logos appeared.

"I'm a little nervous," said the salesman, who seemed worried
I was there to investigate a trademark violation. I explained I just
wanted a car and his shoulders relaxed.

"I am Beer," he said, by way of introduction. "English name is Beer."

Like Rocky, Ray, and Charles, Beer had chosen an English name so he could interact more easily with Westerners. It's also a way to stand out and express individualism in a country where the masses are still referred to as the *laobaixing,* the "common people" or—literally—"old hundred surnames." Some young people, though, choose their names without consulting Westerners, which is how friends of mine have ended up working with young Chinese professionals named Morphine, Popeye, Cinderella, Iliad, Billboard, and Twinkle. Beer had initially chosen a conventional name, Bill, but then changed it to reflect his passion for lager.

"I like to drink beer in big gulps," Beer explained, seemingly guileless. "When I drink with friends, we drink crazily. Seven to eight bottles each."

Beer suggested we go out and get hammered one night. We had yet to even look at a vehicle.

Most salesmen wouldn't introduce themselves as binge drinkers, but Beer wasn't your typical salesman. He was the son of farmers, a fresh college grad from a university in Anhui province, where he had studied electrical engineering and run track. Like Charles, Rocky, Ray, and Chen, Beer was among the millions of people from the provinces who'd come to Shanghai to try to get ahead and make a mark. The flood of outsiders had transformed the city's culture such that there's no single standard for acceptable behavior. This influx frustrates many Shanghainese, who take pride in their own cosmopolitan style and—like New Yorkers—often think they're better than the rest of the country. Beer wasn't clear on what's socially appropriate, but he didn't really seem to care either. When I told him I wanted a Toyota Camry, Beer gently placed his hand on my elbow and steered me toward a Chevy Malibu—as though I wouldn't notice the difference. When I complained, he took me to see a RAV4, which at least was a Toyota. Finally, he showed me a used 2012 Camry. The price tag was more than $31,000.

I didn't like where this was headed, so I walked across the show-room to consult privately with Yang, my assistant, who was serving as a much-needed wingman on this shopping trip. Beer followed, stopped about twelve feet away, and made no effort to hide that he was trying to listen in on what was obviously a private conversation. I glared at Beer. He tried to reassure me.

"I will not understand everything," he said, continuing to eavesdrop.

Beer sat me down at a coffee table and offered his company's standard deal. In exchange for a deposit of 3,000 yuan—about $500—he promised to track down a car that met my specifications. China's business culture is notoriously slippery. The old joke is that the negotiation begins after the contract is signed. I didn't wait for that and began arguing with Beer over the wording of the agreement. Beer insisted on giving me just three days to accept a car he found or forfeit my deposit. I asked for three to five days in case I was traveling outside the country. Beer wrote a five on the contract that looked suspiciously like a three.

"Let's make sure that five is clear," I said, grabbing a pen and reworking Beer's ambiguous digit.

"Sign your name," Beer said impatiently.

"Yeah, I know. I'm going to draw—"

"Sign your name here," Beer continued. He said he had another customer.

"I know!" I said as I wrote a thick five on the contract as though I were carving my initials in a tree.

Beer put his hand on my knee and gazed into my eyes as if he might propose.

"No, please, don't get nervous," said Beer, making me even more uncomfortable.

Unlike Americans, Chinese are not touchy people. Try to hug one and they may stiffen like a board. Beer seemed to be trying to soothe me, make a connection, but I only found it more unsettling. I felt like walking out, but I didn't want to pay even more for a new car. I reluctantly signed the agreement, forked over my deposit, and hoped I hadn't just lost five hundred bucks.

USED-CAR SALESMEN ARE suspect the world over, but Beer seemed especially untrustworthy. When we next met, his attempts at deception would reach the level of performance art. But Beer wasn't all that unusual in Shanghai or China, where many people routinely ran scams and one of the scarcest resources was trust. Society seemed to be sharply divided between an aggressive minority of scammers and the rest, who were largely honest but naturally wary, given the toxic levels of distrust on the streets.

I ran into a scam on my first day back in the city in 2011 while strolling down Nanjing West Road, past the old colonial clock tower that used to overlook the city's racetrack. I bumped into a pair of English-speaking women in their late teens, walking arm in arm as Chinese women often do. The women—who wore jeans and T-shirts and said they were college students—were pretty, friendly, and spoke good English, which they said they wanted to practice.

"Would you like to share some tea with us?" one asked. "We know a nice teahouse nearby."

Chinese people can be very friendly with foreigners, but usually not this friendly. In fact, what I was encountering was not hospitality but the infamous teahouse scam, where con artists lure tourists to witness a "tea ceremony" as a sort of cultural exchange. The marks are then presented with a whopping bill and threatened, sometimes by thugs, if they don't pay. A few years earlier, several French tourists had been hit with a bill for $920 after just an hour of tasting. I politely thanked my would-be scammers and continued to Nanjing East Road, the city's pedestrian shopping street, which is bathed in pulsing neon signs and swarming with touts. Men wearing illuminated strap-on roller skates weaved through the crowds trying to sell their flashing footwear. After a block, a woman wearing a pink polo shirt, denim jacket, and ponytail approached, offering to take me into an alley to buy watches and bags.

"No thanks, I'm a local," I said in Mandarin.

"You're a local? How about a massage? Lady beautiful."

This is the mantra directed at men on Nanjing Road at night: "Watch, bag, lady."

I continued down the street, walking past a replica of a 1930s convertible with running boards where tourists pose for photos, when a young woman in a white windbreaker and white sneakers with socks with blue pom-poms approached to pitch a massage, which I again politely declined.

"No thanks!?" she said, incredulous. Her tone seemed to say: "If you don't want a massage, what are you doing here at this time of night?"

About ten yards later, a woman in a long blue dress walked up and offered me her phone number. In twenty minutes, I had traveled two blocks and been solicited a dozen times. A woman in her late thirties in a blue skirt was the most persistent and shadowed me for nearly a block.

"I make introductions," she said, explaining that she had a quota to meet. She flattered my Chinese and asked four times where I was staying. She said I could choose from the photos on her phone a beautiful girl who could provide a standard massage or a *texu fuwu anmo,* a "special services massage," for $150. I told her no eight times and continued down the block.

"How about lunch tomorrow?" she yelled as she receded into the dark street. "We can be friends."

These encounters have an absurd quality to them, but if men are foolish enough to engage, they usually pay in ways they haven't anticipated. Every couple of weeks, an American tourist calls the consulate here to say he's been lured into a back room off Nanjing Road only to have thugs rough him up and drain hundreds or thousands of dollars from his credit card using a portable card reader and a fictitious business. Then, the thugs photograph his passport and driver's license and tell him if he reports the crime, they'll track him down.

"They're afraid a bunch of hooligans are going to descend on their house wherever they live in the United States," a friend at the consulate explained. "These are guys who are just low-level thugs on the street, but they make them think they have a network of gangsters in the US."

My friend tells the travelers to call their credit-card companies, cancel the charges, and change hotels if they don't feel safe.

"And, in a nice way, I tell them, 'You shouldn't have been looking for sex workers.'"

PEOPLE BATTLE FOR resources in Shanghai every day. In a city of twenty-four million, there isn't enough to go around or quench the ambitions of so many. Traffic is a delicate game of inches, where you tap the accelerator and tap the brake, nosing your way past the competition while taking care to make sure your vehicle never quite touches another. At rush hour, riding the metro may mean stuffing the person in front of you into a subway car like a mattress into a closet. Some people here see life as a Darwinian contest for space and spoils, favoring the most cunning, best connected, and least morally encumbered. Others envision an emerging society in which people consider the welfare of others and the greater good now that many no longer have to worry about the basics of food, security, and shelter. Each day is a battle for the soul of the world's largest country, fought in thousands of small skirmishes.

Nowhere do these two visions of Shanghai life play out more vividly than a couple of blocks from my apartment, along a riverfront promenade where a few days each month hundreds of Buddhists pack the banks to release sea creatures into the river. Amid clouds of incense, monks in saffron-colored robes lead believers in song beneath the blue and silver skyscrapers of the financial district. Wholesalers deliver the seafood in plastic crates that the

Buddhists pour into the waters of the Huangpu. Sometimes the faithful hand carry mud-covered clams, which they drop on plastic chutes that serve as sliding boards. During one release, a child tried to toss a clam over the railing but hit it instead.

"Be careful," his mother advised. "You'll give the clam a headache."

Releasing animals is an ancient tradition among Chinese Buddhists, who believe saving an animal destined to die is an act of compassion. (My wife, Julie, a veterinarian, thinks this is a disastrous idea. If the polluted waters of the Huangpu don't kill the sea life first, she worries, they'll become invasive species damaging an already fetid ecosystem.)

One afternoon, I drove my free taxi to the spot where the Buddhists release the creatures and chatted with the faithful. A retired chef named Shen wanted to make sure every animal was freed, so he climbed over the railing onto a ledge, crouched over the river's surface, and gently brushed the remaining snails into the water.

"We are freeing captive animals," Shen explained. "Why do we free them? They are just like us. We are all living creatures."

Against the backdrop of Shanghai's giant towers, monuments to China's growing wealth and power, it was refreshing to see these selfless acts. But that warm feeling ebbed with the clanging of a beggar banging a spoon on a metal cup as he strolled through the crowd trolling for coins.

"He likes to do this sort of thing," one of the believers said. "He's not poor. We have lots of people like this in China."

Beggars aren't the only people who try to exploit the Buddhists' beliefs. One day, I watched several migrant construction workers in yellow hard hats bike up the promenade carrying buckets full of turtles. One of the Buddhists offered $12 to save one of the reptiles. The worker demanded more, riding in circles while holding the turtle by the tail, taunting the faithful.

The net men were even worse. During some releases, as many as two dozen men position themselves downstream armed with fifteen-foot aluminum polls with nets on the end. As the Buddhists sing and pour fish into the river, the net men scoop them out of the muddy water moments later. The most shameless behavior I ever saw came one weeknight. As worshippers poured fish over the promenade during low tide, a man in a raincoat stood in the river up to his thighs, waiting with a flashlight and net to capture the creatures the Buddhists were trying to save.

One afternoon, I shadowed a net man named Li as he dipped his net into the water, scooping up one fish, then plunging the net back for a second and third time to capture more. Li dumped the fish amid the shrubs along the riverbank, where the net men had rushed around so much they'd carved paths through the foliage.

"Is it very hard to catch the fish?" I asked Li, who insisted he did not resell the fish but ate them at home.

"Easy to catch," said Li, who wore blue slacks and a purple shirt and was in his midforties. "Look at these good fish; why release them in the water?"

A passing freighter gave a loud blast of its horn, and Li returned from the railing with another haul. I asked Li if he thought scooping up all these fish was fair.

"What's fair? What isn't fair?" Li answered, dismissing the question as naive. "There are people releasing fish and people catching them. Nothing is fair in today's society. The more skilled swindlers just cheat the weaker ones."

I could tell by Li's accent and speech that he was a migrant and didn't have a lot of education, but he'd succinctly captured the thinking of many people in China: scam or be scammed. Faith helped guide the Buddhists through the ethical minefield of daily life here. But the government's fear of religion prevented the free spread of its positive influence to people such as Li, who—like the Communist Party—saw many things in zero-sum terms. If people could worship freely, how different China might become.

Back along the banks of the river a retired accountant named Wang, who was helping release the fish, chased Li down and scolded him. She said Li may get some fish today, but he would face consequences in the future.

"The fish are like our parents," Wang said. "Why do we have so many disasters? It's because of our greed. If they catch fish and it makes them happy, then I guess I'm happy for them. But when something bad happens to his family and he wonders why? It's because he did something bad."

"I don't hate them," Wang said of the net men. "I pity them."

THE STAKES OF the fish scam were minuscule compared to those of the frauds some people pulled in Shanghai and around the rest of China. During my years in the city, financial firms bilked investors out of billions of dollars. I only began to appreciate the human cost one sleepy afternoon when I headed up Nanjing West Road for a pick-me-up mocha. Halfway up the block, I ran into a crowd protesting outside the gate of Shanghai TV as a police officer chased them off with a bullhorn. Demonstrations like this in the heart of the city were rare and sensitive for a government that rightly fears organized protests could mushroom into something broader and more threatening. As the cop warned everyone to disperse, I approached one of the fleeing protesters, a middle-aged woman with a helmet of hair, and asked what was going on.

"Don't walk alongside me," pleaded the woman as she stared straight ahead. "The police will detain me."

I walked ahead of her, ducked into a corner, and hid behind a wall. She walked past and I quickly saw why she was afraid: a plainclothes cop in a black baseball cap and a black pollution mask was tailing her. This police pursuit of angry citizens was playing out on Shanghai's equivalent of Fifth Avenue on a workday, which neatly captures China's mix of vibrant commerce and political repression. It seems dissonant from a Western, democratic perspective, but makes perfect sense in the context of China's model of "Market-Leninism"—essentially free markets under increasingly iron-fisted rule. The cop stopped to look at his cell phone and I rushed ahead, crossed beneath an elevated expressway, and walked swiftly until I caught up with the woman outside a Maserati showroom at Tomorrow Square, a sixty-story tower I sometimes used as a landmark when trying to find my way back to the office. I slipped her my business card, then turned back up the street and saw the plainclothes cop, who passed me and continued to tail the protesters. I figured I had rid myself of Chinese state security. As I kept walking, a woman accosted me on the sidewalk.

"Why did you give that woman a card?" she demanded to know as pedestrians swirled around us.

The woman was in her late thirties, pretty, with shoulder-length hair tinted with copper, a popular color at the time. She wore brown sunglasses, a brown leather jacket, and a gray sweatshirt.

"What is your identity?" she pressed me in Mandarin.

I froze and tried to think before responding. Why was she asking? Was she a plainclothes cop I'd somehow missed? If I identified myself as a reporter, I could get the woman to whom I'd given my card into trouble. So, I did what most Chinese would do in this circumstance. I changed the subject.

"What just happened over there?" I asked, pointing to the front gates of Shanghai TV.

She refused to answer.

"I followed you," said the woman.

She was beginning to sound menacing.

"Are you just an ordinary *laobaixing*?" she continued, using the Mandarin word for common people.

I nodded. It wasn't true, but better to play the curious, clueless foreigner, which sometimes wasn't much of a stretch. She had me off balance. I wasn't ready to reveal my identity until I knew hers.

If she's really working for state security, she's terrific! I thought.

Then, in a moment, her facade cracked.

"I can't trust anyone," she blurted out.

Now, I knew, she wasn't an agent.

I invited her to walk inside the building where the NPR bureau is located, but she refused, then burst into tears. We were surrounded by people, but no one seemed to take notice. Seeking some sense of privacy in this jammed city, I walked her to a quiet space between a thick row of shrubs and a display window of a Red Flag dealership, the company that makes the limousines that transport Communist Party general secretaries to Tiananmen Square during military parades. The woman, who gave me her English name, Amanda, explained that she'd invested $160,000—the savings of her family and friends—into a company called Zhongjin Capital Management, a wealth-management firm with an office at a prestigious location on the Bund, the city's colonial waterfront. Police had raided the company earlier in the month, arresting more than twenty company officials. Amanda, who had also worked for the firm, was among more than twenty-five thousand investors who had poured nearly $6 billion into Zhongjin, according to state media. As she told me her story, she shook, cried, and put her hands to her mouth in terror. Desperate to find someplace more appropriate to talk, I led her out from behind the shrubs and we walked another twenty yards down the street, before she stopped and looked over her shoulder, frightened that we were being followed by police.

"There is no trust," she said, tears rolling down her cheeks. "This is China."

The government wasn't providing answers, so Amanda and the other investors had gone to Shanghai TV today out of frustration. Before Zhongjin collapsed, it had sponsored a popular show on Shanghai TV, which is state run. The show featured the company's logo on the screen, so investors had mistakenly read that as a government stamp of approval that their money would be safe. During that afternoon's protest, police had grabbed one demonstrator by the throat and roughed up others. When the protesters threatened to go to CNN, police questioned their love of country.

"You aren't patriotic," Amanda recalled the cops saying.

The Chinese Communist Party rules not only by fear but also through guilt. It had spent decades trying to make people see the party and the country as inseparable, so that to criticize one was to criticize the other. To that end, the party even came up with this martial tune:

> Without the Communist Party, there would be no new China.
> The Communist Party works hard for the people.
> The Communist Party, it strives to save China.
> It pointed the people toward the road to liberation.
> It leads China toward brightness.

Back on Nanjing Road, Amanda was a mess and I needed to get her off the street, so we slipped into the nearest Starbucks. I grabbed some napkins and gave several to Amanda to dab her eyes. I then borrowed a pen from the barista and began scribbling notes on the remaining napkins. Amanda hoped her money was still inside the company and was desperate to get it out. Protesters had posted complaints on Weibo, China's Twitter-like Internet platform, but censors had deleted them. Amanda showed me company documents on her phone but refused to send them through WeChat, the country's go-to social media app, because she didn't want to leave a digital trail. I used my phone to photograph the documents on her phone, doing my best to avoid the glare from the sun streaming in through the windows. Amanda refused to give me a phone number or connect on WeChat. We agreed to meet in a few days at the same place. I stuffed my napkin notes in my socks in the unlikely event cops were waiting outside. I saw Amanda off to the bathroom and then slipped out the back door.

Officially, the government laments the lack of trust between people in China today, and in many respects, that concern is sincere. At the same time, the party's surveillance, intelligence, and censorship systems generate distrust by design, and the party uses this suspicion as a tool of social control. After taking charge in 1949, the party established neighborhood committees in cities. Committee members, often elderly women known as "KGB with little feet," kept an eye on residents, providing political education and helping to "root out class enemies." After the crushing of the Tiananmen Square uprising in 1989, these nosy "aunties" helped search for democracy activists and turned in residents whom the government had accused of engaging in "counterrevolutionary activities."

The Communist Party has also tried to sow distrust of Westerners. In 2016, authorities launched an unusual national-security propaganda campaign by plastering cartoon posters on subway walls. The cartoon told the tragic tale of a state employee who falls for a handsome foreign man. The relationship begins promisingly with the man handing her a bouquet of red roses over tea. Her downfall comes after she gives her foreign boyfriend government secrets on a disk. The final panel shows her crying in handcuffs as police interrogate her.

"I didn't know he was a spy," she says. "I was used by him!"

Chinese friends tell me they pay no attention to this stuff, but over time it may have a cumulative effect on ordinary people. In addition to warning against Westerners, the party was especially focused on discrediting foreign media. In 2016, a member of China's legislature and head of state-owned broadcaster China National Radio claimed that 60 percent of Western news reports smeared China. Li Congjun, the president of the state-run New China News Service, has urged the country to fight against anti-China plotting by foreign reporters.

"Some hostile Western forces and media do not want to see a prospering socialist China," Li wrote in the Communist Party–run *People's Daily.*

That message resonated. When I traveled to Harbin, in China's far northeast, to cover the partial collapse of a new, $300 million bridge, everyone in town pointed the finger at the usual suspect in such cases: low-quality materials and government corruption. I met with a young man, a furniture designer, in Harbin to talk about the collapse. His mother insisted on coming along to the KFC for the interview and frequently interrupted and scowled, trying to prevent him from answering my questions. She wasn't focused on those who'd died or the systemic corruption that had almost certainly led to the disaster. She was bent on preventing her child, whom she saw as unpatriotic, from speaking to a foreigner whose sole purpose, she was convinced, was to malign the reputation of the motherland.

"An opportunist like you is what they need," she told her son before storming out of the restaurant.

The party was trying to manipulate Chinese people into covering up its failures, and the strategy was proving effective.

A FEW DAYS after Amanda had confronted me on the street, we met again at the Starbucks, and she began to pour her story out over several meetings. She was thirty-nine and had run an office supply shop before e-commerce competition had forced it to close. She saw a job ad online for Zhongjin and—although she had no financial experience—landed a position acquiring customers. The company was offering a staggering 15 percent return to investors. What was the secret? Amanda's boss told her they were pouring the money into the Shanghai stock market, which, at the time, was soaring. She assumed the company was trading on inside information, which is common and fuels the market. Amanda decided to test the waters and put some of her savings into Zhongjin. She was able to check her account every day and was allowed to make withdrawals. Over the next six months, the value of her holdings rose quickly. Fast money is seductive, but Amanda had a specific need. Four years earlier, she had learned her unborn son had a deformed right hand. Physicians recommended an abortion, but she refused because she was already in her midthirties and worried she might not be able to conceive again. After the birth, doctors couldn't fix her child's hand. Amanda hoped to use whatever she made from

Zhongjin to take her son to the United States for medical care, and had been taking English lessons to prepare for the trip.

Zhongjin seemed to have the veneer of legitimacy—at least as Amanda and many other mom-and-pop investors perceived it. In addition to advertisements on Shanghai TV and an address on the Bund, Zhongjin had another office across the river in the Jin Mao Tower, a landmark skyscraper a few blocks from my apartment that looked like a cross between the Chrysler Building and a pagoda. That's where Amanda worked and where she began to recruit her family and friends for investments that fulfilled her requirements for customer acquisition. In early 2016, Amanda said, the firm lowered its rate of return to 9 percent. She and other workers saw this as a positive sign, that Zhongjin was being realistic about returns and not making promises it couldn't keep.

"This is a real company," Amanda remembered thinking.

In April, she learned the truth. Police raided Zhongjin, seizing computers and documents and detaining the CEO at a Shanghai airport as he was about to fly overseas. In a tweet, the New China News Service called Zhongjin a Ponzi scheme. Police told investors that only 10 percent of their deposits remained. When Amanda heard the news, she considered jumping off her building. She had convinced her parents, her sister, and her in-laws to invest. Among the losses was the dowry her aunt planned to use for her nephew's wedding the following month. Police had Amanda's work documents from Zhongjin, so she couldn't apply for a new job, and she was nearly out of money. During one chat, Amanda scattered the equivalent of $16 on a coffee table, telling me it was all she had.

"Every time I take a bite of food, I feel very guilty," she said.

Financial fraud was increasingly common in China. Zhongjin was the third firm to collapse in the previous twelve months. Two months earlier, the government had exposed Ezubao, a peer-to-peer lending company, as a $7.6 billion Ponzi scheme that defrauded more than nine hundred thousand investors across the country. While some people were sympathetic to the investors, many others thought they were greedy and naive. Wealth-management firms like Zhongjin emerged in the mid-2000s to provide more financing to private businesses and better returns for Chinese investors frustrated by low interest rates at government banks. But as China's economy weakened, lending continued to boom. China had thousands of wealth-management companies and far more small subsidiaries, all of them lightly regulated at best. Customers said they invested in Zhongjin because there weren't better options. Real estate was widely seen as a bubble. The government's capital controls severely limited how much money Chinese could legally move out of the country for overseas investment. And in 2015 the Shanghai stock market crashed, which Zhongjin executives told their employees only brought more money their way as investors pulled out of stocks.

It was becoming way too expensive for Amanda to keep coming over to Nanjing Road to talk, so I drove my free taxi ten minutes up the north-south expressway to a Starbucks near her apartment. She was waiting when I arrived, wearing a long black raincoat. She sat with her legs crossed, her arms and shoulders pulled in as if trying to protect herself. Already thin, she appeared even more drawn. She wore no makeup and had dark circles under her eyes. Police were pressing her to answer questions about the company, but she was afraid to cooperate because cops had followed up interrogations with other employees by detaining them for up to a week. The day before, authorities had called her husband to apply more pressure. He was urging her to quit the protests and talk to the police.

"It's bad," she said of her relationship with her husband, whom she had already offered to divorce to atone for wiping out the family's savings. "Family problem, financial problem, a survival problem," Amanda continued, beginning to cry.

I reached into my backpack and handed her a tissue.

As the investors pressed the government for answers or some sort of help, they encountered deceit and trickery everywhere. Amanda and fellow investors had planned to protest in front of Shanghai's city hall, but police showed up half an hour before, a sign they had infiltrated the investors' group on WeChat. The investors argued over who inside the group had turned police informant.

"*This* one is a spy," Amanda said, repeating speculation she'd read in the private WeChat conversations. "*That* one is a spy."

When cops weren't running interference inside the group, con men were posting messages there saying they had a way into Zhongjin and that, for a fee, they could get the investors' money back.

When Amanda and I met again near her apartment, her emotional state was even worse. She said she worried police would detain her just for talking to me.

"I came to say goodbye," she said as she sipped a cup of green tea. "If I meet you here, they can easily find and arrest me. They can track me and use video cameras."

I thought Amanda was overreacting—but then I hadn't lost my extended family's life savings. It was also another example of how the government created an atmosphere of uncertainty to extend its grip, instilling paranoia and encouraging people to police themselves. It was time to go, so I walked Amanda to the garage and explained the free taxi concept, so the signs on the hood and doors wouldn't throw her. She walked around the car, reading them.

"Cool," she said in English.

I drove her back to her home and pulled into what seemed to me a private spot. Amanda pointed to a CCTV camera in front of a nearby Communist Party school. I continued down the street and parked beneath some trees. Amanda showed me an investor protest video on her phone and we set another time to meet, though she was reluctant. Then she stepped out of the car and disappeared into her apartment complex.

A WEEK LATER, I drove to our Starbucks at the agreed time and brought along one of my free taxi passengers, a psychologist named

Fifi. In the past couple of months, I'd been driving Fifi to see her patients and thought that, given the pressure Amanda faced, she might benefit from talking to a professional. We waited for thirty minutes, but Amanda never showed. Fifi said that although she had never personally tangled with the authorities—most Chinese hadn't—she could understand Amanda's fear. Sensing the beginning of an interesting conversation, I pulled out my notebook and began jotting down quotes. Then I took out my tape recorder and quietly put it in my lap. Fifi recoiled.

"When you began taking notes, the level of my fear raised a little bit," said Fifi. She was forty-one, had a round, friendly face, and favored clothing in bright colors such as watermelon— which wasn't something you saw often on the streets of Shanghai. "When you took out this tape recorder, it increased again. Whatever I say, I will never have the chance to deny it. This is my voice. That can be used against me and the fear is the fear of the unknown."

The fear of the unknown was powerful in China. On the streets every day, you didn't know whom you could trust and who might try to do you harm. You could never be sure if the food you ate was safe or just how much damage you were doing to your lungs— or the lungs of your children—by breathing the air. Even amid all the new prosperity, being Chinese meant learning to live with uncertainty.

"Has anything bad ever happened to you for anything you've ever said?" I asked Fifi.

"No, not really."

"So, you have no experience of being punished for anything you've said in your life by the authorities?"

Fifi shook her head.

"I think I learned from my environment," said Fifi. "You need to mind your words. You can't say whatever you want. That can be dangerous. People will know this is you."

"But how?" I asked, trying not to sound blasé or flip. "There are nearly 1.4 billion people in China."

Fifi acknowledged that, given her experience and the country's size, the response was not "reasonable," as she put it. It was also radically different from the way she operated in France, where she spent her summers with her husband who lives and works there as an economics professor.

"I'm used to talking about everything in France," Fifi said, "on the Champs-Elysées, Montparnasse, in Biarritz," where her husband's family has a house. "But in Shanghai, it's just different. I have to admit I feel more secure, I feel safer *outside* my country."

"That makes total sense. I censor myself in China," I confessed.

Because the Communist Party had told its people for years that foreign reporters were bent on keeping China down, I made sure most of my posts on WeChat were innocuous so as not to feed the government narrative and spook my Chinese friends, who came from all walks of life and were of varied levels of sophistication. On Facebook, which most Chinese could not access, I posted news stories, including political ones about China's human rights record and skeptical articles about the government's claims to most of the South China Sea. On WeChat, I mostly posted pictures from family vacations in Asia.

"If I posted on WeChat the way I post on Facebook, I'd lose thirty or forty percent of my WeChat friends," I told Fifi.

They wouldn't distance themselves because they necessarily disagreed with the stories I posted, but they might shy away because by Chinese standards the stories were too politically sensitive, and a friendship with a foreign journalist might not seem worth it. Government policies created an atmosphere of fear that made everyone a bit more cautious, suspicious, and protective. They created distance between people and, in the case of Amanda, a calculation that continuing to speak with me entailed too much risk. Which is why she never showed up that day and I never saw her again.

A CERTAIN DEGREE of alienation is woven into the urban experience, but in China there were moments when it defined city life. One rainy day a few years back, Fifi was crossing a road near her home in Shanghai's Pudong district when her knee, which she'd broken five months earlier, gave out and she dropped to the pavement. As she sat in the crosswalk, about five feet from the sidewalk, cars continued to drive past. Fifi feared if she tried to drag herself to safety she might damage her leg even more. A problem solver by nature, Fifi sat on the cold, wet street and dialed an ambulance, then her father. As she sat there waiting for the next twenty-five minutes, Fifi estimated about fifteen vehicles passed by every minute, or several hundred altogether. Not a single vehicle stopped. She said some came within three feet of hitting her. Fifi reckons between fifty and one hundred people passed by as she sat in the road. Some people asked her what had happened and she explained.

"No one very clearly said 'I want to help you' or 'what can I do for you?'" Fifi recalled. "Most of them passed me by, looked at me, and turned their heads away."

But neither did Fifi ask for help, because she didn't trust that another pedestrian would handle her with care. "Even if they are very kind and want to help me, maybe by mistake they will hurt me, because people just don't have this experience. I don't usually see people helping people on the street. They didn't touch me, because maybe they are afraid I will drag them into trouble."

Fifi was referring to an infamous 2006 case in the eastern city of Nanjing, in which a woman in her sixties fell down at a bus stop. The incident was long ago, but it left a lasting impression on many Chinese. A young man offered to take her to the hospital. The woman then claimed he had knocked her down and sued him. A judge in Nanjing ruled that the man should pay about 40 percent of her medical bills, or more than $7,000. The judge figured the man must have knocked her down, otherwise why would he have helped a stranger in the first place? The ruling enraged many Chinese and had a chilling effect on anyone who considered acting as a Good Samaritan. (In fact, two years later, the young man reportedly confessed he had knocked the woman down and paid compensation, confirming the judge's suspicions.) Over the years, other videos surfaced in which people ignored hit-and-run victims on the street, regarding them as they might a dead animal. The most excruciating case came in 2011 in the southern city of Foshan, where surveillance cameras showed a toddler run over by a van and then another vehicle. Over seven minutes, at least eighteen people passed by before anyone tried to help the dying child. Why did people act this way? The answers are complicated, but the behavior is not new. Lu Xun, modern China's most astute social critic, wrote about this phenomenon all the way back in 1933.

"In China, especially in the cities, if someone fainted on the streets, or if someone was knocked over by a car, you'll find lots of gawkers and gloaters, but rarely will you find someone willing to extend a helping hand," he wrote.

In today's China, people are always wary of being scammed, with good reason. Scammers looking for compensation frequently fake road accidents. Dash cams have captured scenery-chewing shakedown attempts, including a bare-chested worker tossing himself against and then under a stationary bus. The most memorable case was a woman who jumped on the hood of a car and repeatedly head butted the windshield so hard she cracked it twice before sliding off the hood. These scams have such a long history in China that they even have a name—*pengci*—literally to "bump porcelain." Some believe the practice dates back to at least the Qing dynasty (1644–1912) when former nobles would stroll in public carrying cheap porcelain. They'd intentionally bump into someone, drop the porcelain, and demand compensation. Chinese attribute the breathtaking car-accident performances to modern greed and low *suzhi*, meaning poor character or inner quality. Not all extortionists fake their injuries. Some legitimately fall on the street but then swiftly search for a scapegoat. Fifi blamed these cases in part on the Chinese medical system, because hospitals demand payment up front from patients.

Yunxiang Yan, a professor of anthropology at UCLA, has studied more than two dozen cases in China in which people tried to extort money from Good Samaritans. He found in most instances the do-gooders were younger professionals, while the extortionists tended to be in their sixties and seventies living on fixed incomes. The extortionists had grown up in the socialist era, when the state paid for medical care, but had grown old in a largely capitalist world, where medical care was costly and many didn't have insurance. Extortionists later explained in media interviews that they had tried to shake down Good Samaritans because they needed someone to pay their hospital bills. But Yan thinks there is a lot more at play here than just the high cost of health care. He attributes the phenomenon to China's yawning income and generation gaps, as well as a clash between an old, rural system of ethics and the reality of a modern megacity, such as Shanghai, filled with people from all over China and around the world.

"How to deal with strangers, how to treat strangers nicely, is one of the biggest challenges in contemporary Chinese society," Yan told me. "The prevailing ethical system in traditional China is based on close-knit community ties, kinship ties. There is a sharp divide between acquaintances and strangers. A number of ethical codes may not apply to interactions with strangers. In other words, taking advantage of a stranger or even hurting a stranger might not be considered as morally wrong because that stranger is not part of the group. Morality is relative. It's also based on social distance."

This was how the cab driver saw me on the road in Charles's village. He didn't know me. I was an outsider, so he had no obligation to treat me with any kindness or respect. Nor did he care if he caused me to roll my van into a rice field because, to him, I was nobody. Many people extended that same logic to crowded cities, where the strangers you bumped into on the streets were actually emotionally very far away. This combination of traditional, community-based ethics and a giant metropolis could lead to behavior that appeared schizophrenic.

"A person might treat some people in the present social group very, very nicely, but turn around when facing a stranger and tend to be very suspicious, hostile, and whenever possible might take advantage of that stranger," Yan said.

Or a person might ignore the stranger as though he didn't exist.

One afternoon, I was driving Fifi to an appointment with one of her clients when we came to a pedestrian crossing where a mother and child were waiting on the sidewalk. On the streets of Shanghai, power is based on size. In all the years I'd lived in China, I had almost never seen a car stop for pedestrians, but being an American I paused at the crosswalk to let them pass. The mother and child stood there staring at me, dumbfounded, not daring to cross. Fifi and I stared back.

"They don't trust that you will stop for them," Fifi said.

It only lasted a few seconds, but our wordless exchange was freighted with meaning. Two different cultures at very different stages of development, two different ways of measuring what we are—and aren't—to one another. Eventually, tentatively, the mother and son stepped into the crosswalk and, never taking their eyes off mine, made their way safely to the other side.

BEER, THE HANDSY used-car salesman, finally found me a 2012 Camry he thought fit my specifications. We took a cab to the dealership, and when we entered Beer started touching me again. He put his hand on my shoulder and then ran it down the back of my bomber jacket. Beer showed me a $29,000 Camry, highlighting the sunroof and the seats.

"Very new," he said.

"This is not leather, though," I said, wincing at the price.

"But it's not cloth," Beer countered.

Naturally, I wanted a test drive. Beer said I would have to put down a 10 percent deposit, which helped keep out the riffraff and ensured the purity of the vehicle.

"Do you want to buy the car that has been tested by other people?" asked Beer, seeming to compare the vehicle to a virgin bride.

"They do that all the time in America," I said. After all, the car had already had at least one owner.

"We want to protect the car. You know, some cars, such as Lamborghini and Porsche and . . ."

"But this isn't a Lamborghini or a Porsche," I protested.

"We know," Beer said, "but we need to protect it."

The car drove well, but I couldn't stomach the price tag and said the words no car salesman ever wants to hear: I'll think about it. Beer launched into his hard sell. He put his hand on my shoulder.

"Hey, mate, don't let me down," he said. "Brother, friend— frankly speaking, I think you are not short of this money."

The sprawling dealership now felt claustrophobic. I rushed out into the fresh air, at least as fresh as air could be in Shanghai. Beer pursued. My assistant, Yang, who had accompanied me on the shopping trip, hailed a cab and Beer asked to ride with us back to the NPR bureau. Foolishly, I agreed. Trying to make conversation, I unwisely asked how sales were.

"Not too good this month," said Beer. "Only two cars. I'm learning slowly, but if I still can't do well, I will be eliminated and have to go home."

It was past lunchtime and none of us had eaten. Beer said he hadn't had breakfast and asked if anyone had food. Yang handed Beer an apple, which he promptly cracked in half with his hands and ate.

"I called my dad last night and told him I am under big pressure," Beer continued, doubling down on his sob story. "After paying rent and food, there is nothing left. Maybe when you're done thinking, I will have been eliminated. Maybe the next time you see me, I will be a homeless person living on the street."

Finally, we arrived at the office and split up. Beer's performance was so shameless, I almost admired it. Then Yang mentioned something I'd missed while we were waiting for the taxi.

"I saw him turn around and shed some tears," Yang said. "He was really disappointed and I felt sorry for him."

Like Beer, Yang is a white-collar migrant living in Shanghai. He appreciates how hard it can be to make your way in this colossal, competitive city. Yang said Beer didn't seem like a bad guy. He just had no tact. Tact or not, I had no intention of buying a car from Beer. Sensing my exhaustion, Yang called a few Toyota dealerships and found me a new Camry with a sunroof and leather seats for just $27,000 including insurance. I returned to the dealership where Beer worked and got my $500 deposit back for the car search. Before I left, I asked the manager how many cars Beer had sold in the past month. Six or seven, his supervisor said—not the two Beer had claimed. Where did Beer rank among salesmen? The manager said neither top nor bottom, but in the middle. And he assured me that Beer was at no risk of losing his job.

CHAPTER 5

"A Virtuous Circle
Needs to Have a Beginning"

Johanna, Max, and Fifi

W HEN I THOUGHT about Beer and his relentless hustle, Fifi sitting on the wet pavement as hundreds of cars sped by, and
the net men scooping dozens of fish from the river, it was
tempting to see aspects of Shanghai—and China more broadly—as
dystopian. If double-digit economic growth rates had resulted in
a society in which people were just out for themselves, what was
the point? And who would want to emulate China? But economic
growth and opportunity had positive effects on people as well. As
more Chinese traveled, they encountered different political and
value systems that sometimes made them see their homeland in a
different light. When these new perspectives collided with more
traditional thought, it could spark revealing conversations about
otherwise taboo topics, such as democracy. I stumbled into just
such a debate the day after Christmas one year while riding in the

front seat of a cab—not mine, but a regular Shanghai taxi. Behind me sat Li, a woman I knew who'd recently been released from a year in prison, which she'd served for scuffling with a cop while protesting her treatment by the government. Li had invited me to attend a hearing to overturn her conviction and we were on our way to lunch. A few blocks into our cab ride, Li began ripping into the government, saying China needed democracy and the rule of law. In my experience, quite a few Shanghai cabbies agree with Li, but not the one behind the wheel today, who immediately leaped to the Communist Party's defense.

"China is already very good," said the cab driver, a working-class Shanghai guy in his forties who sounded like the Chinese equivalent of the brash Ralph Kramden from *The Honeymooners*. "It's been thirty years since we began reforming the economy and opening up the country to the world. How long did it take the West to become prosperous? It took the West fifty to sixty years to get things right."

The driver turned to me, trying to win me over to his way of thinking.

"She's a bit biased," he said dismissively. "Too one-sided."

The driver saw freedom through the lens in which the party had framed it: the freedom to have enough to eat, afford a home, and work as one wishes. And by those reasonable standards, the party has performed very well.

"Take me for example," the cabbie continued. "I drive my own taxicab. If I want to make twelve hundred dollars a month, then I work more hours. If I want to make nine hundred dollars, then I work fewer hours. It's that simple."

He also thought Li didn't appreciate how much better living standards were today, pointing out that in the past he might have had to work for several years to afford a color TV, when a month's salary today would pay for several.

"It's very good!" he said. "Society is progressing."

Many people share the cabbie's pragmatic optimism. The party also benefits from the low expectations it set in the 1950s and

1960s when Mao nearly destroyed the country with the Great Leap Forward and the Cultural Revolution. Since I'd first come to China in 1997, the party had surpassed all economic expectations. Li, though, continued to disagree, as did her attorney, Johanna, who was also sitting in the backseat and had just argued her case ably in court for the past several hours.

"Material goods are much more plentiful," responded Johanna, thirty, who was stylishly dressed in an olive-green jacket with carved wooden buttons and wore a silver cross, a sign of the Christian faith she shared with other human rights lawyers. "But what about the fear in your heart? Do you think you can really plot the course of your own life? Or do you need to listen to the government and wait for it to change its ways?"

Johanna, who had high cheekbones and wore her hair in a bob, was as gutsy as she was unusual, a young, female lawyer fighting human rights cases in a country where the government had been throwing people like her in jail. She was also among an increasing number of people putting their values and beliefs first and helping those far less fortunate. As we continued toward the restaurant that December day, we passed skeletal trees and crossed a canal, providing a momentary glimpse of the soaring towers across the river in Lujiazui, the financial district. The cabbie continued his argument, pointing out that China was much freer than it had been just a few decades ago and that the government was nowhere near as brutal.

"They used to decide when you died, today or tomorrow," he said. "Now, this isn't a problem. You shouldn't think too much."

The driver continued beneath a gigantic elevated highway that blotted out the sky. The surface above was so smooth, it looked as if we were inside the belly of a whale.

"You think we should wait for them to discover more of a conscience and just passively wait for it to happen?" asked Johanna.

"I'm more hopeful," responded the driver. "If you want to make something happen overnight, that's asking too much. Take it slow.

If you feel discomfort in your heart, don't say it out loud. China is like this."

Li had heard enough. She'd spent more than a dozen years petitioning officials for compensation after they'd knocked down her Shanghai home to make way for an apartment building. She was among tens of millions of people who'd lost their homes in China's modernization drive.

"My mother's home and property were snatched by the government!" she said angrily. "We petitioned officials to fight for our rights. In the struggle, we have faced crackdowns, detentions, a jail sentence, and retaliation. We ordinary people only ask for a home and a simple life. Do you think we are asking too much?"

The driver said nothing and a long pause followed—six seconds, which seemed like an eternity.

"Do you think we are asking for too much?" Li repeated.

The cabbie shook his head. He didn't believe Li's story that she'd lost her home, never received compensation, and had been secretly detained and then jailed for complaining about it.

"That can't be true," the driver said. "It's impossible."

"It's probably because you've never come across something like this," Li said.

"Have you?" I asked the cabbie.

No, he said.

"No wonder," said Li, smirking in the backseat.

I asked the driver how he would feel if the government treated him this way.

"It's impossible this would ever happen to me," he answered. "It's impossible in Shanghai."

So it seemed. The government had crafted Shanghai as a glamorous advertisement for its state-capitalist authoritarian model. The riverfront skyline was a futuristic scrim designed to astound everybody from provincial Chinese to foreign investors. But at least hundreds of thousands of homes like Li's had been destroyed to make way for China's Emerald City.

"Demolition by force was banned, wasn't it?" the driver said.

On paper, yes, the driver was correct. There was a law requiring compensation for people whose homes were demolished, but Li had lost her home before it was enacted, so to her it made no difference.

"They claim forced demolition is not allowed, but they are still secretly doing illegal things," Li said. "They come to demolish homes in the middle of the night. Are you aware of these things?"

A year earlier, a fifty-five-year-old Shanghai man named Shen decided to squat in a new home built on the site of his old one, which had been demolished and for which he said he had not received compensation. Police took Shen away and returned him hours later in critical condition with bruises around his neck, according to one of his friends. Shen died soon afterward. Police denied they'd beaten him.

The driver told Li to have faith in the government and assured her it would deliver justice.

"Eventually these people will be punished by law," the driver said. "I am telling you."

"We just finished a court hearing and discovered they are not punished," said Johanna, who'd lost Li's appeal despite gaping holes in the government's case.

Confident minutes earlier, the cabbie now seemed less certain.

"There will be punishment," he said quietly.

When we arrived at the restaurant, I asked the cabbie his name. He'd just given a rousing defense that would have made the Communist Party proud, but he refused. If he was ever connected to this conversation, he feared the government he'd just praised might punish him in some way. Even standing up for the party carried potential risks. The cabbie's defense of the government made sense given his experience, age, and knowledge, which has been carefully restricted by the government. Only a tiny percentage of Shanghai's twenty-four million people have ever felt the full wrath of China's authoritarian government, and the party has worked effectively to keep people largely ignorant about the fate of those who do. The state-run press never reported on the death of Shen or on Li's many detentions. This is one reason why people outside of China tend to have a dimmer view of the party than many Chinese do.

LI HAD DEVOTED her life to demanding compensation from the government. Sometimes she traveled to Beijing in the vain hope of enlisting help from officials there. Police routinely hauled her back to Shanghai where they threw her in a secret detention center, known as a black jail. Human rights activists estimated China had hundreds of black jails housed in converted schools, hotels, and mental-health facilities.

A couple of years before Li went to prison, she took me to see the black jail where authorities had held her half a dozen times. It was a vacation cabin in a sprawling public park along the banks of the Huangpu. We went to visit on a hot summer day and Li carried a parasol, as Chinese women often do, to shade herself as we strolled along wooded paths amid the buzzing insects. After passing through a stand of bamboo, we came to a cluster of quaint little cabins that resembled Hansel and Gretel's cottage. Nestled in a grove of fir trees, they had red tile roofs and wood trim. Some had patios that overlooked a pond. The cottages looked cozy and inviting, except for two things. The windows were covered with heavy glass and thick metal bars. We walked up to one of the cottages where Li had been held and looked in through an open window. Two men sat inside at a desk. I called out, and a skinny man in green camouflage appeared at the door. I asked if anyone else was inside. He claimed there wasn't.

Then, in Mandarin, I asked if this was a black jail. The guard's eyes grew wide, and he retreated inside and shut the door. Li spotted a middle-aged woman in a blue blouse behind another barred window inside the cottage, with yet another guard. I asked the woman why she was being held. She looked stricken and waved me off. She didn't want any more trouble from the guards, who shut the window and closed the blind.

"I know her," Li said, explaining that the woman was a fellow petitioner who had also traveled to Beijing to complain to the central government. Li said the woman had exposed corruption in the company where she had worked.

Concerned the guards might call in reinforcements, Li and I walked swiftly to the nearest park exit and jumped on a bus and then into a taxi that sped down an elevated highway to the center of town. Less than thirty minutes later, we pulled up to a red light at the Garden Bridge, a steel colonial-era bridge that straddles Suzhou Creek and looks out on the skyscrapers of Lujiazui. A tour guide holding a flag led a group of Chinese tourists from the provinces through the crosswalk in front of us. I wondered what they would have thought if I'd told them that less than seven miles away government-hired thugs were holding middle-aged women hostage in vacation cottages in a public park. Would they have believed me?

The protest that landed Li in prison a couple of years later occurred outside a district government building, where she had banged on a stainless-steel bowl to bring attention to her demand for compensation. According to the court record from her trial, a police officer tried to persuade Li to stop banging the bowl and, when she refused, grabbed it from her. Police say Li then tried to get it back and scratched the officer's chest, causing some minor injury. The court found that Li had responded to the cop violently and obstructed government administration, and sent her to prison. In her year behind bars, she'd lost weight and now appeared older and drawn. But she was still undaunted. Even after her release, Li was back in court trying to overturn her conviction and clear her name.

The Shanghai No. 2 Intermediate People's Court is a narrow, gray, concrete building that juts up at least fourteen stories and looks like a Chippendale Highboy designed by Stalin. At the top is a sculptural relief of the scales of justice, an unintended ironic touch in a nation with a 99 percent conviction rate. Inside the tiny courtroom, in front of a jury that spent most of their time focused on their cell phones, Li's lawyer, Johanna, raised doubts about the government's case, which was weak to begin with. She pointed out that the police officer had scuffled the same day with another protester who could've caused his alleged injuries. But the court refused to let the second protester testify. Johanna suggested they look at surveillance footage of the other conflict, but "this evidence disappeared very mysteriously," she noted to the judge.

Then there was the problem of two different medical reports. The first said the officer had suffered some redness and swelling. A second one claimed skin had been torn off, but the photo of the injury did not show the officer's head. When Johanna demanded to have the doctor testify, the court refused.

"I want to remind the prosecutor that eliminating reasonable doubt is your responsibility, not mine," said Johanna, who added that protesting on the street was the only way for someone like Li to express her demands.

"She has no power, no wealth," Johanna said. "The street is her only medium. Whether she did this outside the district government or anywhere in the streets, whether she was hitting a bowl or doing any other things, this was her very last weapon. How will you deal with these people in the future? Just using the criminal law? Putting them in cages?"

This was a good question. Public protests had been growing for many years. One way to handle discontent is through a legitimate legal system, where citizens can sue the government and get a fair hearing. But the party fears that if it allows the courts to operate as a check on political power, as they do in free countries, the government will cede more power to the people and its critics. The rule of law could bring more order and stability to Chinese society, but it is a threat to the Communist Party—as are lawyers like Johanna. "We all hope officials and the people could enjoy a virtuous circle, not continuing in a vicious circle like this," Johanna continued, addressing the court. "But a virtuous circle needs to have a beginning, a just beginning. We hope this trial could be a starting point."

Johanna told me she was confident she was winning the case. As she made her points, the judge frequently nodded. But in the end, as in all political cases in China, the judge did what he was required to do and affirmed the original conviction.

"When he was announcing it, I saw the frustration on his face," Johanna said.

Li was frustrated, too, but she accepted it with characteristic equanimity.

"I feel very sad about the result of today's trial, but it was long expected," said Li as we dropped pieces of pork and cabbage into a bubbling hot pot at the restaurant afterward. "The authority's power is too scary. After all, it's like trying to use an egg to break a rock. We knew the result would be defeat, but you still need to struggle, you can't give up."

JOHANNA'S IMPROBABLE PATH to becoming a human rights lawyer began more than a decade and a half earlier when she was a teenage girl in a small town in north-central China's Henan province. Like most children her age, she grew up revering Deng Xiaoping, whose policies transformed China's economy and set the country on a path to spectacular growth. She was just twelve when Deng died in 1997, an event that left her deeply upset.

"We thought Mr. Deng was like a god," Johanna told me.

Johanna's family ran a store that sold cooking oil and giant bags of flour. Local officials liked to shake down small businesses, and on a couple of occasions they seized some of the family's inventory under false pretenses. Johanna hated them for it. But instead of trying to figure out how to beat officials, she decided to try to become one. Johanna went off to study law at university, thinking it would lead to a government job where she could climb the ranks and protect her family.

And, she added, "be more powerful."

"Powerful to protect yourself or powerful to impose your will?" I asked.

"I think both," said Johanna, providing a glimpse into how many Chinese thought.

In a one-party state with no rule of law, becoming an official provided the opportunity to protect family and friends as well as to exploit others and skim money, just as Charles's uncle had from the village road project. Johanna wanted to become a judge or a prosecutor, so after graduation she took the public service exam, but she failed repeatedly. Her brother, who was studying physics in Munich, suggested she study overseas. Hunting around the Internet, Johanna stumbled upon Sweden's Lund University and a master's program in international human rights law, a concept about which she knew nothing. Johanna had grown up in a collective, hierarchical society that emphasized obedience to parents, elders, and official power. She googled "human rights." The concept was a revelation.

"Wow! Human rights! It sounded so good," Johanna said. "Before I went to Lund, I knew something was wrong [with Chinese society], but I couldn't tell clearly what was wrong or how to change it."

Johanna spent the next two years on campus in Lund, reading, attending classes, and opening her mind. When fellow classmates criticized the Chinese government, she rose to its defense, even though in private she agreed with their arguments.

"I now realize my problem at the time was I could not separate the country from the party," Johanna said. "I thought the party was the country and the country was the party."

Police outside Shanghai TV had conflated the two to try to instill guilt in Amanda and other Zhongjin investors to keep them from talking to foreign reporters like me. To criticize publicly was to make the party and therefore the nation lose face. Under that definition, self-censorship and silence were patriotic acts.

After Johanna returned to China, she focused on workers' rights and collective-bargaining issues, which can be politically sensitive because the government doesn't permit independent unions. That work put her in touch with a small but aggressive community of human rights lawyers who were targeting—among other things—China's notorious reeducation-through-labor camps, where the government could typically put people away for one to three years without trial. At the end of 2013, the government officially abolished the system and said it had released the inmates. However, that wasn't entirely true. After the inmates left, police went out and re-abducted adherents of Falun Gong, a banned spiritual meditation practice that opposed the party. The cops then threw the Falun Gong practitioners in other detention centers. I had even chatted with some of them.

"Actually, they didn't want to let us go," a man named Zhuo told me. He'd served a year in a reeducation-through-labor camp in northeastern China's Heilongjiang province. The day of his scheduled release, government officials picked him up in a car and told him they would take him home. Instead, they took him to a "legal education center"—really an empty office—where he was forced to watch Communist Party videos and pressured to renounce his belief in Falun Gong.

Concerned about this bait and switch, Johanna's colleagues traveled to a legal education center in Heilongjiang and protested the detention of those held inside. As the lawyers prepared a written complaint to the local prosecutor's office, police detained them too. This was classic Chinese police-state thinking. Lawyers try to use the law to protect the rights of people you're holding? Grab the lawyers. That inspired more lawyers to travel to Heilongjiang and sleep outside the detention center in subfreezing weather to protest their colleagues' incarceration. Johanna flew up to lend her support.

Before she went to Heilongjiang, Johanna had never tried to take on the Chinese state, nor had she ever felt the party's fury. In fact, at the time she was a little like the Shanghai cab driver whom she'd later engage in a democracy debate. She wasn't sure if all the bad things she'd heard were true or just exaggerations.

Around 2 a.m. one morning while Johanna was asleep in her hotel room in Heilongjiang, ten armed police broke down her door. They ransacked her room, tossed her clothes onto the floor, and took flash photos of her as she stood in her pajamas. They then bound her wrists behind her back with packing tape, threw a black hood over her head, and hustled her onto a bus to the local police station. As Johanna told me this story, I figured she must have been terrified, but she said she wasn't.

"I was a little bit excited," she said. "I never believed this would happen, but it was happening, so now I knew it was true."

In an opaque society where seeking the truth can be like wandering blindfolded through a maze, epiphany can trump terror. Johanna had begun to see what the party was capable of when threatened, something the taxi driver and most people back in Shanghai had never experienced. At the station, the cops put Johanna in a room with a jail cell, and she slept on a wooden bench with the hood over her head. After sunrise, a pair of cops interrogated her.

Why had she come there?

Who had paid for her trip?

Johanna explained she'd come to support her colleagues and had paid for the plane ticket herself. They pressed her to leave town and promise never to return. She refused. The next morning, she told the cops they had to release her under the law. They told her if she signed a document she could leave with the other protesters they'd detained. After a couple of drafts, Johanna signed a document saying she wouldn't come back. But the police only released Johanna and another lawyer; they held a group of civilian protesters for ten more days. These were classic party divide-and-conquer tactics designed to instill shame and sow discord.

"I felt I was tricked," Johanna told me. "I feel I betrayed my friends. I was so sorry."

Johanna said police beat one of her fellow detainees by punching him in the face through his black hood. They also smacked him on the head with water bottles and slammed his head against a wall, leaving him with a concussion. Altogether, police beat four lawyers until they suffered a collective twenty-four broken bones. The experience changed the way Johanna thought, but instead of intimidating her it angered and inspired her. She took a case defending a church whose steeple had been torn down as part of a campaign to crack down on Christianity in Zhejiang province. Then Johanna took Li's appeal in Shanghai. As conditions worsened for human rights lawyers and government critics, Johanna still saw hope.

"Some say the Chinese have low *suzhi*"—there was that phrase again, meaning "poor character"—"because our natural instinct is to enjoy privilege and we like the feeling of superiority," said Johanna. "This problem does exist, but it's not something rooted in our character that can't be changed."

People like Johanna were fighting for the rule of law. She saw it as the best way to manage conflict in an increasingly complex society filled with people who had rising expectations for their livelihoods, their civil rights, and the performance of their government. The party saw this as a zero-sum game, where ceding genuine rights to the people meant less power and less room to maneuver. Instead of seeing Johanna as a trailblazing civic activist, the party saw people like her as a danger.

DEFENDING THE RIGHTS of the powerless wasn't the only noble pursuit the government didn't seem to appreciate. Teaching genuine politics—as opposed to dogma—wasn't welcome either, as Fifi learned in her first job out of college. I got to know Fifi, the psychologist, as I drove her around Shanghai to sessions with clients. Fifi, like Johanna, was an unusual breed in China: an idealist. She grew up in Shanghai, where her father managed thousands of workers at a factory that made clothing for Nike and other Western brands. Her mother started as a chemist in a water-treatment lab and later worked her way up to a job as an accountant. Fifi said her parents reminded her of China and America. Her dad, she said, was like China: hardworking and trustworthy but also stubborn—rarely showing vulnerability, refusing to say sorry or admit when he was wrong. Fifi's mother, she said, was like America: "cool," an independent thinker, unafraid to stand out—traits she passed on to her daughter. During the Cultural Revolution, when everyone was forced to wear blue-and-green tunics, Fifi's mom stitched colorful pieces of cloth around each button on her jacket, a small ripple of rebellion in a sea of conformity.

Fifi attended Shanghai Normal University—"I'm not normal," she joked—where she studied politics and law. After graduation, she landed a job at a well-regarded high school, where she hoped to transfer what she'd learn to the next generation of Shanghai kids. When she began teaching in 1997, China was still relatively open, and Fifi was able to discuss politics, including sensitive topics such as the 1989 Tiananmen Square democracy movement and massacre. Fifi wanted to teach her students how to think on their own and for them to know the truth about their country's history. But the regime sees critical thinking and the pursuit of historical truth as threats. Over the years, Fifi found that fewer of her students were interested in or even comfortable talking about politics. Some would ask her to shift away from open class discussion and return to the textbook so they could study the specifics they needed to get high scores on their tests and the *gaokao*, China's make-or-break college entrance exam.

"Some students told me, 'Fifi, maybe it's too dangerous to talk like this . . . and we need to pass exams,'" said Fifi, who struck me as something of a modern-day Diogenes, searching for truth and trying to spread it under a system bent on enforcing mass amnesia. As time went on, she was also struck by how little students knew about the bloody events of 1989, when tanks had rolled into the Chinese capital and soldiers had killed hundreds, perhaps thousands, of civilians.

"It's incredible that you can delete history," she said.

Several years into Fifi's teaching career, then Chinese president Jiang Zemin introduced his own sociopolitical theory called the Three Represents. The idea was that the party should represent society's "advanced productive forces," "advanced culture," and the interests of the "overwhelming majority of the people." In laymen's terms, as best I could tell, Jiang meant the party should focus on the people driving China forward: the growing middle class, business owners, and professionals. Fifi thought the whole thing was ridiculous.

"I said my own benefits don't need to be represented by other people," said Fifi. "I want to represent myself. Why did they think the party could represent me?"

Instead of forcing her students to memorize Communist Party gobbledygook, Fifi encouraged them to take a hard look at what the party said and what it did. In her ninth-grade law class, she focused on China's constitution, pointing out that—at least on paper—it protects the right to such things as freedom of association.

"Do you ever see us use this freedom?" she asked the students.

The correct answer is no. If the party allowed people to organize freely, rival parties could quickly form to challenge it. The question could have led to an interesting back-and-forth on theory, practice, and constitutionalism, but Fifi said most of the kids kept asking what they should memorize for the next test.

"I intended to start a discussion, but it's almost impossible," Fifi said in exasperation. "The students are not very comfortable with that. They need to have certainty."

This role reversal—a daring teacher trying to engage pragmatic, risk-averse students—foreshadowed a coming generational shift.

Instead of questioning authority, many in the next generations, which had only known prosperity under the Communist Party, would focus more on enjoying the fruits of economic growth than on critiquing the system that produced it.

"It's like you're in a river," said Fifi. "If you are a piece of wood, you follow where the water flows. It's very easy. But if you are a rock, water constantly flows over you. Of course, it's more tiring. This is how I feel."

Like many independent thinkers in China, Fifi found solace and camaraderie among a small group of friends: four like-minded colleagues at the high school with whom she talked about news, politics, and life. The Gang of Five was like a family. During public holidays, they traveled the country together. When school was in session, they gathered for coffee, pored over copies of *Southern Weekend* (a daring investigative newspaper back then), and debated the issues of the day, sometimes loudly.

"When people walked past, they felt we were very weird," Fifi recalled. Others wondered "why we weren't discussing beautiful clothes and shoes."

Even though no one at the school much believed in Communism, joining the party provided advantages when it came to getting ahead. One teacher in the group decided to apply for party membership, then became disillusioned and changed his mind, which turned into a crisis. Rescinding an application to the party wasn't like canceling a gym membership. By changing his mind, the teacher had humiliated the party and the principal, who was also the school's party chief.

"For them [the party], it's a very serious thing," Fifi explained one afternoon while I drove her to an appointment. "It's something more serious than the commitment to marriage. It's like you proposed to someone and then you regretted it."

The school principal spent three hours trying to talk the teacher into continuing with his application.

"How can you have this thought?" the principal asked, incredulous. Joining the party "is a great, glorious, and good thing."

I was perplexed by this scenario, which to me seemed comic. Why was Fifi's principal compelled to spend three hours trying to persuade an ordinary teacher to follow through and join the Communist Party? After all, at the time the party already had over seventy million members, faced no organized opposition, and had a vast spy network at its fingertips. Why couldn't this small matter be dispatched quietly and privately?

"How can it be private?" Fifi shot back in that familiar how-long-have-you-lived-in-China tone. "As soon as it has something to do with the party, it's not private anymore."

The fact was, the Communist Party was deeply insecure. Although it had designed an economic system that had produced astonishing growth rates and overseen the construction of stunning cities, the party could not risk people knowing all the terrible things it had done during the Great Leap Forward, the Cultural Revolution, and Tiananmen Square, nor did it feel it could withstand a free press. And, it turned out, it was even afraid of being spurned by a pudgy, soft-spoken history teacher.

The dispute was resolved—as many are in China—with a lie. The teacher, ever respectful, said if he joined the party he could no longer be objective about history, which would be a disservice to his students. So, for the sake of the children and his own intellectual independence, he would rescind his application.

"Eventually, he convinced the principal," Fifi recalled, "and the principal said, 'It's good that you think this way.'"

Fifi concluded the story and burst out laughing.

LIVING UNDER THIS system began to become more complicated for Fifi when she met her future husband, Remi, during an academic exchange in Shanghai. Remi was in his forties and teaching economics at a university in Paris. Fifi was in her late twenties. When she first met Remi at the high school where she taught, she was most drawn to his voice and manner. Fifi said he didn't lecture people, as some men do, but was an engaging listener who enjoyed thoughtful exchanges.

Remi says he instantly knew when he first laid eyes on Fifi that she was the one for him. He invited her and her boss to a popular expat restaurant the same day. Remi, who had grown up in France's champagne region, told them he had champagne in his veins and treated them to a glass at an outdoor table. Upon returning to Paris, he asked to come back to Shanghai for Christmas, less than two months later. The pair had spent just a few hours alone and hadn't even kissed. Fifi needed more time. In the meantime, though, they each broke up with their respective boyfriend and girlfriend. Fifi had had many Chinese boyfriends but wasn't especially fond of them. Like her mother, she was fiercely independent, and Fifi said Chinese men often seemed to be looking for someone more vulnerable and pliant.

"Chinese men want to be needed," she told me. "Of course, I need men, but not in that way. I need men to communicate with, understand me, support me, be proud of me, and see the real me. They want me to listen to them, follow their advice, or show that I am so weak I can't live without them."

Remi was different. He was a shy intellectual who read and traveled voraciously and made Fifi feel safe. During his first visit, he and a fellow Frenchman accompanied Fifi on Shanghai's jammed metro, where they stood on either side, instinctively shielding her from the crush.

"For the first time in my life, I felt appreciated and looked after," Fifi said. "I think I'm spoiled by Western men. How can I go back into the arms of a Chinese man?"

Remi returned to Shanghai that spring and met Fifi's parents. The couple proceeded to date long distance for the next three years. Fifi hid the relationship from her friends and colleagues for fear they would think she was just pursuing Remi to get a visa to France, a not uncommon strategy at the time among some women. The couple married in 2006 and continued to visit each other in Shanghai and Paris and meet across the globe. To spend more time with Fifi, Remi came to Shanghai, but it proved a difficult fit. Like many visitors, Remi couldn't stand the air pollution and incivility. When he tried to engage Chinese students, he offended some, crashing up against classroom censorship. Even though most Chinese are keenly aware of the weaknesses of their political system and the problems of Chinese society, they don't like foreigners lecturing them about it, as Johanna, the human rights lawyer, had experienced at school in Sweden. During one classroom address in 2008, Remi criticized Beijing's insipid Olympic slogan, "One World, One Dream."

"China doesn't make people dream," Remi began, taking a jarringly direct approach in a culture where politeness between Chinese and foreigners can be highly ritualized. "Let me tell you why." Remi talked about how people protesting the recent violent crackdown in Tibet had disrupted the Olympic torch relay in Paris, and how it was important for Chinese to know more about what was happening in their country and how those policies were viewed overseas.

"Sir, you can't say something like that," a student said.

At another school, Remi continued to run into opposition, not just to his ideas but also to his right to express them.

"There was a female professor who stood up and was so furious," Fifi recalled. She said, "I cannot understand someone talking to our students like that."

"I'm sorry," Remi said angrily. "You invited me to give a speech. I can't say something I don't believe in. I cannot tell a lie."

This made getting along in China much harder. In the West, speaking truth in a politics class was the point. In China, truth telling could be seen as everything from rude to a systemic threat. Contradictions were everywhere and people knew it, but they let

it slide. For instance, the party continued to claim the mantle of socialism, even though it had used market forces to rescue the country from three decades of its own bad economic policies. Now,
after several decades of staggering economic growth, why make a
fuss over the hypocrisy?

For Fifi, this was a problem. Her school's emphasis on test taking
over analytical thinking wore her down, and eventually she quit and
went into psychology, where she felt she could make a difference.
The atmosphere also had an impact on Remi. His experiences in
China, from the political repression in the classroom to the incivility on the streets, led him to tell Fifi he could never live in Shanghai
as Fifi had hoped, which left them to wonder how they could build
a life together.

BEYOND DEFENDING PEOPLE'S rights or teaching politics, there were
many other less controversial ways to try to make China a kinder,
more civil place. As the economy grew, financial pressures eased for
many, providing more breathing space to think about others and
try to make a difference, even with small gestures. Accustomed to
the rough-and-tumble of Beijing when I had worked there as a
newspaper reporter nearly two decades earlier, I was struck by a
growing compassion I saw in the heart of Shanghai. In my years
in the capital, I rarely saw anyone give money to a beggar. People
were much poorer then, and most beggars worked in gangs, sometimes renting babies for the day to boost revenue. In a significantly
richer Shanghai, many years later, people were still suspicious but
did more to extend themselves. Walking home one evening in the
financial district, I saw a well-dressed professional woman try to
coax a young beggar off the street to buy her a meal. Strolling to
lunch one day on Nanjing West Road, I came across a beggar in ragged clothes, dragging himself along the sidewalk. He was paralyzed
from the waist down and told me he'd lost the use of his gnarled
limbs in a tractor accident. The man recognized a guilt-inducing

juxtaposition and set up his bowl in front of the Maserati dealership at Tomorrow Square, near where I'd first bumped into Amanda. I watched from a distance as one young white-collar worker after another dropped coins into the beggar's plastic bowl. Many were women, and some crouched down to ensure the coins made less noise and drew less attention. A Western couple walked past without stopping, the man putting his hand over the woman's eyes. Within an hour, thanks to his fellow countrymen, the beggar had $5 in donations. A decade and a half earlier in Beijing, the bowl would've sat on the sidewalk mostly empty.

As people's lives were transformed economically, some looked for different ways to give back. Max, a barber from Yunnan province in China's southwest, provided free haircuts to elderly shut-ins. One spring day, I picked up Max at his salon, Maxview, and drove him half an hour west to a decrepit apartment complex called Apricot Plum Garden, a series of grimy, low-rise apartment blocks next to a canal, not far from where Max used to live. Max was a soft-spoken thirty-six-year-old who dressed like a provincial hairstylist in a black jacket, collarless shirt, dark pants, a bright red belt, and black leather shoes with no socks. Carrying scissors, combs, and electric razors in a small yellow duffel, Max entered the complex's common room to the clacking of mah-jongg tiles and applause from some of the elderly residents he looks after.

"Young Hu is a very good person," said Sun, a middle-aged woman who works for the local neighborhood committee, referring to Max by his surname, Hu. "There are very few young people like this doing charity work and he sticks to it. It's really not easy."

Max, Sun, and I made our way up the dusty stairs of an apartment building. From behind a reinforced metal door, we could hear the mournful sounds of a *pipa* (a pear-shaped Chinese lute) and a high-pitched singing voice. Inside sat an eighty-three-year-old woman watching a traditional Chinese musical performance on TV. As we entered, we smelled gas, and Sun moved quickly to turn the stove off. The elderly lady has a son in his fifties who visits once a week to cook for her, but like many old people in the complex she is mostly alone. Max sat her in a chair in the kitchen next to her tiny dining table and went to work on her unruly mop of hair, which looked like cotton candy in a windstorm. She showed her gratitude by flashing a big, toothy grin as Max swept the clippings off the wood laminate floor. The woman's apartment was well taken care of and her double bed neatly made.

"The conditions here are better than a lot of apartments," Max told me, keeping his voice down.

Max's fourth client that afternoon was a ninety-two-year-old woman who had a luxuriant mane of gray hair and eyed me suspiciously from the moment we entered. Sun explained that the last time Max had cut the woman's hair, a TV crew had followed along without fully explaining what they were doing. Later, neighbors told the woman they had seen her on television. Sun said the woman had suffered during the Cultural Revolution, so she was especially cautious with strangers. The woman glowered at me and asked that the tape recorder be turned off.

"Auntie, this is a friend," said Max, trying to allay her fears.

To calm her down, Sun made up a story that Max had told me he gave free haircuts but I didn't believe him, "so they came along today to check it out."

As we prepared to leave, the elderly woman continued to complain about the earlier visit by the TV videographers.

"That was arranged by the TV station, the government, not arranged by me," Max told her. "It was arranged by the neighborhood committee," which Sun oversees.

We left the apartment complex, Sun headed back to her office, and we walked along the edge of the canal, which was carpeted with lily pads, eventually crossing an old arched stone bridge. Max said Sun, who had shadowed us the entire visit, was careful to only show us the nicest apartments and controlled whose hair he cut.

"They don't want outsiders to see old people in the worst conditions," he said.

This would be bad in a Western context, but even worse in a Chinese one, where Confucian values require that children show respect to and look after aging parents.

"Everything in Chinese news is fake, because all you see are the good things," Max continued. "Even if you film negative things, the government will block them."

Last year, Max went to cut a woman's hair and found her alone and unconscious. She was later revived. Max said the woman relied on the kindness of neighbors and a grandson who paid for a part-time caregiver, who cooked her meals and changed her diapers. When Max tried to help some elderly people whose families no longer spend much time on them, he faced resistance.

"They say, 'We don't even care, how come you care?'" Max recalled. "Once, a sister"—Chinese often refer to people as "brother" or "sister"—"from the neighborhood committee told me: 'Don't buy stuff like quilts in the future, because their children would get mad.'"

Max's final client of the day was his most intriguing. His name was Sun—no relation to the neighborhood committeewoman—and he was retired from a state-owned textile factory. We climbed six stories to Sun's apartment and he invited us in for tea.

"I told him your son is in the US," said Max, trying to make conversation.

"What does your son do in America?" I asked.

"He is probably in the White House," Sun replied.

"In the White House? What does he do specifically?"

"I don't know the details. Probably teaching is his primary focus."

"Inside the White House?" I repeated.

"Probably. We don't ask him about specific things. Because . . . basically, they can hear what we say. America is pretty impressive. There is surveillance. They know every move in our family."

"How do you know they monitor you?" I asked.

"We can hear it! When we are talking on the phone, we know there is a device. The tone and frequency change. They all know what we've said. They all know."

I knew what Sun was saying could not possibly be true. The White House didn't hire teachers from China, and American intelligence didn't monitor retired factory workers in Shanghai. But I couldn't yet tell if Sun was putting me on or if he genuinely believed this.

"Did anyone tell you they knew the content of your phone conversations?" I asked.

"If we have a conversation at noon, they will know in the afternoon. *Ta Kung Pao* [a Hong Kong newspaper] reports right away."

Why would Hong Kong media report private phone conversations?

"Who knows?" said Sun, his voice going quiet. "We discuss nothing!" he continued, raising his voice again. "Actually, I'd protested several times about human rights and freedom."

Max wrapped his barber's cape around Sun's neck and began trimming his hair. Sun was living a paranoid fantasy, but he relayed it in such a matter-of-fact tone it was almost convincing. Sun said his son had been overseas for six years, and on his rare trips back he stayed at the Xijiao State Guest Hotel, a grand five-star hotel where President Obama, the Queen of England, and Mao and Deng had all stayed. Sun said China's leaders were all very proud of his son's accomplishments.

"Hu Jintao"—China's former president—"sent me a message saying: 'You cultivated talent for the country.'"

Max finished cutting Sun's hair and we thanked him for his time and began to trudge back down the six flights of stairs.

"You think it's real?" Max asked when we arrived at the first landing.

"What do you think?"

"I think it's not very real," Max said. "He's pitiful."

"Why do you think he says these things?"

"In his heart, he hopes his son or his life could turn into what he now describes. He is living in his own illusion. He's been acting like this for two to three years. The son hasn't been home for many years. He probably misses the child very much."

We were now back out on the street, walking down the sidewalk lined with London plane trees, which resemble American sycamores.

"When did his son leave?"

"I've never met his son since I've known him."

"Do you know if he really has a son?"

"Even his friends have never met the son. He probably has a son and he is probably in a foreign country."

Max anticipated my next question.

"Why do I keep coming to see him?" Max said. "He needs people's care. He needs people to treat him like family. He needs someone to talk to, even if what he says is fake."

LIKE RAY, ROCKY, and Charles, Max came from a simple background. He began life in a poor village and came to Shanghai to make something of himself. While Christian faith helped account for the kindness and generosity of some people I knew—such as Chen, the pajama salesman—Max was not religious. He had developed a sense of altruism through his travels.

Max grew up in the 1980s in a village of about thirty families in Yunnan province in China's far southwest. Unlike the vast majority of the population, he's not ethnic Han Chinese, but Hani, one of China's fifty-five ethnic minorities, by definition an outsider. The Hani have a collectivist tradition, and families help each other build homes and harvest crops. Max spent his early years in a mud-brick hut with a grass roof. The family grew corn, rice, and sugarcane, and Max lived a farm boy's life: swimming in rice fields where he became covered in mud, chasing grasshoppers and

frying the ones he caught. He walked to school forty-five minutes each morning before dawn holding a flashlight or a wooden
torch. The nearest movie was at least a twenty-minute walk down
a mountain road to another village. There was no theater, just an
outdoor basketball court with a projector and a six-by-twelve-foot
screen, with one end tied to a backboard and the other tied to
a house. The first time Max glimpsed an image of Shanghai was
watching *Shanghai Tan,* or *The Bund,* starring Hong Kong heavy
Chow Yun-fat as a student protester in the 1920s who leaves prison
and remakes himself as a Shanghai gangster. The film and its spectacular colonial-era setting made a deep impression on young
Max, who was stunned by the size of Shanghai.

"I thought to myself, I want to see this city," Max recalled.
"I couldn't believe it really existed."

Max said when he was younger, he got into fights, skipped class,
and was asked to leave by five schools. He finally dropped out after
his freshman year of high school. Max's older brother staked him
to a barbecue restaurant, which went bust after Max allowed too
many friends to eat and drink for free. Max's village lies north of
the Golden Triangle, where the borders of Thailand, Myanmar, and
Laos converge. It's one of the world's biggest opium-producing
regions.

"Drugs were so widespread," recalled Max, whose friends included addicts. "When you went to public toilets, people were
injecting drugs with needles everywhere. Among those who grew
up with me, five died of drug overdoses."

Max's brother worried he would turn to drug dealing, so he
ordered Max to leave the county and earn a living. On the day
Max left, his mother gave him $60.

"You need to learn to eat bitter," she said. "You need to be
grateful."

Eat bitter not only means to bear hardships—in Max's case, it also
meant to grow up. Max, then nineteen, made his way to Chengdu,
the capital of southwestern China's Sichuan province, where he

earned money cleaning tables and dishes in a restaurant. In southern China's Guangdong province, he worked in a factory that attached magnetic snaps to leather bags, but the factory ran into financial trouble and the boss ran off, leaving Max out three months' salary. Max lived in a park for a week, sleeping on a wooden bench and washing his face and brushing his teeth in a public bathroom.

Wandering China in search of work can be tough, as Charles had found the day he worked as an ox in Xinjiang. But during his journey, Max was also struck by the kindness of strangers. He walked around to barbecue stands, collecting empty beer bottles and selling them for about a penny each for recycling. One day, a Thai man silently handed him a box with a dozen beer bottles, some unopened, put his palms together, and bowed toward Max. Later, when Max was sleeping outdoors in the southern metropolis of Guangzhou, a man named Li invited him into his apartment, fed him, and let him use his shower. Before Max left, "Brother Li," as Max called him, gave him a 50-yuan note—worth about $6. It was enough money to feed Max for days.

"It blew my mind," Max said.

At the time, there was a lot of robbery and theft in Guangzhou, and Max couldn't fathom why a stranger would help him, asking nothing in return. Max found a job soon after, and when he returned to Li's apartment to repay him, the man had moved on—as migrants often do—and had changed his phone number. Max never spent the money. Years later, Max keeps the bill hidden away in a safe place in Shanghai.

Having seen the city on screen as a child, Max finally made it to Shanghai one day in 2008 and headed straight for the Bund. He climbed the stairs to the riverside promenade. Behind him stood the city's colonial past, including the granite facade of the old Peace Hotel, its pyramidal roof glowing green beneath the floodlights. As he reached the top of the stairs, the full scale of the glass-and-steel towers of Lujiazui came into view. Max stared across the water at the winking lights of the Oriental Pearl Tower, which looks like a rocket ship from a Buck Rogers comic book. He spent the evening watching freighters plow up and down the river as the Pearl Tower's two big spheres—the upper one home to a revolving restaurant, the lower one housing an indoor roller coaster—changed color from red to blue to green. The city was infinitely more modern than the one he'd seen projected on the screen that hung from the basketball backboard all those years ago. Thinking he might only be in Shanghai a few months, Max spent the night on the promenade, occasionally dozing on a wooden bench and using his backpack as a pillow. Many others slept along the Bund that night as well, and Max assumed they simply had nowhere else to go. In fact, they were waiting for dawn and, when it came, they rose to photograph the Pearl as the rising sun flashed off the nearby skyscrapers. Max had finally made it to the city he'd dreamed of since childhood.

"I felt a sense of achievement," he told me.

Using the money he'd saved, Max enrolled in a top school for hairstylists, eventually opening his first salon a few years ago, where he built up a clientele of about 160 paying members. Max posted photos on WeChat of his charity work cutting the hair of the elderly. One day on the phone, his mother, who cannot read or speak Mandarin, asked, "Is it true that you don't have enough business so that's why you provide these free services?"

In fact, Max provides free haircuts in part as penance for leaving his parents behind in the countryside and being what he sees as a most unfilial son. Like Charles, he had to leave his parents behind to make something of himself in the big city. While Max was away, his father died. He felt terrible about not being there and became a vegetarian to atone for his sins. He said when he cuts the hair of the elderly, "I am thinking about my parents. After I finish, I feel better, there is less guilt in my heart."

Max is the flip side of Beer, and the net men along the banks of the Huangpu, and the scores of people who walked past Fifi as she sat on the wet pavement nursing her injured knee. He's not scrambling after the next sale or the next fish. He's using his budding success to pay forward the kindness of the strangers who looked after him when he was down and out in southern China.

"I wasn't able to say thank you in person" to Brother Li for the six dollars, Max said. "Because of his actions, I'm doing this charity work, things that allow me to give back to society. Although I don't have lots of money to help people, at least I can cut hair, right?"

CHAPTER 6

A Woman Missing in the Mountains
Crystal and Winnie

═══════════════

I N THE SUMMER of 2015, after I'd been driving the free taxi for more than a year, I received a cryptic note on LinkedIn. "There's a story you might be interested in and I need your help," a Chinese American woman named Crystal wrote from her home in Michigan. Blind queries rarely led anywhere, but I wrote back anyway. An email followed. Crystal had grown up outside of the city of Harbin in northeastern China and now worked in information technology in central Michigan. She was returning to China in the fall for her little brother's wedding but was planning to first fly to Yunnan province in the southwest to hunt for her little sister, Winnie, who'd vanished two years earlier in the mountains near the Lao border. Winnie had married a farmer, who she said had beaten her. She had fled their home and then disappeared.

At the time of Winnie's disappearance, Crystal had just started a new job, so she paid for her father and brother-in-law to fly down to Yunnan to look for her sister, but their investigation had led nowhere. In the past year, Crystal had finally saved up enough money to travel back to China in hopes of jump-starting the search.

Why had this woman reached out? She was an NPR listener. She'd heard my free-taxi stories and was especially interested in my road trip with Rocky and Charles. If I could drive people home for Chinese New Year, perhaps I could accompany her into some of the dicier parts of China's borderlands on a missing person case.

"By reading and listening to your reports," Crystal wrote, "I know you can help me."

About two months later, I met Crystal at a small airport in Jinghong, a city in Yunnan province. She was a slim, no-nonsense forty-four-year-old who arrived in jeans, a blue polo shirt, and sneakers. The next morning, we drove to see a lawyer for advice on the law surrounding missing persons and how to approach the police. The attorney explained that although the police were legally obligated to search for people who'd disappeared they rarely made much effort. Too many people went missing in China, and the cops didn't have the resources. Crystal, who'd been living in the United States for six years and had an especially favorable impression of American law enforcement, was appalled.

"Don't you understand?" said the lawyer, shaking his head and laughing. "This is China. We're not in America."

This became one theme of our journey: how different the country of Crystal's birth was from her adopted country. Jinghong wasn't just different from the United States, it was also very different from Shanghai. Instead of skyscrapers, there were palm trees. Instead of hundreds of thousands of cars, there was an endless stream of motorbikes that washed around my rented SUV as I guided it through the city's chaotic roundabouts. After lunch, we headed southeast, crossing the muddy Mekong river toward a remote farming area where Winnie had lived with her husband. Soon, we came to a military checkpoint manned by armed soldiers in camouflage, helmets, and body armor. At the time, military checkpoints were rare in most of China. A soldier asked for my driver's license and where we were heading. I wondered what he was looking for.

"Maybe drugs," Crystal said.

Of course. This was the same province where Max had grown up, just north of the Golden Triangle, a hub for opium and human trafficking. We continued deeper into the mountains, following the snaking path of a river below. Crystal filled me in on her family's history. She'd grown up in the 1970s and 1980s on a farm. Crystal was the eldest. Winnie was eight years younger, the fourth of five children. The seven-member family spent nearly a decade and a half in a one-bedroom mud-brick house with a dirt floor and a grass roof. The family slept on a sheet made of corn husks on top of a *kang,* a combination bed and stove that is heated from below by burning wood or coal briquettes and is common in northeastern China. Beginning at age eight, Crystal helped plant seeds and harvest corn, potatoes, tomatoes, and cucumbers. The family relied on government rations, which weren't enough to feed all five children.

"There was no money," Crystal said simply. "We grew up hungry."

Without enough food to eat, Crystal's mother couldn't produce milk for Winnie. The infant suffered from calcium deficiency, which Crystal thinks affected her little sister's intelligence.

"She was kind of slow," Crystal recalled. "She studied so hard, even harder than anyone else in the family, but she never got good scores."

Had the sisters been born a decade or two earlier, they would have probably stayed in the countryside and lived similar, circumscribed lives under Communism. But Deng Xiaoping's economic reforms created something new: the opportunity to succeed and the chance to fail. Like Rocky and Ray and other bright migrants, Crystal moved to the city, in this case Harbin, the provincial capital, where she studied and became a nurse. Disappointed with her grades, Winnie left school at sixteen and headed to Harbin as well, where she worked as a waitress and then fell into the default profession for many uneducated migrant women: sex work.

"It's really sad," Crystal said. "It's just for survival."

During the Communist era, Mao had all but eradicated prostitution, but after the economy began to open up, it returned with a vengeance. Tens of millions of men moved to the coastal cities on their own to work, creating tremendous demand. Poorly educated women left the farm for the city as well, providing supply. With government restrictions on religion and no rule of law, there were few moral or legal curbs to prevent the rapid spread of sex work. When Winnie moved to Harbin in the 1990s, prostitution was already booming there. In fact, the sex industry had become so big that Harbin had started taxing women who worked as *san pei xiaojie,* or literally "three-accompany girls." These young women served as paid escorts in bars and karaoke parlors, where they accompanied men to drink, sing, and dance. Some also engaged in prostitution and charged much more for the fourth accompaniment: sex.

I first traveled to Harbin in 1998—around the time Winnie was working there—to do a story on taxing these female escorts. One Sunday evening, I visited a nightclub in town. The madam took me to a back room where about twenty young women in tight dresses and high heels sat playing cards and mah-jongg. As I entered, some of the women giggled nervously and glanced shyly at the floor. I scanned the room, looking for someone who might make for an engaging interview. A woman with bright red lipstick and platform shoes tried to hide her cigarette by cupping it in her palm, a clumsy attempt to appear demure. I chose her and we walked back into the main room of the nightclub. She slid into a booth next to me, put her hand on my knee, and began tossing her hair and smiling.

Her name was Zhang and she was from a small city in the countryside, where she owned a flower shop. Over a glass of warm milk, amid the strains of Simon and Garfunkel's "Scarborough Fair,"

Zhang explained how the business worked. Escorts who accompanied men to sing, drink, and dance made tips ranging from $12 to $30, but could earn up to $180 for sex—which, in the late 1990s in provincial China, was a lot of money. Zhang insisted she was not a prostitute but said half the women at the club where she had last worked were. She said she brought in $850 a month. Like other women in this line of work with whom I've chatted, Zhang said she planned to quit by the end of the year, return home, and open a clothing store. In those days, there was a popular saying, "Laugh at poverty, but not at prostitution," because women could make so much money compared to their friends who remained back home in rural towns or worked on factory floors on the coast.

Prostitution exists to varying degrees in most countries, but in China, it seemed to be almost everywhere. When I first arrived in Beijing in 1997, prostitutes would congregate most nights just outside a McDonald's along the city's main boulevard. In Shanghai, a high-end brothel with an atrium fountain and pool tables opened outside our apartment compound next to the school-bus stop.

Some saw the Chinese Dream as unconnected to morality and considered illicit sex part of the package. Mistresses and prostitutes often saw it as a stepping-stone. Many men viewed it as a trapping of success. The major disincentive for men not to seek paid sex was not moral or legal but the remote risk of public shame. The risks for the women, of course, were much greater. During her time in Harbin, Winnie had paid a price.

"A couple of times she called me when I was abroad and she had been beaten," Crystal recalled as we continued south through the mountains in Yunnan. "Her nose was broken."

Another time Winnie called to say she'd escaped from her pimp, but that he was still holding her ID card and she didn't know what to do.

"I just told her, 'run far away, run home, come home,'" Crystal recalled.

But Winnie never did. Instead she moved to the northeastern port city of Dalian, where she climbed the next rung of the career ladder and became the mistress of a businessman. Keeping a mistress is common among well-to-do businessmen and government officials in China. In 2013, a People's University study found that nearly all corrupt officials had adulterous affairs and 60 percent kept a mistress. Working as an *ernai* (pronounced "are-nigh")—or literally a "second wife"—is widely seen as an occupation and includes a contract. Second wives can expect an apartment and a monthly allowance, depending on the tier of the city where they live and their perceived market value. Chinese cities are ranked in tiers based on GDP, population, and government administrative level. Megacities such as Shanghai, Beijing, and Guangzhou are first-tier cities, while Dalian is in the second tier. Among second wives, country girls who've previously worked as prostitutes occupy the lower rungs of what's been dubbed the mistress–industrial complex.

As the late 2000s rolled around, Winnie turned thirty. Her skin was not yet creased, but her youth was beginning to fade and she often looked tired. She took her savings and moved far away to the other end of the country, where she could enjoy anonymity and her money would go a lot further. She bought six small apartments and became a landlord in Jinghong. It was not uncommon for mistresses to become businesswomen. One of the most celebrated examples was Li Wei, a French Vietnamese woman who came to Yunnan as a refugee in the late 1970s. Li worked as a tobacco broker and married a provincial tobacco official. With that connection, she built a network of contacts and parlayed a series of romantic relationships with high officials and businessmen across China into a billion-dollar empire. Known as the "common mistress of high officials," Li had holdings in tobacco, real estate, and advertising and owned more than 180 gas stations in Beijing. She was jailed for tax evasion but reportedly kept much of her fortune and moved to Hong Kong.

"Looking back at her path, the ups and downs of the refugee billionaire has been an example of the 'Chinese Dream,'" wrote the Chinese business magazine *Caijing*. The government responded by pulling the offending issue from the newsstands.

In the fall of 2013, out of the blue, Winnie made a move that seemed to fly in the face of her ambitions. She announced to her family that she'd married a rubber farmer named Luo and moved into his tiny house in a remote village. In the beginning, she said her husband treated her like a queen.

"He would wash my feet and feed me meals and he handed me all the money he made every day," she told Crystal in a series of messages at the time on WeChat, China's most popular social media platform. "I managed all the money. If there was only one bite of food left, he would give it to me."

But Winnie kept her secrets. She didn't tell Luo about the apartments she owned. When she tried to make trips to the city to check on her real estate, he naturally became suspicious.

"He always said I went to Jinghong to look for other men," Winnie told Crystal. "The more he thought about it, the angrier he got. A couple of days ago, he smashed my phone."

Winnie told Crystal that Luo had beaten her twice.

"The second time, I told him that if you beat me again, I would either run away or die," Winnie texted Crystal at the time. "But it happened yet again and I told him, 'Don't beat me! My injuries haven't healed.'"

Crystal tried to advise her little sister.

"Does he know what you did before and is that the reason he watches you so closely?" asked Crystal, referring to Winnie's past. "If that's the case, he'll never trust you. You'd better find a good place and go into hiding to start a new life."

As the sisters traded messages, Winnie grew more distraught. She was now thirty-four. Her dream of finding a lasting relationship and building a new, independent life was slipping away.

"I myself feel empty, always feel empty," Winnie said as she wept. "I simply want to find a man who dearly loves me. Why is it so difficult?"

She said she wanted a divorce but feared facing her husband again. A lawyer had told her that if she disappeared for two years, her husband could then sue her for divorce without her having to appear in court. At times, Crystal could not hide her frustration. Why had Winnie not sought advice from other family members before marrying this man?

"How much bitterness have you eaten?" she said. "You still haven't had enough?

Crystal said that once her life was more settled in Michigan, she would invite Winnie to visit. Winnie boarded a bus and rode ten hours to a small city and checked into a hotel. She wrote Crystal that she was going out to eat and would try to make some friends.

"You take care and let's stay in touch," Crystal said.

"ok," Winnie texted back.

A few days later Winnie checked out of the hotel and vanished.

CRYSTAL AND I continued through the mountains of Yunnan province, shadowing the river as it curved around small towns and then opened out into a broad, flat valley lined with fields where people planted by hand and tilled the soil with hoes. We entered a long, dark tunnel. There were no lights and for a stretch it was pitch-black, like driving inside a cave with no end in sight. As we emerged into the light, Crystal recalled other parts of conversations with Winnie after she had left her husband.

"Occasionally, she said she didn't want to be alive anymore and she's so lonely, she feels like her life is meaningless."

"Is there any possibility she tried to kill herself?" I asked.

"I don't think so," Crystal said, "because she has us and she sounded optimistic when I last talked to her."

It was unsettling that in all the time Winnie had been missing, she'd never reached out to let family members know she was OK. I noted that we'd passed through a military checkpoint and were driving through one of the more dangerous parts of the country.

"Is there any possibility she was trafficked?"

"I don't know," Crystal said. "I did warn her that you need to be careful. I would think even if somebody wanted to traffic her, they'd have to drug her or use some kind of violence, she wouldn't just go with a stranger."

There was one cause for hope. Earlier in the year, a possible sign of life had emerged. Local police had received an alert that Winnie's government-issued ID number had been used at a bank in Dalian, the city in northeastern China where she'd previously lived. The cops thought she was following the lawyer's advice and had gone into hiding for two years. If that was the case, perhaps she would emerge in a couple of months.

"We haven't seen her body," Crystal said. "So I'm thinking she's alive, somewhere."

The next morning, we drove to the local police station to meet the cop who'd been handling the missing person case. In nearly two years, he hadn't accomplished even the most basic tasks, such as getting permission from WeChat to access Winnie's account, which would have revealed with whom she'd last texted or spoken in the days before she vanished. Crystal was frustrated with the officer, but also dependent on him, as he was the only person with the power to get the banking records in Dalian to see who had used Winnie's ID card. Giving gifts, especially to officials you need something from, is a long tradition in China, so Crystal presented the policeman with cosmetics for his wife. Instead of thanking her, the cop backed away from the gift as though it were a snake. Then he rushed over to the window and threw the curtains closed. This seemed a strange response, but then it dawned on me. President Xi was deep into the toughest anti-corruption campaign in Communist Party history, and a cop in a remote corner of the country was afraid of taking even the smallest gift. Since the officer wasn't going to do much to help find Winnie, we pressed him for the name of her husband's village, which he finally gave up. He warned us not to go off investigating ourselves—which, of course, we did.

ABOUT A HALF-HOUR drive out of the city near the border between China and Laos, we came to the turnoff for the village and headed up a one-lane road that was so rutted I thought the rocks below would rip out the gas tank and tailpipe. Gray clouds clung to the green hilltops as we drove along a lush valley carpeted with banana trees and dotted with wooden shacks topped with corrugated aluminum roofs. Along the way, we passed fishponds, farmers weighed down with wicker baskets, and men on motorbikes.

We came to a fork in the road. We were now so deep in the valley that even the GPS was hopelessly lost. To the right stood a flimsy bridge that looked like it would collapse beneath the weight of our SUV, so I turned left. Police had cautioned us about approaching Luo. He'd recently been released from jail for stealing a motorbike and, although we didn't know it at the time, police believed he dealt drugs.

We came across a man walking along the road who wore black shorts, flip-flops, and a black T-shirt with random letters embroidered on the shoulders. We asked for directions to Luo's house and he told us to continue up the road, deeper into the valley. After a half mile or so, we stopped another passerby who told us to turn back, giving us more precise directions that took us to a cluster of one-story cinder-block homes with gray, clay-tile roofs. We met the man in the black T-shirt again who, upon further questioning, admitted he was in fact Luo. He offered us tiny wooden stools, which are common in the countryside, and we crouched down to chat at the threshold of his home. Next to Luo's house stood an open shed that housed his yellow motorcycle, which he used to drive to work in the middle of the night to tap rubber trees. Attached to the shed was a chicken pen made of black nets held down by rocks to keep the chickens from escaping. Luo explained that he first met Winnie one night on WeChat.

"She was drunk and crying in her apartment," he told us. "She'd broken up with her boyfriend. I said, 'It's not worth it. There are many men out there. You can find another.' Then she asked me to see her the next day."

After just ten days, the couple decided to marry. Luo's parents opposed the snap decision and Luo was uneasy, too. But Chinese rubber tappers who live in the middle of nowhere have few prospects, so Luo went ahead. Early on, Luo said, Winnie treated him well.

"But after our marriage, she turned into a different person," he said. "I didn't know what she was thinking. She was very irritable. One night I was out harvesting rubber. She went to a bank to wire money to someone. I asked her who she was sending the money to. She refused to say."

Luo said they argued and she slapped and screamed at him. Eventually, he admitted that he had slapped her once but insisted he didn't beat her in the way she had described to Crystal. Crystal, who had agonized over her text exchanges with Winnie, thought Luo was lying. Glowering, she confronted him.

"Do you know what happened exactly?" she asked angrily. "Where did she go? Or did you kill her?"

After Winnie accused Luo of killing her sister, I expected him to run us off. Instead, he kept talking.

"If I'd killed her, I wouldn't still be here," he said, genuinely taken aback by Crystal's prosecutorial tone. "She really ran away. You guys should not think that I sold her to someone or killed her. I've never done things like that."

Then, revealingly, Luo had questions for us. He said he actually knew very little about his wife and her past. Winnie had told him she had no friends, didn't tell him where she lived in Jinghong, and wouldn't let him see her ID card. She told him she was a real estate agent and she often traveled to Jinghong to meet renters. Nearly two years later, he still didn't know she was a landlord. Luo told us more. He said the day they picked up their marriage license, the clerk asked Winnie to produce a divorce certificate. Luo was stunned.

"Before we got our marriage license, she had just divorced a guy a month earlier," said Luo, incredulous. "When we were dating, she didn't tell me that."

Luo went inside the house and returned with a small booklet that belonged to another man. It was a border pass to travel to four northern provinces in Laos, which Luo said Winnie had left behind. At the time, at least sixteen thousand acres in northern Laos were under poppy cultivation, according to a United Nations survey. I was intrigued by the border pass, but Luo had more questions about his missing wife.

"I want to ask you guys: How many years has she been in Jinghong?" asked Luo. "She never really told me what she's doing. When I asked her, she said, 'Why do you want to ask about these things?'"

"Where do you think she is now?" I asked.

"I don't know. I am guessing she hasn't gone too far away. She is probably hiding in Jinghong."

It was beginning to get dark.

"Since you've come here, why don't you stay here for the night," Luo offered. "Although my family is poor, it's OK."

"Thank you," Crystal said. "We have a lot of things to work on. We are very desperate to find her."

We said goodbye to Luo, walked back to the SUV, and began to make our way out of the valley. I pulled over on what passed for a shoulder to let a tractor rumble by. My wheels came up to the edge of a drop-off, but unlike during my trip to Charles's village, all four tires remained on the road. I was learning.

"I am so tired," said Crystal. "This is so complicated."

"Do you think he killed your sister?" I asked.

"Not really," she said. "I was just trying to get a reaction out of him."

"We talked to him for about an hour and a half, and he kept talking even after we stopped asking questions," I said. "Generally, people who have committed a terrible crime, they want to get rid of you and they sure don't want to talk." Then I asked, "Was he what you expected?"

"No," Crystal said. "I thought he would be a bully, a violent person."

The more we learned, the more questions we had. Why would Winnie marry a rubber farmer who lived in the middle of nowhere?

"I don't know," Crystal said with a sigh as we bounced down the rutted road. "My God, little sister, what did you leave behind?"

We returned to town and went straight to the clerk's office to ask for Winnie's marriage records. Sure enough, she'd married another man and divorced him a month later. Records showed that in a period of six months she had married and left two men. The unions had no obvious financial advantage, as neither man appeared to be wealthy. We tracked the first husband to an address at the local traffic bureau, but no one there had ever heard of him.

Our next lead took us three hours back across the mountains to Jinghong, where Winnie had a friend named Cao. We met him at a local restaurant and the first thing that struck me was just how different he was from Luo, a poor country boy in his twenties. Cao, a businessman who worked in biofuel, was in his midthirties, tall, confident, and gregarious, with the chiseled features of a movie star. He said he met Winnie at an outdoor market one evening in early 2013 and they'd struck up a friendship that mostly involved chatting and taking walks together. He said she'd come to Yunnan as a tourist and liked it so much she decided to move here. She read motivational and self-help books and was good at making investments, but was often depressed, he recalled.

"She gave out a feeling of loneliness," said Cao, who had a wife and son several provinces away near Shanghai. "She was clearly unhappy."

He said he knew nothing of her marriages, but sensed she was looking to settle down and start a family. As we talked over a two-hour lunch, Cao was friendly and charming, often flashing a magnetic smile. But listening back over the tape, we found he'd actually provided very little information. He said he last saw Winnie when he helped her move apartments. She gave him a key. I asked Cao if he could show us the apartment, but he repeatedly said he couldn't remember where it was. Cao said he didn't know what had happened to her but reminded us that this part of Yunnan was dangerous and infested with drugs. He said he'd met a girl in a club here years earlier who'd asked him to sell drugs for her in China's interior, which he said he had declined. He also told us not to trust the cops. Cao said people busted for drugs here generally paid them off with a standard bribe of about $80,000, which could buy two apartments in town.

I picked up the check. On the way out of the restaurant, Cao treated us to some ice cream cones. It was a nice touch.

Running out of leads, I drove Crystal to the airport, where she had booked a flight to Dalian. She was anxious to speak to police there and find out who had used her sister's ID number at the bank.

"I really hope it was her," Crystal said as she prepared to go through security, "so we are just a step away from finding her."

The trip was a disaster. When Crystal went to the local bank, officials there said Winnie had no account. She called police back in Yunnan, who made inquiries and then apologized. They said when the bank was reorganizing accounts, there had been a computer glitch that mistakenly spit out Winnie's ID number, triggering an alert to police in Yunnan.

"No! Please double-check!" Crystal demanded, weeping. "You need to make your best effort. Find my sister, dead or alive."

But there was nothing to be done.

"How could they make a mistake like this?" sobbed Crystal, angry and dumbfounded. "We've accomplished so much in just four days. The police have had almost two years."

She had arrived in China a week earlier, believing her sister was alive. Now, she feared the worst.

"I don't think anything good happened to her," Crystal said, choking back tears, as we spoke over WeChat. "She's a tough survivor. She would think of a way to contact somebody from my family or the police. I think maybe she was killed by somebody."

But who? And why?

CHAPTER 7

Disillusioned with the New China

Chen, Sarah, Charles, and Ashley

═══════════════════════

ONE MORNING IN July, I drove to my bank, the cavernous China Merchants Bank headquarters that sat at the bend in the Huangpu river, where the city's financial district juts out into the water like the prow of a ship. As a silver rain poured down in sheets, I sensed an opportunity. My free cab was a decent draw in dry weather and even harder to resist in a downpour, when all the regular cabs were full. I pulled my car under a glass walkway to shield it from the rain and slapped my magnetic signs on the hood and doors. A young Chinese woman in a pink skirt and white blouse walked out of the bank and asked for a lift back to work. Her card said she was the business development manager at the headquarters of Ferrari Maserati Shanghai. She was in her early thirties and exuded the image of the worldly, modern, professional Shanghainese woman. As I looped around Lujiazui Park, which is ringed by skyscrapers representing China's biggest financial institutions, she told me she had a degree in fashion retail from the University of Manchester. After a few minutes, barely enough time for a conversation, I pulled up to the Ferrari showroom. She thanked me, then darted inside.

When I first came to China in the 1997, there weren't many people like her—and even fewer luxury cars like the ones she sold. In fact, back then, most of my friends didn't even own cars, and Maserati only arrived years later in 2004. Today, luxury cars seemed to be everywhere, especially in the financial district where I lived. One morning, I walked through the parking garage of my apartment complex with a notebook and counted six Rolls-Royces, six Maseratis, five Porsches, four Bentleys, four Ferraris, two orange Lamborghinis, and a McLaren supercar, which sold for more than $600,000. I didn't even count the BMWs—the brand was known as *Baoma*, or "treasure horse," in Mandarin—because in the current context they seemed pedestrian.

That evening, I headed out in my humble Camry to a dinner. Earlier in the week, I'd received a text from Chen, the Christian pajama salesman who'd sent his family to America. Addressing me as Brother Liang, my Chinese surname, he'd invited me to a get-together at his apartment on the other side of the river and seemed deliberately vague about the details. I drove up the long entrance ramp onto the Nanpu Bridge and then beneath the huge, white, concrete arches emblazoned with red calligraphy by Deng Xiaoping, whose economic reforms kick-started the boom that eventually transformed Shanghai's skyline. It was still raining, and fog poured off the brightly lit tops of the city's skyscrapers as if they were sparklers. Just upstream stood the Power Station of Art, a former power plant turned contemporary art museum. Towering over the museum was a smokestack nearly as tall as the Washington Monument, with white and red lights running up and down, forming a huge thermometer that was visible for miles. Once across the bridge, I banked into a disorienting corkscrew that spun me through two revolutions before dumping me onto the surface streets. Two more turns and I was headed down a dark, narrow street, feeling as if I'd entered a different city. The houses and shops to the left were practically abandoned, slated for demolition to make way for high-end apartment towers and office buildings. To the right stood Chen's dingy brown high-rise. When I entered his apartment building, I heard singing filtering down the hallway from behind a door with a metal security gate. Chen greeted me with a smile and ushered me into his living room, which turned out to be the headquarters of an underground Christian church he ran. About twenty men and women sat on folding chairs lining the walls, singing the hymn "Lord, I Would Follow Thee":

> *Savior, may I learn to love thee,*
> *Walk the path that thou hast shown,*
> *Pause to help and lift another,*
> *Finding strength beyond my own.*

Chen's living room was spare. There was a refrigerator, a wall calendar, and a naked lightbulb hanging from the ceiling. With his family already relocated to Los Angeles, he was living the stripped-down life of someone plotting his next move. The parishioners sang in Chinese for what seemed like twenty minutes, repeating the verses over and over again. Then the preacher, a member of the congregation whom parishioners called Master Li, stood up and gave his sermon. It was blunt, clear, and relevant. Today, he said, we live in an age of empty materialism. Only through Christ can we find meaning in our lives. I pulled my iPad out of my backpack and began to look up religious words to keep up. Master Li, who had a round face, a receding hairline, and a wisp of a goatee, decided to incorporate my technology into his teachings.

"When you have something, you always want something more," he said. "Maybe you want an iPad, but later, you'll want a Ferrari, but you'll never be satisfied, unless you love Jesus and follow Jesus."

In the 1980s Deng Xiaoping was credited with saying, "To get rich is glorious," seeming to turn Communist ideology on its head. There is no solid evidence Deng actually said those words, but they were repeated over and over and captured China's pivot toward capitalism. Now, nearly three decades later, Master Li had a very different message: "To get rich is not enough." It was a variation of the message Ray, the Shanghai lawyer I'd met on my Chinese New Year road trip, had delivered after his brother Rocky's wedding. China's success should not be measured in just skyscrapers and GDP, but also in the way people treat one another.

Afterward, the church members in Chen's apartment filled two tables with dishes, including sweet braised pork belly, a tangy orange squirrelfish, mushroom soup, and bitter green melon. We were less than a four-mile drive from the Ferrari showroom where I'd stopped earlier in the day, but we might as well have been on another planet. When the two-storey Ferrari dealership had opened several years earlier, the press release had crowed: "Perfectly situated in the Lujiazui Financial District, the showroom faces the acclaimed 'Oriental Champs Elysées'—Century Avenue. With a neat and modern all-glass facade, the showroom vividly displays the complete Prancing Horse range ... visible to every passing pedestrian and automobile on Century Avenue. The showroom in Pudong will enhance our outstanding network and offer Ferraristi a unique experience and superior services."

At tonight's service there wasn't a Ferraristi in sight, just modestly dressed, working-class and middle-class migrants who had built a secret community of faith in this run-down apartment two blocks from the river. Unlike so much else in Shanghai these days, the service was refreshingly egalitarian. One by one, parishioners stood up, told personal stories, and then connected them to their own interpretation of scripture.

"Here, everybody always discusses the Bible," Chen told me. "If there are things we don't understand, people can improvise to express their views. There is no distinction between you and me, whether you are rich or poor, where you are from, city or country-side. Everybody speaks the same language."

In an increasingly stratified society—where the wealthy were constantly seeking bigger status symbols to set themselves apart—this apartment was a haven where everyone could preach and express their thoughts, regardless of their station. Chen's church not only promoted faith and community, it was also a rejection of the materialism that had enveloped urban China over the past two decades.

Chen was raised a Buddhist but converted to Christianity under the influence of his wife, Gong. Her path to the faith began with her grandfather, who had a Bible he hid in his home. When she was sick, he would take it out and put it next to her head.

"This is a heavenly book that can cure all your diseases," he told her.

Back then Christianity was stigmatized in Gong's village. For instance, Christians who lost parents were barred from engaging in open ancestor worship. That included sweeping their tombs as well as burning incense and "ghost money" to benefit their loved ones in the afterlife. Gong told me a tomb without ashes was a sign of a lack of filial piety and a big loss of face. Christians were so ostracized, Gong said, "you couldn't even find a husband." This reminded me of the political persecution that Guo, Rocky's mother, faced when she tried to start a family. The Communist Party is leery of anything that people might view as a higher power, especially a foreign religion, so it regulates organized faith and oversees a system of state-sanctioned churches. Chen had visited some and found them too big and impersonal, with congregations that seemed less informed and less engaged.

At government churches, "many people don't get a chance to talk," Chen observed. "You don't talk. Only people up on the altar talk."

That wasn't a critique just of the state church, but of the Chinese state itself and officials' distance from those they ruled. Chen estimated there were about six hundred house churches in Shanghai—though no one really knows. All are by definition illegal because they aren't registered or overseen by the government. Chen said Shanghai officials had tightly controlled house churches a few years back but had become more tolerant recently as long as gatherings didn't exceed fifteen people, which this one did.

"Sometimes when there is a big gathering, people from the government may come to ask you questions," said Chen, adding that it had become obvious that police listened to some of his phone calls. "They have files on us. Nowadays, we may inform them in advance if there is a gathering. It seems letting them know is better."

Tolerance for underground and even state-sanctioned churches has varied from place to place over the decades. Chen grew up around the city of Wenzhou, the heartland of Chinese Christianity, often called the Jerusalem of China. Beginning in 2014, officials there cracked down on government-sanctioned churches, sawing the crosses off steeples or burning them off with blowtorches. Over two years, they would decapitate at least 1,200 churches in surrounding Zhejiang province, a sign of things to come.

The government also bans Chinese from attending foreign-run churches. One Christmas season, a man from the religious affairs bureau came to the international church my family attended in Shanghai's Pudong district to videotape the Christmas pageant. The videographer set up his tripod about ten feet from the altar and shot the children as they sang and recounted the story of the birth of Christ. My son, Christopher, then nine, was a reluctant shepherd, his head wrapped in a blue-checked scarf. As the audience focused on the children, the videographer revealed his true intent. He quietly pivoted and panned the audience, zooming in on the Chinese-looking faces in the crowd.

The Communist Party is particularly concerned about Christianity because of its power to move people and potential to drive political change. The party sees the lead-up to the collapse of the Soviet Union as a cautionary tale. When Pope John Paul II, a virulent anti-Communist, returned to his native Poland in 1979, millions turned out to greet him, leaving leaders in Moscow stunned. The following year, Poles formed the independent trade union Solidarity, which drew inspiration from the pope. Solidarity was the first big anti-Communist political movement and eventually negotiated with the Polish government to establish elections. Christianity has also played a role in reform movements inside China. Many Chinese human rights attorneys, including Johanna, are believers, and a number of the leaders behind the 2014 Hong Kong democracy protests were educated in Christian missionary schools.

China's government is also uneasy with Christianity because it brings people together under the auspices of an alternative value system. That's what it did for Chen and me. Chinese rarely invite strangers—let alone foreign reporters—into their homes for meals, but the fact that I drove a free cab and attended a Shanghai church persuaded Chen to make an exception.

"People have a simple saying: 'Don't trust strangers,'" said Chen. "Seeing fellow believers like you feels very intimate. We are like family members. If there are more Christians in one country, the country will become more peaceful."

Chen also repeated something that other passengers had mentioned. Because I was a foreigner, particularly an American, he trusted me more than he would've one of his own countrymen. (This, of course, ran completely counter to the message the Chinese government was trying to send in its propaganda campaigns.) Chen said, from his perspective, Americans were more straightforward than the average Chinese.

"I think the values taught to you Americans since an early age are among the reasons I trusted you," said Chen, for whom the party's official line didn't resonate.

After dinner, I shook the hands of each member of the congregation and thanked them for having me. Chen and a couple of curious fellow parishioners walked me across the street to my car.

"Where are the advertisements?" one asked, referring to the magnetic free taxi signs.

I explained the free taxi was off duty the rest of the evening and I'd put them in the trunk. I wasn't familiar with Chen's neighborhood and had no idea how to find my way back onto the Nanpu Bridge. The men jumped in the car and guided me to the entrance. I thanked them and began the long, circular climb onto the bridge, crossed the river, and then returned to my apartment complex with its garage full of luxury cars. Back in my apartment on the twenty-ninth floor, I stared out through the mist across the river at the towering smokestack with the glowing red-and-white thermometer. Downstream from the bridge, about a mile across the water, I could just make out the lights in Chen's building.

CHEN WAS DISILLUSIONED with China and looking forward to moving to America. He didn't like the authorities spying on his little house church and he didn't like the distrust that sometimes seemed to ooze from the Shanghai streets. But the biggest reason he wanted to go to America was to give his family a freer life and his children a more open, less oppressive education.

Chen was in good company. Many Chinese millionaires—by definition the winners in China's transition to capitalism—were also looking abroad and hedging their bets. At least as far back as 2011, half of the country's millionaires said they were thinking about emigrating or were already in the process of doing so, according to a survey by Bank of China and Hurun Report, a Shanghai-based firm that researches wealth. Many were worried about air pollution and wanted to stash assets overseas as an insurance policy against slowing economic growth, government seizure, or political instability. At the time, many were lining up for what are called

EB-5 investor visas. In exchange for a minimum investment of $500,000 in a US-based project, an applicant could be fast-tracked to a green card in just three years. One Sunday afternoon, I went to a pitch session at a Shanghai hotel for investment in a convention center project near Chicago's O'Hare airport. That's where I met Oliver, who did market research for Western companies in China.

"Everybody worries," said Oliver, who was attending the session on behalf of his brother, a businessman who wanted to move to the United States. "If you have money, you worry. Tomorrow, these assets are going down."

Many businessmen were beholden to local party officials for access to land and permits. Behind many fortunes was an unsavory relationship with the government, which could boomerang if President Xi continued with the anti-corruption campaign that was bringing down officials across the country.

"You get rich working with the government," Oliver said over evening coffees at a Shanghai Starbucks. "But if they don't keep their word, you have nothing." And if things turn sour, "you may lose everything. That probably is the most dangerous situation."

Many well-to-do Chinese already had foreign passports, even some who'd built their public profiles criticizing America and praising the Communist Party. Chen certainly didn't have the money for an investor visa, but he had been determined to get his daughter out of Shanghai and its school system, where teachers hit her and the homework load had caused her eyesight to deteriorate. He had also wanted a second child, which was banned at the time under the country's one-child population policy. Over lunch one afternoon, Chen told me how his family had snuck into the United States. In 2013, Chen had accompanied his family to Hawaii on tourist visas, having been advised that it was the easiest port of entry. Gong, his wife, was more than five months pregnant and showing. They were worried about being turned back, but the immigration officer simply asked why they were visiting. Chen lied and said "tourism," and the officer stamped their passports.

"How did I get through?" Gong remembered thinking. She couldn't believe how easy it had been to enter and was excited to hit the beaches in Hawaii.

"This is America!" she had thought excitedly. "I was like people from the countryside who come to Shanghai for the first time."

The family flew on to Los Angeles, where Gong moved into a house that cared for Chinese immigrants who had come to the United States to have children. Four months later, she gave birth to Yingying. Chen returned home to Shanghai and continued to earn money to support the family.

About a year after I first visited Chen's house church, he called one evening, saying he needed help applying to emigrate to the United States. The next day, he arrived at my office with a sheaf of documents. It wasn't uncommon for Chinese to reach out to foreigners for help with visas and navigating the dizzying bureaucratic process. Chen was terrified of being rejected. The US government wanted proof that his marriage to Gong was his first and only. My assistant, Yang, called the US consulate in Beijing, only to be hung up on. Then I called. My American accent seemed to do the trick, and Chen was able to sort out what the consulate needed. As Chen chatted in Mandarin with the visa officer, I looked over his papers sitting on my desk. They said he was applying for a green card as a relative of someone who had been granted asylum.

Asylum? Really? I thought. *For what?*

I asked Chen. He said his wife had won asylum after telling immigration officers she feared that if she tried to have a second child in China, she'd be forced to have an abortion. In all our conversations, Chen had never mentioned this. He had told me his greatest fear was being hit with a fine of up to $30,000, the equivalent of nearly two years' salary.

Millions of Chinese women had endured forced abortions. A famous lawyer named Chen Guangcheng, who was blind and self-taught, had investigated an area in coastal China's Shandong province and estimated there had been 130,000 forced abortions and sterilizations in 2005 alone. Many years later I spoke with a father in northwestern China's Shaanxi province, who decided with his wife to have a second child to make the couple's aging parents happy. The local family-planning officials demanded more than $6,000 in fines and abducted his pregnant wife. After holding her captive for three days, a family-planning official called the father.

"I told you a long time ago that you should have got the money ready and you didn't do it," the official said.

An hour later, the man's wife called to say she'd been given an injection that had induced labor and the couple's seven-month-old fetus had been stillborn. A relative posted a photograph on Weibo of the mother and the dead fetus lying next to her hospital bed. People were outraged over a policy that was already widely hated and—some demographers would argue—unnecessary.

But that was Shaanxi province, corrupt Chinese coal country, not cosmopolitan Shanghai. Chen lived in the heart of China's financial capital, just upstream from the Bund. I had trouble imagining officials here dragging Chen's wife out of her apartment, strapping her to a gurney, and killing her unborn child. I also knew asylum fraud was common. When covering a government church-demolition campaign back in 2000 on China's southeastern coast, I learned that Christians there routinely coached each other to tell US immigration officers they were fleeing China because of religious persecution, when in fact they were just going for better-paying jobs.

After Chen left my office, I felt guilty about helping him. I was also disappointed. I understood why he was desperate to leave China but had hoped he wouldn't lie about something so serious just to get out. Years later in Los Angeles, Chen and his wife would tell me the whole story.

THAT DAY THAT began with a passenger with a British MBA who worked at a Ferrari dealership and ended in the apartment of a working-class salesman who hosted an underground church illustrated one of the biggest changes I'd seen since I'd returned to China after nearly a decade away. The income gap that had divided people in the 1990s had now become a chasm in what the Chinese government still claimed was a socialist country. When I'd first arrived in Beijing, most people's incomes were rising, but they were still relatively poor by American or European standards. My friends tended to live in drab government-owned apartments and they either biked or took the subway to work. The government's continued shift from socialism to capitalism transformed the economy and people's expectations. In the late 1990s, the government began selling off state-owned apartments to government workers at steep discounts to break the "iron rice bowl." The iron rice bowl provided cradle-to-grave benefits to employees who earned pitiful salaries but received schooling, housing, and health care essentially for free. The system was very generous to workers but destined to bankrupt the country. The massive sell-off of real estate—perhaps the greatest transfer of wealth from a government to its people in modern history—was a huge boost for government employees who worked in cities. Even before we left Beijing, our friends were moving from state-owned apartments to modern duplexes and were fast becoming landlords—the very class Mao had targeted for persecution and even killing in the late 1940s and early 1950s. As China's economy continued to boom in the 2000s, income inequality grew and Shanghai came to resemble its nearest equivalent city in America, New York.

Hunting for passengers in the financial district, I occasionally drove past the lobbies of five-star hotels, which had been empty lots when I'd first traveled from Beijing to Shanghai in the late nineties. On the fifty-eighth floor of one hotel was a bar with outdoor terraced seating and a spectacular view of the city's seemingly endless skyline. Soon after we moved to Shanghai in 2011, my wife, Julie, visited and asked to sit outside, only to be told she would have to pay a table charge of about $500—nearly a month's wages in the city for many workers—before ordering from the drink menu, which included a champagne cocktail for $31.

"I could buy two electric scooters for that price," Julie said. Before leaving, Julie took in the view. Past the Bund, in the gaps between the skyscrapers, she could see a carpet of red-tiled roofs, thousands of apartments without plumbing or heating where people kept warm with space heaters and duvets in winter when temperatures fell to near freezing. Nearly 20 percent of Shanghai—a population larger than the city of Los Angeles—lived in what's called "extreme housing poverty," with just eight square meters of living space per person. One cold December day, I bumped into a woman who was living under these conditions. Her name was Sarah, and she'd stopped to admire the signs on my free taxi and take photos. Sarah had graduated from a university in Nanchang, more than eight hundred miles southwest of Shanghai, and was slogging through a dull, entry-level job selling radio-frequency identification chips to foreign companies for use in credit, subway, and door-key cards. She was living with her father and mother, who had also migrated to the city. As it so happened, her mother worked as a maid at the same hotel with the $500 outdoor table charge. Like millions of migrants who come here, Sarah was both excited and daunted by the city. She posted a picture on WeChat of a building overlooking the river with a giant, illuminated "I Love Shanghai" sign.

"Magic metropolis, unique friends, unforgettable stories," she wrote beneath the picture. "Love it. Embrace it, treasure it."

But for most migrants, embracing Shanghai was far easier said than done. As outsiders, they'd missed out on the vast real estate transfer of the late 1990s, and finding a foothold in the city was difficult for most. Rents had skyrocketed, often forcing several migrant families to cram into a single apartment that had been subdivided. Sarah lived in a windowless room a bit larger than a prison cell with just enough space for a bed, a particle-board table, and a chair. Several families occupied the apartment, sharing a two-burner stove that was often covered with burnt noodles and a layer of yellow grease. The toilet in the lone bathroom was missing the seat, as well as the lid to the water tank. Sarah was desperate to move out, so one Sunday I drove over the bridge to help her look for a new place. She was shy and wore owlish glasses, a white blouse, and a wrinkled navy skirt. Her real estate agents, two guys in their twenties, pulled up to a street corner on a black motor scooter and we followed them to a twenty-five-story apartment block. We took the elevator up to a five-bedroom apartment, which was only marginally less depressing than her current circumstances. The room for rent had a bed, a bureau with all the drawers missing, and a two-foot-wide windowsill.

"Maybe I can grill out there," Sarah said hopefully.

The apartment had one bathroom and no kitchen. The asking price for the room Sarah was interested in was $245 a month.

One of the realtors said the price in Shanghai's neighboring Xuhui district had jumped from about a $1,000 per square meter to more than $9,000 in the past decade. Sarah dreamed of owning her own home in Shanghai one day, but, she said, "in China, twenty percent of the people own eighty percent of the wealth."

Sarah was close. A 2015 report by Peking University found 1 percent of China's households owned one third of the country's wealth, while the bottom quarter had just 1 percent of the wealth. Sarah eventually found a new place to live. One winter morning I helped her pack out of her apartment. She didn't own much, just some boxes of books, some quilts, and clothing. I drove her in the free taxi to her new room, which was high up in an apartment block with a nice view of the city. Sarah, though, was still struggling to figure out what she wanted to do with her life, uncertain if she'd ever be able to find her place in what she called "the magic metropolis."

SHANGHAI AND ITS mythology appealed to migrants such as Sarah. But Charles, whom I'd driven home for Chinese New Year and whose wedding I'd attended, saw the city completely differently. He viewed Shanghai as a means to an end and a symbol of the growing divide in China, which he resented. One Sunday in April, I drove Charles to a long-distance bus station so he could head back home to Hubei for his sister's wedding. Charles's wife had given birth to a son, so I asked a question that ordinarily would elicit excitement in a new father.

"What is your plan for your child?"

Charles paused and sighed.

"That's the one thing that gives me nightmares and insomnia," he said. "What will we do with this baby? Who will take care of it? It's not convenient to take care of it in Shanghai."

As a migrant worker, Charles was subject to a system of soft apartheid, a two-tiered form of citizenship that divided people in China based on their place of birth. Because Charles had been born outside of Shanghai, he and his family could not fully access the same public health and education benefits as local Shanghainese, and his son would have to return to Hubei province for the college entrance exam. Officials figured if they allowed people to enjoy full benefits wherever they moved in China, cities such as Beijing and Shanghai, which were already jammed, would collapse under the weight of migration. So, with no prospect of long-term public benefits, Charles's pregnant wife moved home in 2015—leaving Charles here alone. Charles had grown up in a family similarly fractured by China's household registration system but wasn't sure how to avoid repeating the mistakes of the past. When Charles was young, his father was gone most of the year cutting hair. His return visits filled young Charles with anxiety.

"We knew he was our father and we know what a 'father' means, but he was just like a stranger," recalled Charles, who had become the de facto man of the house, helping his mother plant and harvest rice beginning when he was five or six. Charles's description of his uneasiness around his father during his rare visits home reminded me of little Honghong, who ran from her dad when I accompanied him back to his village for Chinese New Year in 1998.

Charles wanted to live with his growing family, but the need to make money and his migrant status made that difficult. At the same time, he didn't want his son to grow up in Shanghai. Charles feared the boy would become what he called an "edge" person, a migrant kid who lives in a megacity where he's never accepted, but who also never feels comfortable back home in the countryside because he doesn't speak the local dialect. In other words, he feared his son would become a child of nowhere.

"Where do you feel you belong?" I asked.

"I belong . . ." Charles trailed off for a few seconds. "I'm a lonely man in a big city. I think my heart is in my *laojia*," he continued, referring to his ancestral village. "Here is just an ATM, an automatic teller machine. I don't like Shanghai at all."

For many migrant workers, living in Shanghai meant feeling as though you were always on the outside looking in. It could also be exhausting and undignified. Like Sarah, Charles lived in typically poor migrant circumstances: a lone room in a four-story walk-up where he slept on a mattress and box spring on the concrete floor. Next to the bed sat a black roll bag, a reminder that his stay here was always temporary, and a telltale empty milk bottle.

"Embarrassment moment," Charles said as I eyed the bottle on a visit one afternoon.

Charles shared the bathroom with two other families and sometimes had to wait thirty minutes to pee, hence the container within arm's reach.

"It's not exactly the Chinese Dream, is it?" I said, instantly regretting saying something I had not intended to sound mean. "But there are a lot of people who are struggling in the United States as well," I added, "even though it's the richest country in the world."

Both the Chinese Dream and the American Dream were leaving people behind. When I spoke with people in Shanghai, I was struck by how similar the conversations were to the ones I'd had in America just a few years earlier in the lead-up to and during the global financial crisis. People complained about how hard it was to afford property, especially in big, desirable cities; the intense competition to find good jobs; and the high cost and difficulty of accessing quality health care. Remove the language barrier, and many working-class Chinese and Americans could finish each other's sentences. Of course, there were big differences. For one, the United States had lost several million jobs to China, but some of those have now moved on to lower-wage countries or are being performed by robots.

With little money to spend on entertainment, Charles spent much of his free time on self-improvement. Stacked on a shoebox near his bed sat an English-language biography of Charles de Gaulle and another on Franklin Roosevelt. Charles rose each morning and spent an hour before work sitting on a broken chair at a worn, wooden desk, where he dipped a brush into a bowl of black ink and practiced writing Chinese characters on rice paper. I had never studied calligraphy, but Charles's characters appeared graceful and elegant.

He'd calligraphed a Tang dynasty (618–907) poem called "The Swordsman" and taped it to the wall over his bed.

> *I have been honing this sword for a decade;*
> *Its frosty edge has never been tested.*
> *Now I am holding it and showing it to you, sir:*
> *Is there anyone suffering injustice?*

"The sword is myself," Charles explained one evening. "I want to achieve something, make some contribution."

I was struck that the speaker in the poem seemed to be a lone figure devoted to righting wrongs. The poem would prove prophetic.

Charles's striving also reminded me of one of the final scenes in *The Great Gatsby*. Gatsby's father arrives for Jay's funeral on

Long Island and discovers his son's handwritten schedule for self-improvement, which included these notations:

Study electricity, etc. ....7.15–8.15 A.M.
Practice elocution, poise and how to attain it.......5.00–6.00 P.M.
No wasting time at Shafters.
Read one improving book or magazine per week.
Be better to parents.

WHEN I RETURNED to China in 2011, the state of Internet freedom was mixed. The government had blocked most major foreign social media platforms, but China's most popular one for news, Weibo, was still surprisingly wide-open. Weibo was like a dam break of gripping stories about public corruption, injustice, and social unrest that provided endless easy leads for foreign reporters. For instance, that forced-abortion story in Shaanxi province first emerged on Weibo.

Weibo had even become a platform for ridiculing the Communist Party. One of China's most notorious political cartoonists, a man who went by the pen name Rebel Pepper, routinely posted his cartoons on the platform. One of his best cartoons mocked a propaganda campaign extolling the virtues of Lei Feng, a model People's Liberation Army soldier who was devoted to his fellow workers and the party—and who had been dead for half a century. The campaign included a ninety-minute, televised, Broadway-style extravaganza, with a chorus of marching construction workers, flight attendants, and police officers belting out lyrics such as "Study Lei Feng, good role model. / Loyal to the Revolution, loyal to the Party." Rebel responded with a cartoon inspired by *Finding Nemo*, in which a giant angler fish with menacing teeth dangles a glowing picture of Lei Feng before a school of smaller fish who stare adoringly at the light, unaware the angler fish is about to eat them.

"The government still uses this sham image of Lei Feng to confuse gullible people," Rebel told me.

As I pondered the remarkable political openness online, I began to wonder: What kind of an authoritarian regime was this?

Xi Jinping seemed to be wondering the same thing and concluded that all this freedom was undermining the party. Soon after he took control in 2012, the government began cracking down on Weibo, deleting the microblog accounts of rabble-rousers like Rebel Pepper, who, fearing detention, fled to Japan and later to the United States. Xi's crackdown made it much harder to know what was going on throughout China at any given moment, which frustrated Charles in his next job.

Months after we drove Charles home for Chinese New Year, Yang spotted a job posting for a news assistant with a Dutch newspaper in Shanghai. He knew Charles was looking for more money and something more stimulating than working as a salesman, so he suggested Charles apply. I provided a reference and Charles landed the job, which he saw as a big opportunity. Charles had a long commute, so on several occasions I drove him back and forth to his workplace in the city's former French Concession. One of Charles's responsibilities was finding interesting stories in the Chinese press. But by this time—Xi had been in power for four years—the space for satire and muckraking had shriveled. Over dinner near his home one night, Charles complained about how boring and useless Weibo had become. Between bites of greasy pork balls and spicy chicken with peanuts, he opened his phone and scanned the platform for interesting news. He came upon a story that described how police had detained two girls in the southern city of Shenzhen for twenty-four hours because they weren't carrying their government-issued ID cards, which isn't required. The story, which was about basic legal rights, didn't rank among the top stories. Instead, the hottest trending post at that moment was a famous actor consoling his wife for losing out on a film award.

"I don't really look at Weibo anymore," Charles said. "Now, it's just entertainment."

Nearly a year into the job, Charles seemed to be becoming disillusioned with foreign journalism as well. He complained that his boss didn't talk to him much and that foreign correspondents sometimes got facts wrong.

"They are not that good, generally, but I read their things," he said dismissively.

As Xi's government continued to tighten the screws on free expression, Charles told me he had even censored his own diary entries, frightened that government agents might one day find them, which I told him was highly unlikely. Recently, he said he'd decided to be more candid between the pages.

"Keeping something in my mind is a heavier burden," he said.

I was curious: What had Charles been bottling up that he now could no longer suppress?

"I can't talk to you about this," Charles said, shaking his head. "Three years from now we can talk, because I think this is very serious."

"Are your thoughts too sensitive?" I asked.

"No, it has to do with work," he said.

And that is where we left it.

F. SCOTT FITZGERALD created Jay Gatsby as a symbol of America's Gilded Age in the 1920s. Nearly a century later, he embodies the drive and excess of China in a similar era, one defined by ambition, wealth, and an absence of values. Like Charles, Gatsby was a hustler, the son of a poor farmer from the provinces who came to the big city to reinvent himself in a time of profound opportunity and inequality. Like Winnie, his road to reinvention involved moral compromise and great risk.

In a case of impeccable timing, a remake of *The Great Gatsby* starring Leonardo DiCaprio hit Chinese screens in 2013. A Shanghai publishing house also issued a new bilingual translation of the novel and organized a screening of an earlier version of the film, starring

Robert Redford, at a Shanghai art museum. This was at least a year before I started driving my free taxi, so I caught a cab to the screening. Afterward, I chatted with audience members and asked if they saw similarities between America in the Roaring Twenties and China now. Lily, a recent grad in economics from a US university, focused on one scene in which Tom, a wealthy businessman, gets into a fight at a party with his working-class mistress, who wants him to leave his wife, Daisy. The mistress shouts Daisy's name over and over until Tom smacks her in the face, bloodying her nose.

"Tom, he's rich, he can do whatever he wants and buy whatever he wants," said Lily, who recognized Tom's reckless indulgence in many wealthy Chinese men. "When they get very, very rich, they may have several wives and they don't care about their families and don't care about how their children grow up."

China's boom had fueled the mistress-industrial complex that provided opportunities for women like Winnie. For many rich men, a mistress was a possession to flaunt. I saw it in my own apartment complex, which had a reputation as a place where wealthy men set up their mistresses. Now and then, a chauffeur drove the son of an auto-dealer magnate to the front door of my building in a Rolls-Royce—sometimes it was a black one, other times a white one—to visit his mistress and their young child. The doormen, with whom I often shared information, had looked up the vehicles on the Internet and said each cost more than $1 million. The chauffeur could've taken the scion into our underground garage and parked his Rolls with all the others, but then no one would've seen it, which would've defeated the purpose.

"Many people are becoming more and more materialistic today," Lily continued, as people filed out of the Gatsby screening. "Many people are trying to realize their American dreams, to buy some really good cars or live in a luxury house, but sometimes people in the end find they are like Daisy and Tom and they lose their humanity, and they just care about money, and they find their lives are empty."

Those words sounded just like Winnie's when she realized her dreams of a secure, steady life were slipping away. "I myself feel empty, always feel empty," she'd told her sister Crystal after trying to put her life as a mistress behind her in the days before she disappeared.

I wanted to hear more about what Chinese thought of *The Great Gatsby*, so we put out a request on Weibo looking for other people who'd read the book. We received a reply from Ashley, a graduate of Peking University, the Harvard of China, who'd read *Gatsby* twice. Ashley lived in Beijing, where she worked as a management consultant. She said among the scenes that struck her were Gatsby's parties at his mansion in West Egg: "By midnight the hilarity had increased," Fitzgerald wrote. "A celebrated tenor had sung in Italian, and a notorious contralto had sung in jazz, and between the numbers people were doing 'stunts' all over the garden, while happy, vacuous bursts of laughter rose toward the summer sky."

Gatsby's party reminded Ashley of a far more extravagant one at a yacht show on the island of Hainan. Partygoers posted photos of Ferraris, Maseratis, and half-naked women on multimillion-dollar yachts. One photo showed men and women in their underwear amid balled-up sheets and sofa cushions. Netizens, as citizen Internet users are known in China, claimed one of the models pictured at the party had earned over $90,000 at sex parties and that, at another similar event, participants went through two thousand condoms. There was no way to verify the claims, but given the sky-is-the-limit atmosphere in China, some were apt to believe them.

"We have a new upper class in China who kind of live a life like Gatsby's, the parties, the fancy cars, the girls," Ashley said. "It is a shock. Most people kind of hate it. They don't like this kind of 'end of the world' image."

It wasn't just the excess that bothered people. They also wondered where the fortunes came from that fueled it.

"They don't think they earned their money through decent means," said Ashley. "They think they did deals with powerful people and they don't deserve the money."

I had that sense strolling through my parking garage. A number of the Ferrari and Lamborghini owners didn't even bother with license plates, suggesting they were so confident in their connections with the government that they didn't have to worry about cops. I also felt that some of the drivers didn't deserve to be behind the wheels of these vehicles. One night I stood outside my building and watched a twenty-five-year-old repeatedly attempt and fail to parallel park an Aston Martin worth several hundred thousand dollars. As in other cities, the rich in my compound drove like the roads were theirs. As they wound down the narrow corkscrew ramp into our parking garage, they often crossed into the oncoming lane, assuming drivers of more modest cars would just swerve and give way. That strategy was not always effective. One day I was walking down the ramp to my free taxi and saw a white Maserati with its left front smashed in. It had crossed the white median and crashed into a Ford coming up the ramp. The Ford won.

Gatsby was published in 1925, four years before the stock market crash and the beginning of the Great Depression. Ashley worried China's society and economy could be headed toward a similar fate. The economic growth rate, while still high, had been declining for years. Labor costs were rising, local governments were continuing to build "ghost" cities where many buildings sat empty, and state-owned companies and local governments were racking up huge amounts of debt.

"I don't know where and when the bomb is going to explode, but when that bomb goes off, the world economy will go with it," said Ashley, whose warning sounded especially ominous coming from a twenty-three-year-old. "It's going to be very cruel."

Ashley came from a Communist Party background and was an unusually thoughtful critic of Chinese society. Growing up in western China as the daughter of two Communist Party officials, she'd been a gifted student, scoring among the top forty people on the college entrance exam out of more than 270,000 in her province. During high school and college, when China's Internet wasn't as tightly controlled, she'd read and been influenced by the work of the post-Tiananmen generation, democracy advocates who'd been in the square in June 1989, such as Liu Xiaobo, a literary critic and human rights activist who went on to win the Nobel Peace Prize. In 2008, Liu coauthored "Charter 08," a blueprint for democratic reform that would make the government more accountable to the people. Charter 08 called for the separation of legislative, judicial, and executive power, genuine freedom of association—not the Communist Party lip service that Fifi had tried to teach her students about—the rule of law independent of political parties, a fair social security system that no longer favored urban residents, democratic elections, and an end to illegal arrest and detention. Charter 08 would've ended the party's monopoly on power, so the government sentenced Liu to eleven years in prison.

As a party insider, Ashley knew how the system worked. Friends had told her how police had invited them to *he cha,* or "drink tea," a euphemism for a soft interrogation masquerading as a friendly chat. The same year Charter 08 was released, the government began to tighten control of the Internet, blocking YouTube after protests in Tibet. Following riots in Xinjiang, China's far-northwestern territory, the government censored Facebook and Twitter as well. Ashley instinctively resented this and thought one of the Communist Party's fatal flaws was its insistence on serving as referee and participant in many aspects of life, including the economy. Despite the country's spectacular economic growth, Ashley saw limits to how far her homeland and its people could go.

"A great portion of people in China are oppressed, and you can't expect the country to live to its full potential," she said. "You decide the American or Western values are more attractive than the ones you live under. There are better schools, better quality of life, and you just want to live there."

I first got to know Ashley before I drove the free taxi, so there was no chance to offer her rides, but I liked her and found her perspective educational, so we stayed in touch. She would turn out to provide a unique perspective as I watched her homeland change. Disappointed with a China that had never been so prosperous, Ashley would move to America for work and study, seeking a freer life where she could read and say what she wished. In the coming years, we would chat online and meet up in Chicago, during her summer internship there, as well as in London and Paris, where she would spend a semester abroad for her American MBA. Over time, political earthquakes in the United States and China would begin to change her view of both.

CHAPTER 8

The Dark Side of the Chinese Dream

Crystal and Winnie

FOR MANY CHINESE, pursuing their dreams means moving. Rocky, Ray, Charles, and Max all had to leave family members behind in the countryside for a chance at a better life in Shanghai. Crystal traveled even farther. After leaving Harbin, she worked as a nurse in Malta and South Korea. Now that Crystal had found her footing in America, she felt compelled to find the little sister she'd left behind in her rush to escape.

After our search in the mountains, Crystal attended her little brother's wedding in Harbin, where she had hoped to deliver better news to her family. Before returning home to Michigan, she flew back to Yunnan province with a blood sample from her father to provide DNA in case police ever found a body. She asked the police if they knew what had happened to the owner of the border pass to Laos that Winnie had left behind in the farmhouse she briefly shared with her husband. An officer who was helping handle the case checked his police computer and found that the man had died in a traffic accident.

Crystal also met up with Cao, Winnie's handsome friend who'd bought us ice cream. When we talked to Cao, he had claimed not to remember where Winnie lived. This time around, he agreed to take Crystal to the apartment where Winnie had stashed her belongings nearly two years earlier as she prepared to go on the run. The apartment sat on the fifteenth floor of a high-rise overlooking downtown Jinghong, a collection of cookie-cutter housing blocks occasionally interrupted by construction cranes and pointy, Thai-style roofs. The architectural accents were a reminder of how close the city lay to Myanmar, Laos, and Thailand. Although the apartment was in the middle of the city, the crow of roosters echoed from below all day long. A manager at the apartment complex said police had never visited the building until recently and—even then—had never entered the apartment to examine the contents, which included a personal computer, cell phone numbers, photos, videos, and personal notes. In other words, the cops weren't interested.

The apartment was a time capsule of a life interrupted, crammed with woven plastic bags, the standard suitcase for Chinese migrants. After two years, some of the bags, which were stuffed with clothes, had dry-rotted and were ripping at the seams. Atop one sat a black high-heeled boot. The apartment was sparsely furnished with a pink sofa and a coffee table with a pack of cigarettes and lighter on top. There were rental contracts and bags of keys for the six apartments Winnie owned. A collection of CDs suggested a musical taste that stretched from Madonna and Britney Spears to Enya, George Winston, and Windham Hill Records—a soothing, hypnotic style of music that seemed suited for someone who had fled a big city for a quieter one in the tropics.

"Something caught my attention," Crystal told me, after she looked around the apartment. "It was a divorce certificate from Winnie's first marriage. It was just lying on the coffee table."

In the apartment, there was also a photo of Winnie with copper-tinted hair staring blankly at the camera with her first husband, a portly man seven years her junior. In the photo for her second marriage—taken just months later—she appeared no more enthusiastic. Her husband, Luo, the rubber farmer we'd interviewed in the remote village, wore a blue-checked shirt and a look of surprise, perhaps because he was marrying a woman he'd known only briefly.

The apartment was also littered with artifacts from Winnie's past. There was a pile of instructional DVDs on stripping and exotic dancing and a book filled with the personal confessions of prostitutes, including those who had tried to leave the life but failed. Winnie was an inveterate note taker and scribbled numbers, names, and ideas all over stationery from the Shangri-La and Kempinski, luxury hotels in Dalian where she had apparently spent time with clients. Cell phone photos, presumably taken by the businessman for whom she had served as a mistress, showed Winnie posing naked in an airy duplex in a Dalian high-rise.

But the contents of her home also suggested a woman trying to turn a corner. Winnie had profited from one of the side effects of the China boom: men with money willing to spend it on pleasure. Now, she seemed to be trying to leave her old life behind and reinvent herself as an independent businesswoman. Her library was a collection of self-help and educational books. One was called *The Must-Have Book for Cultivating Character,* and offered a chapter on public speaking. Another was entitled *Try Your Best to Let Other People Like You.* Additional titles included one by Alibaba founder Jack Ma on how to start a business, another on Western economics, and still others with titles such as *From Mediocrity to Excellence, The King of Marketing,* and *Lessons on Managing People.* The collection reminded me of Jay Gatsby, the American gospel of self-improvement, and the Tang dynasty poem taped on Charles's wall.

Winnie had financed her real estate spending spree through loans and the sale of an apartment in Dalian for $64,000. As she began to build her portfolio of properties, she visited dozens of apartments in Jinghong, videotaping many on her phone. She seemed to have designs on even bigger properties, shooting video of a sprawling, unfinished villa in a Spanish-revival housing complex that looked like it belonged in Southern California. And she'd obtained a flyer for a local bar for sale and had been chatting online with a supplier of beer-making equipment.

Reinvention is now as much a part of China's mythology as America's. In her own way, Winnie was trying to make a change and pursue success as her big sister had. What set Winnie apart, though, was her earlier path. She had made her money beyond the gleaming skyscrapers, in the shadows amid the gritty reality of Chinese city life, and she hadn't been entirely able to leave it behind. For all the Chinese who had succeeded on their merits, such as Ray and Rocky, there were many others who had gotten ahead working the seamier side of the China boom. Winnie's story—and perhaps her fate—was the dark side of the Chinese Dream.

Among her belongings were several SIM cards and health-care records indicating that she had operated under an alias for years. On top of the coffee table sat a computer satchel and on top of the satchel a medical document.

"It was a pregnancy test," Crystal told me.

Six days after she divorced her first husband, Winnie went to a local hospital and took a pregnancy test that came up positive. But two things were odd about the test. The document gave her age as twenty-four, when she was actually a decade older. The second thing was this: the month after she tested positive for a pregnancy, she went to the hospital under her alias and had her IUD removed, which would seem to rule out that she could have been pregnant in the first place. Unsettling details mounted. When Winnie had first gone missing, her father and brother-in-law flew to Jinghong. They met Cao, who never revealed he had a key to Winnie's apartment, so they hired a locksmith to open it. When they left, they sealed the door with a thin strip of tape as though it were a crime scene. Now, nearly two years later, Crystal photographed the door to the apartment and sent the image to her father and brother-in-law to compare notes.

"My father immediately noticed the tape was changed," she told me. "It was a sign that somebody had opened the door and gone into the room."

The only person she knew who had a key was Cao. Her father and brother-in-law said that when they were in the apartment two years earlier they had seen a note between Cao and Winnie, which now seemed to have disappeared. In fact, in the meantime, someone had hidden that note and a second one inside one of the more than a dozen bags filled with clothes. Both notes read like personal contracts between the couple.

"Cao and Winnie must be together for their whole lives," read the first note, which appeared to have been signed by Cao. "If they don't stay together, Cao's family must break up and his family members must die."

The note implied that if Cao left Winnie, he would curse his own family and wish for their destruction. The note also included Cao's home address, presumably so Winnie could visit his wife and expose their affair if he reneged. The other note was less dramatic.

"If we break up, no matter what, regardless of what caused the breakup, even if it is your wife, I will allow you to go back immediately," Winnie wrote, "but Cao cannot find any other woman."

On Winnie's computer, there were photos and videos of Cao and her together. In contrast to the static wedding photos with her actual husbands, these showed a couple that seemed in love. There were selfies of the two cuddling together. Winnie shot a video of the two driving at sunset, with Cao appearing in profile, a cigarette hanging from his lips, his head silhouetted against the setting sun. He turns and stares at Winnie, his mouth forming a slight smile.

There were videos of the couple having sex, which Cao knew could serve as ammunition if Winnie ever chose to expose their relationship. Winnie also had photos of Cao's wife. She was a plain-looking woman who wore her hair in a ponytail, in contrast to Winnie, who was thin with long, tapered legs and whose taste ran toward red miniskirts and black nail polish. Winnie seemed to torture herself with images of Cao's family. Among the photos was one of Cao's wife with their son in a park next to a field of bright yellow rapeseed.

"Toss and turn, can't fall asleep late at night," Winnie typed across the bottom of the images.

The most striking photos among her collection, though, were a series from her earlier days in Dalian when she was a mistress. One particular image seemed to capture her aspirations for the future and the humble roots from which she'd come. On a Saturday morning in early spring, she stands on a curving, stone quay along the edge of the ocean wearing a burgundy flowered scarf and a gray, pinstripe, double-breasted overcoat with the collar pulled up. She looks away from the camera, trying to strike a pose that suggests mystery and sophistication, her long, curly hair with blond highlights covering her face like a curtain. However, the tone she tries to strike is undermined by what sits in the far right of the frame, something she doesn't see: a migrant worker with a crew cut wearing olive fatigues, standing in the back of the flatbed of a blue, six-wheeled truck, the kind you see all over rural China. The worker and the truck effectively photobomb Winnie's fashion shoot, subverting the image of wealth and sophistication she is trying to cast. For Winnie, the past is always present.

In another image taken later that morning, Winnie lounges on a hillside amid fir trees in a residential community of American-style wooden villas with stone chimneys and decks that look out over the water. Nine years later, her big sister Crystal will move into a similar home overlooking a lake in central Michigan with her new husband, an attorney, completing Winnie's unfulfilled dream.

ARMED WITH INFORMATION about the pregnancy test and the notes between Winnie and Cao, Yang and I flew back to Jinghong to investigate further. One morning, we made our way to the hospital that performed the pregnancy test. Yang had called ahead, and we were directed to a lab where I met a young female physician in a white coat and explained the situation in Mandarin.

"Please take a look and can you tell us if it is real or fake?" I asked, showing her a cell phone photo of the document.

"Where was this test done?" asked the physician, sounding skeptical.

This hospital, I explained, noting the name of the doctor who had performed the test.

"It's not done by us," she said dismissively. "Our department doesn't have a doctor by this name or an ID number like this. This report is fake."

Another physician called up Winnie's medical records and found an earlier, legitimate pregnancy test, which had been negative. He said Winnie appeared to have created the positive test using a Word document.

"Why would someone forge a pregnancy test?" I asked, having a pretty good idea what the answer might be.

"Some girls want to take some leave from their jobs," said the female doctor. "Others lie to a man, saying, 'I'm pregnant,' to get a sum of money. People faking medical reports to get out of work is fairly common."

That was true. A year earlier, online stores in China had been busy producing fake doctor's notes—even extensive falsified medical records—so people could get out of work to watch the World Cup. Faking illness to get out of work would explain a lot of false medical records, but not Winnie's. She didn't have a job. Yang asked if a layperson would be fooled by Winnie's fake pregnancy test. Was it good enough to trick someone who wasn't a medical professional?

"They'd believe it," the doctor said.

We reached out to Cao again. On sensitive stories, I almost always prefer face-to-face interviews, so I can read a person's expression and body language. But this missing person case was growing darker by the day. What had begun as a hopeful search was taking an increasingly ominous turn. When we had chatted with Cao over lunch a month earlier, he'd lied repeatedly about his relationship with Winnie. We decided it was safer to call him on a burner phone and not tell him where we were. I feared that once he knew why we were calling, he would hang up. In fact, he spoke for forty awkward minutes. I began by explaining we'd seen the notes threatening his family with ruin if he ever left Winnie.

"She wrote it," Cao insisted, even though the signature appeared to be his.

Why?

"I don't know, but from the very beginning, I'd said that we were just friends and I have a family. Later, after she spent some time with me, I didn't know what she was thinking. One day, she wrote this note. If you hadn't mentioned it, I would have forgotten it."

Actually, a note threatening one's family most people would remember.

As Cao continued to refer to Winnie as a friend, I wondered if he was trying to disavow the affair.

"Did you love her?" I asked.

"I certainly loved her."

"Did she want to marry you?"

"Yes, she wanted me to get a divorce," said Cao, adding that she had pressed him over and over again. "She said if I got a divorce, I should give an apartment to my wife as compensation."

Cao said he had stood his ground and finally decided to break it off.

"I couldn't continue this relationship with her because if we kept going like this, she would sink deeper and deeper emotionally, right?" he said.

When Cao broke the news, he said Winnie was speechless and wept.

"I told her two or three times, she tacitly consented," Cao recalled. "After the breakup, she always treated me as a friend. I helped her move once. After the move, I never heard from her again and haven't contacted her since."

In the months before Winnie disappeared, Cao's wife and son came to Jinghong to see him, and Cao warned Winnie not to call too often while his family was in town. She obliged for a while, but eventually called and demanded he come see her. She said if he didn't, she would go to his apartment and expose their affair.

"There was nothing I could do, so I went over there," Cao said. "Once I was there, I didn't return. I had to lie, right? Men do lie, right? So, I said to my wife I was working at a certain place."

His wife later called one of Cao's employees, whose story about Cao's whereabouts conflicted with Cao's, and the cover story quickly unraveled.

"Later, I told her the truth and, in the end, she forgave me," Cao said simply.

Cao said this happened in mid-July. Winnie dated her fake pregnancy test a week later. We told him she had had a positive pregnancy test.

"This I don't know," said Cao, unconvincingly.

Then I told him it was fake.

"Awwwww!" Cao responded, sounding like someone who had finally learned the answer to a lingering question.

Cao repeatedly refused to speculate as to why Winnie would've forged the document. After dodging the question for several minutes, he acknowledged that, had he been the target of the fake test, the obvious motive would've been to force him to marry her. If the test wasn't targeted at Cao, as he suggested, then whom? Cao said, as he often did, that he had no idea. Then he tried to distance himself from the woman he'd said he loved.

"We only occasionally spent time together because I work every day. So, I can only say I know a little bit about her. The rest of her life, I don't know. You make a fake [pregnancy test], whether it's for me or another person, it's pretty immoral. It's very bad."

Cao said he last saw Winnie not long before she vanished. Given the heavy drug trade and human trafficking in this part of China, Cao said he assumed something terrible had happened.

"I think after such a long time, I guess she could have stopped contacting me, but she should contact her family members, right? She's either been taken hostage or someone has murdered her."

WE HAD A few phone numbers from Winnie's papers and decided to try them on the burner phone. The first number was out of service. The second, Winnie had put on flyers she'd distributed to try to rent some of her apartments. We didn't want to spook anyone who might answer, so Yang took the phone and I listened in on headphones. The phone rang three times.

"Hello?" a man answered.

"Do you have any apartments to sell or rent?" Yang asked.

"Who are you?" the man answered.

"I want to buy an apartment. A realtor gave me your number."

"What?"

Yang repeated the question.

"You dialed the wrong number."

"Is this a Jinghong number?" Yang asked.

"Where are you?" asked the man, who sounded like he was in his forties.

"I want to buy an apartment in Jinghong."

"I am asking where are you right now?" the man pressed.

"I'm now in Jinghong."

"Where are you in Jinghong?" the man asked again, now sounding suspicious and aggressive.

"In the center of the city."

"How do you know this is my number?"

"A realtor gave it to me."

"Which realtor?"

Yang tried to finesse the question.

"Where are you from?" the man repeated.

"I'm from outside the province."

"OK. Where are you right now?"

Yang, sensing danger, declined to say.

My heart began beating faster. These were not the questions of someone trying to hang up on a misdialed call or someone who might have been randomly reassigned Winnie's phone number. This was the longest wrong-number conversation I'd ever heard. I felt like we were speaking to someone who must have known Winnie.

And he wanted to find us.

Now.

"Buying an apartment, I am telling you, I don't have an apartment," the man said.

Then, he added this: "Can we meet up? OK?"

"If you don't have an apartment to sell," Yang said, "we can forget about it."

There was a long pause and then the man hung up.

Yang and I looked at each other wide-eyed.

"What did you think of that conversation?" I asked.

"He sounded very suspicious and asked a lot of questions about me."

"He wanted to know exactly where you were," I said. "That's very dangerous. If you didn't have an apartment to sell, why would you want to meet someone who had dialed a wrong number?"

If it hadn't been clear earlier, it was now: we were entering uncharted territory, and the story of Winnie's disappearance was growing more chilling with each new detail. We were investigating the disappearance of a mysterious woman with at least one assumed identity who had disappeared after apparently faking a pregnancy test. She'd been involved with a married man and had threatened to expose their affair. Even more alarming, she'd wished for his family's destruction if he left her.

Meanwhile, our leads were drying up. The man who owned the border pass to Laos that Winnie had left behind in the farmhouse was dead. Police said they couldn't find her first husband and had no interest in pursuing the case. Now, we'd called one of her phone numbers only to speak to a menacing voice that urgently wanted to track us down. I spoke with NPR security personnel, who thought continuing to look for Winnie was unwise. We told Crystal what we were learning, and even she no longer thought it was safe to keep digging.

I never did find out what happened to Winnie. The facts, though, supported a general theory. She'd moved to Yunnan to turn her life around and fallen in love with a married man. She wanted just what her big sister had, a stable life with a good income and a lifelong romantic partner. She went to great lengths to secure that, even faking a pregnancy and threatening to expose the affair. That would be a dangerous course of action anywhere. But here, on the edge of the Golden Triangle, where Winnie was just another anonymous migrant with no family and the cops were crooked, it seemed reckless. Nor had Winnie entirely turned over a new leaf. She had continued to compartmentalize her life, jealously guarding information and using multiple SIM cards. As her relationship unraveled with Cao, she seemed to spin out of control, marrying two men she barely knew and leaving each of them within a month. Instead of achieving her Chinese Dream, Winnie had descended into a Chinese noir.

When I returned to Shanghai, I went to visit Wei, a private detective I knew who'd made a career investigating adultery. Wei, who was nicknamed the Mistress Killer, estimated he'd investigated more than 1,600 cases. Many people looked at the phenomenon of mistresses through the lens of economics. For poor country girls such as Winnie, being a mistress was, at least in theory, a fast track to financial independence. But Wei saw his booming investigative business as a measure of the rot at the core of what some called the China miracle. Market economics had thrust the country forward at warp speed, providing previously unimaginable temptations, but the construction of a moral framework to help people grapple with such extraordinary change had lagged far behind. China's radical transformation was more than most people could absorb or navigate, and tragic stories like Winnie's were a price of progress.

"China's huge economic success has concealed people's falling morals and spiritual degradation," Wei told me. "Its exterior looks shiny and splendid and the entire world is watching, but actually its inside is rotten to the core."

I asked Wei what he thought had happened to Winnie. Given his years tracking adultery cases, he said, people who took the sorts of risks Winnie did often ended up the same way.

"She's dead," he said.

Before Crystal returned home to America, she made one last attempt to find the little sister she'd left behind. She rode a bus nine hours through the mountains of Yunnan to the hotel where Winnie had last been seen. She put up flyers in the city market and asked people if they'd seen anyone fitting her description. The journey was grueling. The bus passed through military checkpoints and along twisting roads with no guardrails. She couldn't understand the other passengers, who spoke local dialects. The driver routinely crossed the double-yellow line even though he couldn't see if a vehicle was coming in the other direction. As she prepared to fly back to the United States, I asked Crystal what she had learned in her nearly three weeks in China.

"I miss my life in America," she said as she laughed and sniffled at the same time. "I think I was spoiled by the civility of America." Her voice began to crack. "Here, I just felt I'm nobody."

She also couldn't shake the sense that she'd failed her baby sister. Crystal had made it out and built a happy life in America, while Winnie spiraled downward thousands of miles away. Under Communism, most people's lives in China had been pretty similar, but under capitalism, there were winners and losers. Some, like the owners of the cars in my compound's parking garage, won big, while others, like Winnie, lost and paid with their lives.

CHAPTER 9

Making China Great Again

Ray, Charles, and Fifi

━━━━━━━━━━━━━━

AFTER A DECADE of political malaise, one of President Xi's biggest challenges was winning back support for the Communist Party from the Chinese people. He'd seen how the Soviet Union had become so corroded that it had collapsed from within and told the party that it risked the same fate. With socialism largely discredited, the party no longer had ideology to bind together a huge population that Sun Yat-sen, China's first president, had famously called "a sheet of loose sand." So, Xi emphasized Chinese identity and nationalism as ways to bring an increasingly restless population with rising expectations closer to the party, while focusing their anger on external enemies and historic wounds. The fruits of this effort could increasingly be found in the pages of state-run newspapers, on movie screens, and in music videos. You could never be sure where you might encounter it next.

One spring evening, I attended an arts performance by a local elementary school. It was not a typical Shanghai school but a progressive, outward-looking one. Under Xi's increasingly nation-alistic, authoritarian rule, the school seemed almost countercultural, an antidote to the repression that had driven Fifi out of teaching and sent so many of the colleagues of Johanna, the human rights lawyer, to prison.

The two-hour show, which students had been working on in dress rehearsal since eight that morning, was bilingual and a near pitch-perfect blend of Chinese traditional music and dance and more spontaneous, fun-loving, Western-inspired numbers. It left the impression of a China in harmony with the Western world. The show opened on a vast stage with students singing their alma mater as they waved their hands in the air "We Are the World"–style. The next number, a tune called "A Profusion of Flowers in Full Bloom," began with girls in green dresses sitting in spotlights onstage plucking Chinese zithers, each note sounding like a drop of rainfall. Recitals of classic poems followed, including an homage to rural life from the Tang dynasty called "Commiseration for the Peasants." The program continued with a nod to some of the re-alities of contemporary life here. Several students walked onstage, coughing and complaining.

"Why is the pollution so bad?" asked one of the students.

Soon, they were joined by more students with sponges who pretended to clean the environment by giving the earth a shower. At first glance, this seemed to be an encouraging sign that people were talking openly about pollution and children were developing an appreciation for environmentalism.

"Cherish what we have," they sang. "Keep our water clean. Create a better life."

But the child's awkward question—"Why?"—went unan-swered. To address it honestly would mean acknowledging that the party had allowed industry to poison the air and shorten the lives of hundreds of millions of people to boost economic growth and maintain industrial employment, ensuring political stability and, ultimately, the party's grip on power. And that was certainly not the stuff of feel-good student variety shows. The energy picked up when six kids in white-and-red-striped shirts and tan pants took to the stage with drums, guitars, and keyboards and broke into the Beach Boys' "Fun, Fun, Fun." A group of screaming girls in pink and green skirts raced onstage as a camera at the end of a crane panned the performers, projecting their black-and-white images onto a big screen as if they were on *American Bandstand* circa 1964. As the girls shimmied and waved their hands in the air, three boys zipped past on skateboards.

"And we'll have fun, fun, fun 'til daddy takes the Tesla away," the kids sang.

Several numbers later, the kids rode bicycles around the stage singing an anthem of global inclusion.

"A world full of equals, so different in each case," they sang, as best I could make out. "We're prepared to help each other, any time, everywhere, every place."

Then five girls in red hot pants did a dance break to the disco classic "I Will Survive." At some point, someone quoted President Xi saying the world had a shared destiny.

The show was terrific and this Shanghai school seemed to have come up with an image of global appeal that had largely eluded the Communist Party since the 2008 Beijing Olympics. The performance showed an open, fun-loving China that embraced Western pop culture while still paying homage to ancient Chinese traditions. Tang dynasty poetry and Chinese zithers combined with Brian Wilson and Gloria Gaynor: soft-power genius.

With the opening of the penultimate number, though, the show took a turn. Red light bathed the stage and fifty students walked out in khaki shorts and skirts, white short-sleeve shirts, and red scarves tied around their necks. The children, who stood at attention like little soldiers, were dressed as Young Pioneers, a mass organization run by the Communist Youth League. The kids began recounting a story of resistance against the Japanese invasion of China in World War II called the "Five Heroes of Wolf

Teeth Mountain," which every schoolchild knows by heart. Amid a blast of horns and drums that sounded like cannon fire, five boys dressed as soldiers in Mao's Eighth Route Army stood on boxes that symbolized the mountaintop and struck dramatic poses. One took aim with his rifle while another held his fist defiantly in the air as the boys reenacted the David and Goliath military tale. In 1941, a handful of Communist soldiers tricked the Japanese Army into pursuing them up Wolf Teeth Mountain in Hebei province, southwest of Beijing. The Japanese wasted valuable time chasing what they thought was the main force. When the heroes ran out of ammunition, they jumped from the cliffs, according to Communist Party history. Three died, but two clung to tree branches and survived to tell the story. Tonight's dramatization played out over eight minutes, with the five students finally jumping off the boxes.

Screens on either side of the stage spelled out the message in Mandarin and English: "Five national heroes bravely resisted the foreign invaders with their lives, to defend the territorial integrity of the motherland and the national dignity. Through poetry recitals and performances, the students have shown high respect for the national heroes, expressed great pride in our country and the strong values of world peace."

But the patriotic theme did not end there. Again, red light bathed the stage and the Young Pioneers returned, carrying flowers for the martyred soldiers. Then the children turned to the giant screen and knelt down. A giant, red Chinese flag whipped in the wind, followed by soldiers saluting and goose-stepping. One of China's new aircraft carriers appeared, followed by images of fighter jets on the flight deck and soaring through the skies. The images continued with paratroopers diving out of planes and tumbling through the air.

Why choose a wartime event from nearly eight decades ago as the climax for a Shanghai elementary school arts performance? To better bind the nation together through a shared sense of national pride and historic victimization. In fairness to the Communist

Party, China has a lot of material to work with. The country's most hated nation is Japan, which earned that enmity through barbarous behavior during and after its invasion of China in 1937. Most Americans are familiar with the Nazi horrors of World War II, but the Japanese committed terrible atrocities as well. Many years ago, I interviewed a man who had been subjected to biological-weapons experiments by the Japanese Army's infamous Unit 731 in Harbin. Late one winter night, warmed by a coal fire, he described how doctors infected him with bubonic plague and then, after he failed to die, laid him out on a surgery table where a physician planned to cut him open without anesthesia to see how his organs had responded to the infection. As he prepared to cut, the Japanese surgeon recognized the man from several years earlier when he had helped build a Japanese clinic nearby.

"He is my friend," the surgeon said and, in a rare reprieve, told assistants to take the man away.

"Without a word from him, I would have died," the old man told me as tears formed in eyes buried beneath folds of skin.

This history continues to define the fraught relations between the world's second- and third-largest economies. The Chinese remain in dispute with Japan over the Diaoyu Islands in the East China Sea, hence the reference in the elementary school production to defending "the territorial integrity of the motherland." The images of aircraft carriers, fighter jets, and soldiers reminded the audience how China's rapidly growing military, funded by the country's economic boom, protects the nation from old enemies like Japan, which exploited China's weakness in the past.

"Five Heroes of Wolf Teeth Mountain" was a great way to hammer home these points using a well-known story that has been recounted in paintings, movies, plays, and museums. Inconveniently, not everyone in China bought the entire Wolf Teeth narrative, which included the claim that the five heroes had killed or wounded at least ninety Japanese soldiers. Some years back, a historian named Hong Zhenkuai questioned how many enemy troops the Communist soldiers had actually killed and whether the troops had leaped from the mountain or slipped, which doesn't make as good a story.

Conservatives and party-run media attacked Hong as unpatriotic and accused him of what the government here calls "historical nihilism," which means challenging the party's version of history that it uses to help justify its rule. Sons of two of the five heroes sued Hong, who lost in court. The verdict said he failed to portray the five men positively and cast doubt on the event based on "insufficient evidence."

"Thus, it also damages the Chinese nation's spiritual values," the verdict read.

Hong was not surprised by the result and chalked it up to the government's return to a more authoritarian Communist political culture under President Xi.

"We've been seeing the political winds shifting to the left, and leftists want to safeguard so-called red culture," Hong told the *New York Times.* Hong's Weibo account was disabled—just like cartoonist Rebel Pepper's—preventing him from defending himself. Hong said that people should respect war heroes who resisted the Japanese, but they should also respect the facts.

"Although it is understandable that propaganda might have been exaggerated back then for the sake of encouraging the military and the public to resist Japan's invasion, by now people want to know the historic truth," he wrote in *Caijing* magazine.

One of Hong's attorneys said the result of the trial was based on politics, not the law—just as Johanna, the human rights lawyer, had argued unsuccessfully for her client Li in Shanghai.

"It shows the authorities' lack of confidence," the historian's attorney said.

At a time when the leader of the Communist Party was more powerful and popular than he'd been in decades and the country's global profile had never loomed larger, the government was frightened by a historian who'd questioned some details in one of the party's many founding myths. It was a sign that, no matter how powerful the party appeared abroad and even at home, the foundation on which it stood was softer and less secure than it seemed.

How much did "historical nihilism" actually worry the party? In 2018, the Chinese government enacted a law against questioning the country's historical heroes.

"It is prohibited to misrepresent, defame, profane or deny the deeds and spirits of heroes and martyrs, or to praise or beautify invasions," the government's New China News Service said, summarizing the law. It also said anyone who does so may be investigated for the commission of a crime.

ONE AFTERNOON, I drove over to Ray's new law office in Shanghai Tower in Lujiazui, the financial district. It was the city's tallest building at 2,079 feet, but the government consortium that owns it had been offering discounts and incentives to fill up the massive floor space, which was still mostly empty. We sat in a conference room and looked down at the luxury stores across the road. The facade of the Louis Vuitton store sparkled like diamonds while the digital ticker that ran across the footbridge over Century Avenue spit out stock averages from the Dow and the Nikkei. As we took it all in, Ray thought back to a childhood photo from his village in Hubei province, with Rocky, then just two years old, standing on a muddy road next to a mud-brick shed.

"It looked like the kind of hut you see in reports about old tribes in Africa," said Ray, who wore a pink shirt and a tailored gray suit. "Twenty years ago, in this area," he said, referring to Lujiazui, "there was nothing."

That was pretty accurate. Back then, the Louis Vuitton store and nearly all the surrounding buildings didn't exist. The Jin Mao Tower was the area's lone skyscraper, rising above a wasteland of two-story Chinese homes that were later razed and then covered with grass as though they had never been there. I photographed the Jin Mao when it opened in 1999. It was so tall—1,381 feet—I had to lie down on the grass to fit it into the frame.

Today, Ray said, "it's a totally different world."

After a tour of his law offices, Ray and I got into the car and I drove under the digital ticker overpass, into the tunnel beneath the river, and then up onto the Yan'an elevated expressway, where we passed some of the colonial buildings that had defined Shanghai in the city's earlier, Western heyday. To the left stood the Great World, a 1930s entertainment complex that had been home to acrobats and magicians and had a tower that looked like a wedding cake. To the right, across People's Park, stood the Park Hotel, a brown-brick, Gothic tower. At twenty-two stories, the Park was once Shanghai's tallest building, but today from the expressway you barely notice it, wedged between the city hall and the urban planning museum. Shanghai has retained many colonial landmarks but also built around and over them.

The city ultimately owes its Western architecture to British drug dealing. In the nineteenth century, the British smuggled and sold opium into China to solve a huge trade imbalance that had developed between the two countries. Faced with an epidemic of addiction, China fought back and destroyed some stocks of the drug, leading to the First Opium War, which the British easily won. As part of the peace treaty, Britain forced Shanghai to become an open port where they, the Americans, and the French created settlements that they cast in their own image. Most Shanghainese take pride in their colonial architecture and see it as a sign of the city's cosmopolitan heritage, but the buildings are also reminders of what the Chinese government refers to as the century of humiliation, when foreign powers, including the Japanese, carved up China.

Building was the signature activity of China's resurgence, and the most remarkable and controversial recent projects weren't made of glass and steel but reef and sand. Since 2013, the Chinese government has built at least 3,200 acres of new islands hundreds of miles from its coast in the South China Sea, an important international waterway through which one fifth of the world's trade passes. Ray is politically moderate and disagrees with some Communist Party positions, but he backs the government on its island building in the South China Sea. From his time studying law in Illinois, Ray developed a deep affection for the United States, but that did not outweigh his patriotism. Like many Chinese, he admires America's freedom and rule of law but opposes what he sees as the US attempt to contain China's rise and hold the country back. In particular, Ray thinks the United States should stay out of the dispute between China and its neighbors over its near seas.

"Politicians always argue that China will challenge the power or challenge the current status of the United States, but that's not true," Ray insisted as I worked my way down the crowded expressway at rush hour. "China is only trying to protect its own rights."

Ray believed that China had legitimate, historical claims to the islands. He didn't see his country as a rising power throwing its weight around, but as a victim that had been exploited by smaller nations when it was weak.

"In the last century, China had to focus on its own problems, like the Cultural Revolution, and didn't have the resources to take care of the islands," Ray said. "A lot of countries at that time just stole the islands, one by one."

Now, China was finally powerful enough to create its own islands where there had just been reef and could enforce its claims as part of the nation's rejuvenation, Xi's Chinese Dream. To illustrate how smaller countries had exploited China, Ray cited a case in 1999 when the Philippine Navy, which is very small, beached a former US World War II transport ship called the *Sierra Madre* on a coral atoll in the Spratly Islands, which China and the Philippines both claim.

"They promised China they would withdraw the ship as soon as possible," Ray said. "But finally, they sent more troops, settled on the ship, and claimed the island was theirs."

In 2013, China sent a coast guard cutter to patrol the area around the rusting hulk where a dozen lonely marines held out, spearfishing for their food. For the record, the *Sierra Madre* is 120 miles off the coast of the Philippine province of Palawan and more than seven hundred miles from China's Hainan island. Ray said the United States played favorites, never chastising the Philippines, a US ally, for beaching the *Sierra Madre*.

"Now, when China wants to enforce its claims against other countries, America shows up and says, 'No, you cannot do this! It will change the balance of power in the Pacific,'" Ray said. "America is just like a big boy in class that just bullies others, that does whatever he wants."

I had learned that arguing America's position in a country where there is no free access to information and an educational system that emphasizes a history of national humiliation was rarely productive. Had I been willing to debate Ray during our commute, I might have pointed out that no other country had built so much, so quickly in the South China Sea as China had. And, although President Xi had pledged not to militarize the islands, the government had built radar stations, constructed airstrips that could handle bombers, and installed surface-to-air missiles with a range of 125 miles. Not so long ago, Xi's predecessor, Hu Jintao, had publicly vowed that China would have a "peaceful rise." But in military meetings between China and the United States, the Chinese made their intentions clear.

During one exchange back in 2011, the Americans raised China's construction of artificial islands during a meeting in Beijing. "Why are you continuing to build?" the US admirals asked, according to one in attendance. "This is a hostile act."

One of the Chinese admirals became angry; he stood up and leaned over the table.

"We are a rising nation," he said sternly. "You are a nation in decline. This is our turn. It's always been our sea and we're going to start enforcing it now, and you guys just need to get used to it."

The Chinese said they wanted the US Navy to leave the South China Sea, even though it is international waters. The United States government thought Beijing was trying to turn the South China Sea into a Chinese lake, which posed a challenge to the US Navy's role overseeing the Pacific since the end of World War II. Chinese ships continue to shadow US naval ships when they approach China's artificial islands. The fear is that miscalculation on the high seas could lead to conflict between the world's two most powerful countries. In October 2018, the United States said a Chinese ship aggressively maneuvered around an American destroyer and came within forty-five yards of hitting it. China and the United States are defined by their differences, including political systems and approaches to basic rights. But their similarities also run the risk of bringing them into conflict. Both countries are nationalistic and have a belief in their own superiority and manifest destiny.

As Ray and I headed away from downtown, we passed some of Shanghai's quirkier buildings. One was shaped like a giant boot. Another was blanketed in LED lights that created images of bubbles rushing to the roof as though the building were a sixty-story glass of champagne. I wasn't driving my free taxi today because I wasn't allowed to. In an effort to reduce traffic, the city government had banned cars like mine—with low-priced, provincial license plates—from driving the highways at rush hour. (The more I drove the streets of Shanghai, the more I began to appreciate how Charles and other outsiders felt like second-class citizens in the city.) To drive Ray today, I'd had to borrow my assistant Yang's BYD sedan with its privileged Shanghai license plate. Yang, who was in the backseat, asked Ray a question about the South China Sea.

"You said the US is like a schoolyard bully," said Yang. "But to a lot of China's neighbors, China is also like a bully. So, you should also see the problem from their standpoint, right?"

"Yes, I can understand that," Ray said. "Because people are not used to a stronger China. For the past one hundred years, China was weak. China could not protect its rights. But now China has the resources and ability to protect its rights, so people don't like that. You know people always like a weak country, a weak China. Now, China has more power, so he has to stand up, not be quiet and sit in a corner. I believe when these things get settled, people will get used to a new China."

One of the things that struck me about conversations around the South China Sea was how certain many Chinese people were that nearly all of it was China's. The reasons were tied up in history and the education system. In 1948, China's Nationalist government published a map of its claims to the South China Sea that included a giant, U-shaped, nine-dashed line that stretched from the south of Taiwan, past the Philippines, all the way down to Malaysia, and then up the coast of Vietnam, encompassing almost the entire body of water, which is three hundred thousand square miles larger than the Caribbean. If a map could be translated into a single phrase, it might read: "It's all ours!" In fact, that's what Chinese schools teach students. An eighth-grade geography textbook calls a bank named James Shoal—or Zengmu Ansha in Mandarin—"the southernmost point of the country's territory." James Shoal is in fact more than 1,100 miles south of China's mainland and only fifty miles from Malaysia. It's also seventy-two feet underwater. To mark China's submerged territory, which isn't territory at all, a Chinese marine surveillance ship dropped a marble "sovereignty stele" engraved with the characters for China over the bank in 2010. When Zheng Wang, who runs the Center for Peace and Conflict Studies at Seton Hall University, was teaching a course at a top Chinese university, he presented students with a 2013 article in *China National Geographic* magazine, which said, "The nine-dashed line is . . . now deeply en-graved in the hearts and minds of the Chinese people." Wang asked his class if they agreed with that statement. Most raised their hands.

HAD CHARLES BEEN in that class, he would have raised his hand, too, but he insists he is now much less nationalistic than he used to be as a college student. As I drove him home from work one afternoon, he shared an entry from his diary in 2006 when he criticized one of his roommates for being insufficiently patriotic. The roommate was watching *Final Fantasy,* a Japanese cartoon, around the time that the United States and Japan were holding joint military drills focused on the Diaoyu Islands in the East China Sea, which both China and Japan claim, and which Japan calls Senkaku. Charles told his roommate to stop watching.

"A classmate and I criticized him for introducing Japanese culture to our mainland, for letting Japanese culture invade China," Charles said. "I was that kind of Chinese. I almost forgot I had that kind of mindset."

"Why would you see a cartoon as an invasion?" I asked. "You haven't fought a war with Japan in many, many decades."

"We speak based on what we learn from media, from textbooks," Charles said.

Back in college, Charles read *Global Times,* a jingoistic, state-run newspaper. In 2012, protests against Japan broke out after Japanese activists landed on one of the disputed islands and raised Japanese flags. The next month, the Japanese government bought some of the islands to prevent Japanese nationalists from developing them. China's state-run press, though, portrayed the move as a landgrab and fanned the flames.

"Tokyo has chosen the wrong opponent at the wrong time and the wrong place," warned *Global Times,* quickly reminding readers of Japan's brutal past. "Japan inflicted the deepest atrocities on China in its modern history, which was full of humiliation. If China were to pick a target country to wash out the old shame, Japan is the best choice."

The protests against Japan at the time varied in intensity. I walked with demonstrators in Shanghai. They marched through the streets with pictures of Mao that read "Liberate the Japanese Islands" and hand-drawn signs that said "Kill Japan." But many of the marchers were laughing and seemed to be enjoying the day off from work. In other cities, though, protests turned violent. In Shandong province, demonstrators set fire to a Panasonic factory and a Toyota sales outlet. Out to the west in the city of Xi'an, a protester pulled a man from a Toyota and bludgeoned him with a bike lock, sending him to the pavement bleeding and unconscious.

The *People's Daily* website ran an editorial supporting the protesters.

"No one would doubt the pulses of patriotic fervor when the motherland is bullied," the editorial said. "No one would fail to understand the compatriots' hatred and fights when the country is provoked; because a people that has no guts and courage is doomed to be bullied."

Charles didn't think much of the protesters.

"I thought people were just being used like pawns," he said.

What had changed his thinking?

Charles said that during summers off from college he had no money and nothing to do back home in Hubei, so he watched state TV from morning until night. Finally, he had an epiphany.

"This whole thing, the TV set itself, is designed to make you stupid, including the news of course."

While still in high school, Charles had discovered Google, which the government had yet to block. Unlike Chinese state TV, Google opened up a whole new world of information. Charles didn't have much to do, so he decided to educate himself.

"We call it the insatiable desire to know more, or to know the truth, thanks to my boring life," Charles said. "That's the reason I know something besides mainstream domestic media."

It was through Google that Charles found the banned book *Tombstone* and learned the truth behind the Great Leap Forward and the great famine, which killed more than thirty-six million people. The author, Yang Jisheng, who was from a neighboring county of Charles's, wrote that he learned his father was starving in 1959 and returned to their village, not realizing the scope of what Mao had wrought.

"Upon reaching Wanli, I found things radically changed," Yang wrote. "The elm tree in front of our house had been reduced to a barkless trunk, and even its roots had been dug up and stripped, leaving only a ragged hole in the earth. . . . My father was half-reclined on his bed, his eyes sunken and lifeless, his face gaunt, the skin creased and flaccid. He tried to extend his hand to greet me, but couldn't lift it."

"Every time I think of that, I get very angry," Charles said of the Great Leap Forward as we drove beneath a canopy of London plane trees in Shanghai's former French Concession.

I recalled that on our ride to Hubei for Chinese New Year, Charles had tried to describe the book to Rocky, who hadn't read it and didn't seem interested. I wondered, if Google were still available in China today and hundreds of millions of Chinese had had the opportunity to read *Tombstone,* would they still look at Mao's portrait in Tiananmen the same way? More importantly, would it change the way they saw the party? Based on the growing censorship in China, it was clear the party wasn't willing to risk it.

Even if Charles was skeptical of the anti-Japanese protests, he was still patriotic and, like Ray, supported China's territorial claims. Charles had traveled for a story to Hainan, China's southernmost province, to visit government researchers who laid out evidence that Chinese had lived on some of the islands in the South China Sea long ago. Charles even brought back conch shells purported to come from the South China Sea. He said he had no doubt who owned the islands.

"I'm Chinese and the South China Sea is ours," he said.

The Philippines had challenged China's claims and taken the case—which the United States supported—to an international tribunal in The Hague, which was expected to rule in the next month. I asked Charles how he would respond if the tribunal ruled against China (as it did).

"Our government has expressed its standpoint crystal clear," he said. "We will boycott this arbitration."

"There are a lot of things that you read here that you don't believe," I said, "so why do you believe this?"

"We have been under a siege led by the US," said Charles, who saw his country as surrounded by unfriendly neighbors and considered the South China Sea islands a buffer.

"But why have you built much, much, much, much bigger islands than anybody else has?"

"Because we can," Charles said simply. "We are rich."

When Chinese leaders looked east from Beijing, they saw American troops, ships, and aircraft in South Korea, Japan, and Guam. Like other rising powers in the past, China wanted a sphere of influence. After so many decades of poverty, chaos, and "national humiliation," the Chinese government was now able to enforce its will in ways that would have been unthinkable as recently as the 1990s. This was the new reality. It was also another element of Xi's New Era, and it filled some otherwise moderate Chinese, such as Charles and Ray, with patriotic pride, just as the president surely had hoped.

GIVEN THE POLITICAL climate in Chinese education, Fifi, the psychologist I shuttled around town to see clients, was glad that she had left her teaching job, but she missed her old school chums and the sense of camaraderie. One day in 2018, she met up with two of them on campus. They all beamed when they saw each other and seemed transported back to a more open, hopeful time when people could share ideas more easily in China. Over coffee at a wooden table in the faculty café, the conversation turned nostalgic, and the two remaining faculty members talked about how much the school had changed since the late 1990s. One, a female administrator, said there was no way to have the sort of freewheeling conversations they had enjoyed back then.

She felt there was a generation gap between her and the current crop of students, as well as many teachers. The school had recruited a new breed of instructors from the provinces who were skilled at teaching to the national college entrance exam but had no interest in encouraging independent thought. The administrator, who was warm and direct, said the educational system was not focused on developing critical-thinking skills, leaving students unable to develop strong theses or make sharp arguments. She said student essays often amounted to little more than fragments of ideas. Recently she'd told her students to read a book or watch a movie and give their opinions. Of those who completed the assignment, only 15 percent expressed their own original ideas.

"Most just copied and pasted from the Internet," she said.

Was intense academic pressure and refusal to teach critical-thinking skills part of a survival strategy to make sure young people would have neither the energy nor the tools to question the party?

"Correct," said the administrator simply. "Correct."

Chinese leaders knew that if schools taught the next generation to think on its own, the party would only shorten its life span. Recently, the administrator had gathered with other school leaders to discuss a new school slogan. Some thought it should emphasize active thinking. Others thought it should stress students developing their own opinions. Then everyone agreed that would only provoke the party.

"The second choice will be more dangerous," the administrator said.

In Fifi's time away, the school had expanded and the facilities had improved dramatically. There was an elevator, an escalator, an underground basketball court, a weight room worthy of a five-star hotel, and a faculty lounge with a giant fish tank and a flat-screen TV. But along with government money came government propaganda. A new giant outdoor screen beamed messages to the students and faculty on a loop. Against the digital backdrop of a hammer and sickle, it touted the recent party meeting where Xi Jinping's political theories had been enshrined in China's constitution as Mao's had.

"Study in-depth and implement the 19th Party Congress," read the sign greeting people as they strolled onto campus. "Strive to build a strong, prosperous, democratic, civilized, harmonious, and beautiful modern socialist country. Stay true to the original self. Work for the people's happiness. Keep the mission firmly in mind to rejuvenate the nation."

The party was redefining the grand bargain it had struck with the Chinese people after the blood and bullets in Beijing in 1989. In the wake of the violence, the government had allowed people far greater personal freedom and the opportunity to get rich, as long as they did not challenge the party. Now, the party seemed to want the people to believe—or at least pretend to believe—what the party said.

The faculty members had to return to work, and Fifi needed to head to lunch. Before they split up, they spoke briefly of their dreams. The history teacher, who years earlier had spent hours trying to rescind his Communist Party application, said he dreamed of a cleaner China.

"When I read news of an animal or plant species going extinct, I feel pain," said the teacher, who had moved to another campus and now spent his time tending turtles. "We've destroyed so many animals."

The administrator grew quiet and looked a bit sad.

"I don't have a dream," she said. "That's my problem."

CHAPTER 10

President Donald J. Trump

Ashley, Ray, Chen, and Gong

I
N 2016, AS I prepared to move my family to London for a new assignment, I met up with Ashley, the *Gatsby*-reading social critic, at a Starbucks near my office in Shanghai. She was about to head to the United States to get an MBA on full scholarship, and she intended to settle there. Ashley said she was going to America not only for the education, but also because she wanted to get away from China's pervasive corruption and thirsted for an environment where she could read and say what she wanted. As the daughter of Communist Party officials, she'd grown up observing garden-variety graft play out at home. When she was young, her parents went out until late at night giving gifts of cigarettes, money, and Maotai, a high-priced white liquor, to help her mother land a new job. As her parents developed connections of their own, people started bringing them expensive liquor and cigarette boxes stashed with the equivalent of hundreds of dollars in cash to help get their kids into the party. Ashley didn't judge her parents.

"It's just something people expect you to do," she said, "and I just don't like it. It goes against my integrity. In China, people know it's wrong, but they also think it doesn't matter."

By China's corruption standards, the behavior of Ashley's parents barely rated as a misdemeanor. In the decade or so I had been away from China, officials had stolen with both hands, threatening popular support for the Communist Party. A 2008 study by the People's Bank of China found that more than sixteen thousand Communist Party officials, businessmen, and CEOs had disappeared with more than $130 billion. President Xi began cracking down soon after he came to power in 2012 and, unlike past campaigns, the impact had been huge. Since 2013, the government had punished more than 1.3 million lower-ranking officials for corruption.

"Some people who used to come to our place a lot ended up in prison," said Ashley. "It's shocking."

Ashley's move to America turned out to be something of a shock as well. Five months after she arrived on campus, Donald Trump was elected America's forty-fifth president. Ashley didn't like Trump's policies or his leadership style.

"The sole purpose that drives me from China to America is because I don't want to live in an authoritarian state anymore," Ashley told me in exasperation after Trump's victory. "I want to live in a free country. I feel very unlucky for a minute to jump from a very bad place to another very bad place. And this is just the beginning of it. I know how powerful propaganda can be over time, so I'm still not sure about the future."

This observation in early 2017 by a woman who had grown up inside the Communist Party would prove prescient. But after the first few months of the Trump administration, Ashley became less anxious. She thought the United States had not fundamentally changed and the system of checks and balances had held firm, with the courts initially rejecting Trump's ban on people coming from seven majority-Muslim countries.

"The moral compass is still very strong inside people's hearts," Ashley said hopefully. "We should probably have a lot more confidence in the American people and to trust them to try to bring this country back to where it should be."

BACK IN SHANGHAI, Ray, like Ashley, initially seemed more amused than bothered by President Trump. Many Chinese found Trump's blunt talk a refreshing contrast with the traditional, hyper-controlled public personae of their own leaders.

"I really like him," said Ray, laughing as we chatted, about ten months into Trump's presidency. "Usually, people in Asia don't speak this way."

Ray respected Trump for looking out for the American worker, but thought some of his approach made no economic sense. It was still early in Trump's term, and the president was focusing on bringing back jobs in manufacturing and coal. Instead, Ray said, the president should target fields that pay better and where America has a natural competitive advantage, such as education, finance, design, and entertainment.

"That's a dangerous path," Ray said of Trump's focus on blue-collar energy and factory jobs, "because if you focus on old-fashioned industry, you will damage the advantages of our great United States. Don't be a second-tier country."

I was struck by Ray's use of the phrase "our United States," as though America wasn't just any country, but one that at least some people beyond its borders felt they still had a stake in. For Ray, the United States stood for something larger than mere national self-interest. He was also concerned about Trump's "America First" strategy, his disdain for the world order, including multilateral institutions, such as the World Trade Organization, that the United States had helped build.

"I really love the United States," said Ray, who looked back on his time studying in Illinois as one of the best experiences of his life. "I believe a powerful and global United States is good for the world. For the last forty or fifty years, the whole world has benefited from this system. Just like the Chinese government always says, 'We don't want to tear up the system. We just want to play a more important role.'"

And, Ray added, "we should get considerable respect."

It was easy to criticize Trump's policies, but there were areas—especially the relationship between China's government and US business—where the president had a point. American business leaders had once been hard-core supporters of the Chinese Communist Party, because it had given them preferential treatment while helping to develop an economy that had driven so much growth for multinationals. But over the years, American business soured on the Chinese government, which demanded some American companies turn over technology in exchange for access to the China market or allegedly used hackers to steal it.

"Foreign business used to be China's best friend," said James McGregor, chairman for greater China with APCO Worldwide, the global public-affairs and strategic communications consultancy. Now, "in private, it's universally negative. Under recent policies, the government has been completely 'screw you.' A 'win-win' means China wins twice."

One morning when I was still working in Shanghai, I hopped a cab and headed toward a three-acre compound hidden in plain sight amid restaurants, karaoke clubs, massage parlors, and grocery stores in the city's sprawling Pudong district. The complex centered around a twelve-story office tower with satellite dishes on the roof. Signs on the outer wall warned people on the street not to film or photograph. When I showed up, a plainclothes cop in a blue down coat was pacing the sidewalk out front, scanning the street and speaking anxiously into a cell phone. Hours earlier, Mandiant, the US cybersecurity company, had revealed the compound was home to the People's Liberation Army Unit 61398, which Mandiant said had launched cyberattacks on American companies, stealing hundreds of terabytes of data, including technology blueprints, proprietary manufacturing processes, business plans, and partnership agreements.

"They've compromised over 141 corporations across twenty different industries and stolen just a wealth of intellectual property," Dan McWhorter, who oversaw Mandiant's threat intelligence business unit, told me.

As in the past, the Chinese government denied it was in the business of industrial espionage.

The US government saw it differently. Two years later, the director of national intelligence estimated that Chinese cyber espionage cost America $400 billion annually. Inside jobs have also been a problem for many years. In one recent case, police caught engineers at a Taiwanese chip company concealing laptops and USB drives, which authorities say they planned to use to smuggle American tech secrets to China to help launch a $5.7 billion government-backed microchip factory. In 2017, members of the American Chamber of Commerce in Shanghai listed intellectual property rights as the area of reform most important to their companies' growth. Last fall, in an unprecedented move, US agents lured a suspected Chinese government spy to Belgium, where he was extradited to the United States to face charges of economic espionage. Ray, who happens to be an intellectual property rights lawyer, says IP protection has improved a lot in China, which other IP attorneys say is true when it comes to most commercial disputes. After all, Chinese companies don't want their intellectual property stolen either. But when it comes to strategically important industries, McGregor says, Beijing does whatever it takes to gain an edge.

During his first eighteen months in office, President Trump took aim at America's allies, calling the European Union a foe and berating fellow NATO members for not paying their fair share on defense. As Trump pursued his America First agenda and US global influence ebbed, Washington seemed to be ceding the field to Beijing. Ray, though, was still optimistic about the United States.

"Presidents come, presidents go," Ray said.

"So, you're not that worried about America?"

No, he said. He wasn't.

"You should have faith in the United States Constitution," said Ray, who had studied constitutional law when he was getting his master's in Illinois. "The founding fathers did an amazing job. It provides liberty and it protects the American people."

Ray noted that China doesn't have a system of checks and balances like America.

"President Xi is a good leader, a great leader, right?" Ray continued. "But the next one, I don't know. But if you have a bad president in America, you have a good constitution. Even if you have one or two bad presidents, that's OK, it's not a big deal."

Actually, it was a big deal. George W. Bush's invasion of Iraq, the global financial crisis, and the early Trump administration had damaged the United States' standing in China and the world. But Ray was right about one thing. Americans—unlike Chinese—have the power to vote.

"Actually, I'm worried about China," Ray said, catching me off guard. "When we have a very good leader, like President Xi, we will make very good progress. But if we have a bad one, that will be a terrible thing. You heard about Bo Xilai, right?"

I had. In fact, I'd covered his wife's murder trial in Anhui province back in 2012. Bo was a smooth, charismatic politician who had run the southwestern megacity of Chongqing like a mafia state. He'd jailed businessmen and political opponents and instituted the public singing of Mao-era songs—actions that left many people in China unsettled. Bo was aiming for the top tier of party leadership but was brought down after his wife murdered a British businessman who had allegedly blackmailed the couple over corruption.

"If he'd become president—holy shit!—we'd have gone backwards fifty years as if it were the Great Cultural Revolution," Ray said.

"You have a very good democracy," Ray said. "You have a very good, educated, and industrious people. America is the people, not the president. I have faith in you!"

A year after this conversation, the Democrats won the House of Representatives in a midterm election that was widely seen as a rebuke to the president.

CHEN, THE HOUSE-CHURCH running pajama salesman, eventually got his green card and moved from Shanghai to Los Angeles County to join his family there. His wife, Gong, had set up a one-bedroom apartment for the family in a suburb east of LA. In the months after Chen's arrival, he seemed to relish living in the United States, based on the photos he posted on WeChat. As Gong drove the family's Corolla around greater LA, Chen shot pictures through the windshield of images that seemed exotic compared to the perpetual-motion machine that was Shanghai: quiet, palm-lined streets with lawns and bungalows beneath clear blue skies, a squirrel perched on a roof gutter, and a giant, outdoor Christmas display with reindeer and strings of lights that spelled "Feliz Navidad."

A year and a half later, I flew to Los Angeles to see how Chen and his family were doing. In a nice touch, Gong, who drove for Lyft, picked me up at the airport and drove me to my hotel. I spent much of the next few days hanging out in the family's first-floor garden apartment, learning about their transition to living in America. It had not been easy. Gong had given birth to their second daughter, Yingying, in a special house for expectant Chinese immigrant mothers. Finding a stable living arrangement on a meager budget without her husband around had been challenging. At one point, Gong and her two daughters lived in their Toyota, spending the nights in a McDonald's parking lot, where her elder daughter, Jiali, could use the Wi-Fi for homework and wash up in the bathroom sink before school. Now, two years into their reunification, the family was doing better. Chen was working as an electrician and Gong was studying for her barber's license. They had brought Jiali here to save her failing eyes and get her out from under the heavy Chinese academic workload. Although Jiali was still withdrawn and sometimes had trouble making eye contact, she found school less of a burden in America. She had a 3.5 GPA and was thinking about colleges in the University of California system.

President Trump's attempt to ban immigrants from majority-Muslim countries had jolted the family. Even though China was not among the banned nations, Gong felt insecure because she was a mere green-card holder with asylum status. That spring, the couple planned to return to China for the wedding of Gong's son from an earlier relationship, but Gong was worried. US immigration officials might ask why, if she was so afraid of persecution by Chinese authorities for violating the one-child policy, she would return to China. She also feared immigration officers might block her from reentering the United States, as politics in America now seemed unpredictable. Scared of being cut off from her family, Gong decided to stay in California and missed her son's wedding in China.

One Sunday after we attended local Chinese church services, the family treated me to their favorite pan-Asian buffet. As we dug into a mix of dishes, including pork ribs, sushi, and dim sum, they talked about their disappointment in Trump and his anti-immigration policies.

"If it were Obama, he wouldn't do this," said Gong.

"Obama is more relaxed and polite," Chen said.

I asked Jiali what she thought of America's new president.

"He makes fun of women," said Jiali. And, she added, "he's a racist."

I asked if she worried about the future for immigrant families like hers.

"I think we're OK," she said, "for now."

I understood the fear Chen and Gong had about going to a wedding in China and not being able to return to the United States, but some of Trump's policies were designed to prevent people like them from entering America under false pretenses. A few years ago, they had flown to Hawaii hiding Gong's baby bump and lied to immigration officers so they could give birth on American soil and begin to beat a path toward citizenship. Sitting on the floor of their apartment one evening, I finally got up the nerve to ask about the asylum application—the one based on fear of persecution under the country's one-child policy—that Chen had shown me years earlier in Shanghai and that had won them the right to live here. Chen knew I was asking because I was skeptical.

"It's real," he said somberly. "It's real."

Yingying was playing on the floor of the living room. Jiali was out at a movie with friends. Sitting at the plastic folding table the family used for meals, Gong paused and began to explain what had happened. After Jiali was born, Gong felt compelled to have a son for Chen, as is Chinese tradition, but the law forbade it. If she did have another child, Gong feared she'd be sterilized and hit with a crushing fine. She said family-planning officials had sterilized her mother back in 1983 after she had had a fourth child. Gong's sister had been forcibly sterilized as well.

In 2002, Gong decided to risk it anyway and became pregnant. As the baby was growing, so was the barbershop Gong ran in their Shanghai neighborhood. After years of struggle, she was beginning to get ahead. Then a little after nine o'clock one night a knock came at the door of their apartment, which sat behind her barbershop. Chen had gone out to buy seafood, and Gong assumed it was her husband returning home. When she opened the door, she saw a local family-planning official named Zheng, who had brought along four hired thugs.

"Are you pregnant?" Zheng asked.

"I don't know," Gong lied.

"Let's go to the hospital and find out," Zheng replied.

"I don't have any money," said Gong, suspecting this was just a shakedown.

"It won't cost you a dime," Zheng said ominously.

Gong isn't sure how Zheng learned of the pregnancy, but she thinks one of her clients ratted her out for the $80 fee the family-planning office routinely paid informants. Zheng and the thugs drove Gong to a nearby hospital and told her to go to the bathroom and pee on a stick to see if she was pregnant. Gong thought about escaping through the window, but she was on the second floor and the drop to the street was simply too far, especially in her condition.

"If I were back in the countryside, I could've gotten away," she told me.

Gong returned with the positive pregnancy test and realized resistance was futile. The men took her into an operating room and used yellow rubber medical tubing to bind her hands and feet to a surgical chair. She was given an injection to induce an abortion. There was no offer of anesthetic.

"If you move your ass, we will tear up your organs," Gong recalled one thug warning her.

As the thugs watched Gong, her legs spread apart, she cursed them using an old, graphic Chinese insult.

"*Jiao ni sheng haizi mei pigu yan,*" Gong said, which literally means "may your child be born with an unperforated anus."

The thugs became angry, and Gong refrained from cursing them further.

"They had surgical scissors," Gong recalled. "My life was in their hands."

Gong said before the doctor began performing the abortion, her mind went blank and she felt helpless.

"After the surgery, I felt my body was gutted and empty," she told me. "My heart was dead."

Chen sat in a purple folding chair and stared, expressionless, at the wall as Gong recounted her story. He gripped his head with his hands and then, overwhelmed, stood up and walked into the dark bedroom.

After the abortion, around 11 p.m., the family planning officials sent Gong home as if nothing had happened. Later, on the street, she spotted one of the thugs who had tied her down. He pretended not to know her. She avoided making eye contact as well.

"I know them all," she said of the thugs. "You can't kill them. China is like this, especially for ordinary people. We don't have the right to speak up."

"China is like this."

"This is China."

That's what Amanda had said when she was breaking down on the sidewalk back in Shanghai, frightened she would be arrested for protesting the collapse of the wealth-management company in which she'd lost her family's life savings.

In the following years, Gong's salon business continued to grow, providing some of the savings the family would eventually use to move to the United States. One day at an outdoor market, Gong ran into Zheng, the family-planning official who had overseen the forced abortion.

"Looks like your barbershop is doing well," Zheng said. "I'd like to come by for a haircut."

"I'm too busy," Gong replied.

As Zheng selected fruits from a bin and tried to bargain the vendor down, Gong paid for her $4.50 worth of fruit with a note worth nearly $8 and told the wholesaler to keep the change. This was what passed for revenge in a country where ordinary people had few rights and little recourse.

After the abortion, Gong continued to have health problems. Her fallopian tubes were partially blocked, and every time she was intimate with Chen she got an infection, but she didn't give up.

She continued to save her money and decided on in vitro fertilization, which is illegal in China but can be done on the sly at
certain hospitals. Once she learned she was pregnant again, the
couple decided to go to America, where one of the parishioners
in their house church served as an agent for homes that took care
of Chinese women preparing to give birth. The year was 2013 and
the timing was perfect. Gong's barbershop was slated for demolition to make way for development. The $140,000 she received
in compensation provided the seed money to begin a new life in
America. Gong doesn't think much about the abortion anymore
and hasn't shared her story with many people. More than a decade
and a half later, she still suffers from infections and doesn't have sex
with Chen very often because it's just too painful.

"Our husband-wife life isn't harmonious," Gong said, speaking
in typical Chinese euphemism.

Thinking back on her life, from the forced abortion in Shanghai to her years as a single mother in LA working long hours and
sleeping in her Toyota, Gong was struck by her own survival.

"I'm surprised after I've eaten so much bitterness, I still haven't
died," said Gong, sounding genuinely puzzled.

Several years after Yingying was born, the Chinese government
changed the population policy to allow two children per couple.
China's fertility rate is now among the lowest in the world, and
officials who years earlier had forced women to abort their babies
now want them to have more. The reason is simple: China's population is aging too quickly and the country now faces the crisis of a
rapidly shrinking labor force. Some demographers now say China
never needed the one-child policy in the first place. They argue
that, as China became more affluent and urban and raising a child
became vastly more expensive, people would have naturally had far
fewer children, which is exactly what happened.

CHAPTER 11

Losing Hearts and Minds

Charles and Ashley

A BOUT A YEAR after I said goodbye to Charles in his tiny room in Shanghai, I video called him one morning from London. Charles, who was back visiting his family in their apartment in Hubei province, sat down in a wooden rocking chair, put in his earbuds, and laid out a litany of bad news. His father, Shenhua, who'd never recovered from carbon monoxide poisoning when he was a migrant worker, had died a month earlier from stomach cancer, and Charles's grandmother had passed away as well. His father-in-law, who never thought Charles was good enough for his daughter, had suffered a stroke, and Charles had had to lend his in-laws nearly $3,000 to help with medical care. But there was some good news. Nearly three years since I'd served as chauffeur at their wedding, the couple was expecting a second child. I offered my congratulations.

"Too early," Charles said of the timing.

The pregnancy was unplanned, another burden for a man who—now that his father was gone—referred to himself as the lone pillar propping up his family.

"These children won't be able to contribute anything to the family for the first twenty years," said Charles. He noted that there was one advantage: the children would be so close in age, his wife could raise them and then go back to work earlier. Charles's reaction sounded cold, but his financial insecurity as a migrant worker—even a white-collar one—sometimes made him view his life as he might a ledger.

Charles, who wore a buzz cut and a sleeveless T-shirt, looked like he'd put on some weight. I tried to engage him in a conversation about President Trump, who he had predicted would win the American election, but Charles wasn't interested and his face remained expressionless. Charles's boss, the Dutch correspondent, was nearing sixty-five and would soon retire. Charles wasn't sure if a new correspondent would want to keep him. Charles is curious by nature and full of intellectual energy, but he seemed beaten down by the loss of his father and the loan to his father-in-law. I'd never seen him like this.

"I'm not yet desperate," he said, because he still had his news assistant job, the highest paying of his career.

I hope he feels better, I thought after we hung up.

Before Charles boarded the train back to Shanghai, he posted a picture of his luggage, which contained a book and some hard-boiled eggs and potatoes from family members.

"Feeling sad, leaving home," Charles wrote on WeChat.

You "need to make money," wrote his sister, whom he helped support. She added a smiley face.

A few days later, Charles wrote: "After turning 30, I live in fear every day."

A COUPLE OF weeks later, I flew home to the United States for the summer and stopped in Chicago to visit Ashley. She had finished her first year in business school and was doing an internship at an investment bank. We met in a park outside her apartment, a block from the Chicago River and walking distance to Lake Michigan. Ashley had just finished a spin class and arrived in a pair of lime-green running shorts, flats, and a white T-shirt with a cartoon cat on the front casting a side-eye glance—an appropriate image that captured Ashley's natural skepticism.

We strolled along the lakefront beneath some shade trees as sail-boats tacked back and forth along Lake Michigan. Ashley was one of three interns at the investment bank and optimistic about land-ing a job after graduation. She hoped to spend the fall in Paris on a semester-abroad program. I wondered how much Ashley might make in her first year out of business school, but hesitated to ask. In the 1990s, asking salaries in China was not considered impolite, but social norms—like so much else—were always changing and some of my recent salary inquiries had drawn appalled stares. In this case, though, I couldn't help myself.

"One hundred and twenty-five thousand a year," Ashley answered.

This was more than her parents' salaries combined.

We crossed Lake Shore Drive and waded into the crowds at Taste of Chicago, a giant summer food fair in Grant Park, where clouds of smoke from grilling sausages and frying popcorn shrimp filled the air. As we pushed through the sweaty mass of people, Ashley fanned the smell of fatty American food away from her nose. I sometimes forgot that many Chinese move to the West in part to get away from crowds.

"My mother doesn't want me here," said Ashley, adding that her parents didn't approve of her career choice or her move to America.

"But you could be making a lot of money," I offered.

"Money isn't as important to them. They are traditional Chinese."

Ashley's family was well connected in the Communist Party. One of her aunts served as chief of staff to the Chinese equivalent of a US cabinet secretary. Many American parents would be delighted with Ashley's professional and financial accomplishments. At twenty-eight, she was in the process of doing in one generation what usually took at least two or three in other countries.

We strolled along the Chicago River, had some dim sum, and then headed up to her sixteenth-floor sublet with a view of Lake Michigan, where our conversation returned, as it often did, to politics. Ashley recalled watching the results of the 2008 US presidential election with excited American students at Peking University who were stunned to see their country elect a black president and seemingly put race behind it. Eight years later, Ashley spent election night in a Chinese restaurant near her campus in America, but she paid little attention to the TV because she assumed Hillary Clinton would win. After Pennsylvania and Ohio turned red, Ashley returned to her apartment and watched online as Trump took the presidency.

"Yikes, this actually happened," she thought.

In the few months since we'd last talked, President Trump had accused—with no evidence—the Obama administration of spying on him in Trump Tower and fired James Comey after apparently failing to extract an oath of loyalty from the FBI director. He'd also announced plans to withdraw the United States from the Paris climate agreement. A decade earlier, Ashley had had a fairly idealistic view of the United States, but that had begun to change in 2014 when she spent a year working in Washington, DC.

"I started to see the ugly side," she said. Ashley was struck by how ill-informed many Americans were, and she began to question a fundamental premise of American democracy: that an informed citizenry will make the right choice at the ballot box.

"I think if you give people power, you have to prepare for stupidity, because most people are ignorant," Ashley said as we sat on her futon in the sparsely furnished sublet. "That's just the truth. They're very easily manipulated by politicians."

"In terms of Trump and the electorate, did it make you rethink democracy?" I asked.

"I think it does," she said. "Of course, it's difficult for me, because that's part of the biggest reason for me to come here, but it's overrated."

"What's the overrated part?"

"People can be trusted. That's not true. This whole idea from the eighteenth century that everybody is born equal or should be treated equal, it's very nice, it's very kind, but that's not reality. Obviously, not everybody is born equal, and how you form your opinions about things is mostly determined by your social status. You want people to have the power to determine their own fate, but that's just not right at some point. But also, you can't decide it for them, because that's also not right. So, you're just caught in a dilemma."

Trump's election and the policies he was pursuing were changing the way Ashley saw America and making her more cynical about democracy. I wondered if it might also change her plans to settle here.

"I don't think so," Ashley said.

Then she paused.

"You know what? It might. I'm not going back to China, but I might go somewhere else other than the States."

"Where would you go?"

"Probably Europe or somewhere else. I thought when I moved here I was pretty much just going to settle down," she said wistfully. "There's no way back, but here isn't very satisfying."

There were more Chinese students in America than students from any other country. America had welcomed them for decades, not only for the tuition dollars they brought but also in the hope they would absorb American values of free speech, rule of law, and democracy and take them back to help change China. The strategy had yet to bear fruit. But with Trump in the Oval Office, American ideals were becoming an even harder sell abroad. Instead of being inspired by their time in the United States, students like Ashley were becoming disillusioned.

Ashley's path forward was uncertain. For now, she'd given up on her homeland, where the prospects for freedom were the dimmest they'd been in more than two decades. As if to emphasize that point, as we chatted, one of the leaders of the Tiananmen Square protests, Liu Xiaobo, whose writings had fired Ashley's idealism during her college years, was dying in custody in northeastern China. Liu, whom I'd interviewed years ago about his time in a reeducation-through-labor camp, was in prison for pushing for peaceful democratic change. The Chinese government refused to let Liu travel overseas for treatment, and he died several days after Ashley and I spoke. The leader of the Norwegian Nobel Committee, Berit Reiss-Andersen, said the Chinese government bore "a heavy responsibility for his premature death," which was a polite way of saying the government had ensured his demise by refusing to let him seek better medical treatment outside of China.

After a year as a student in America, Ashley was disappointed in her homeland and her adopted country. She was also beginning to come to terms with something she hadn't anticipated: "Moving here is not going to fix everything."

SEVERAL WEEKS LATER, as I boarded a plane back to London, I received the following note from an email account I didn't recognize: "This is Charles. I will go home today as my boss starts his one-month-long vacation. I would like to have a video chat with you, do you have time later today (say sometime between 7pm to 10pm Beijing time)?"

Something was up. This was unusually formal for Charles. I called him on WeChat video the next morning as he was climbing the stairs to his family's apartment in Hubei. Charles got straight to the point.

"My boss, the old Dutch guy, has been writing fake news for at least two years."

Charles had hinted about troubles at work on our final drive a year earlier in Shanghai but didn't seem to want to tell me what was bothering him. Now he explained. His boss, Oscar, had worked as a reporter in China for nearly a decade. During the two years Charles had worked for him, Charles said, Oscar had never shown him a published version of a single story they'd produced, despite several requests. Charles wanted to see the results of their work, so he went to the website of Oscar's newspaper and eventually tracked down the stories. Charles didn't read Dutch, so he ran them through Google Translate. The translations weren't perfect, but Charles was able to spot small factual errors. There was more. Oscar had decided to do a story on the government crackdown on golf courses, which was part of President Xi's anti-corruption campaign. Businessmen often treated government officials to rounds of golf and drinks. Many courses had been built on farm-land obtained in corrupt real estate deals, so golf had become yet another symbol of Communist Party excess. Charles and Oscar went to visit a Shanghai golf course, but Oscar was turned away. In the printed story, though, Oscar wrote that a caddie at the club told him President Xi had golfed there in 2007, which could've made China's president look like a hypocrite.

"In order to make these golf stories about anti-corruption more vivid, he just made up a rumor about our highest leader," Charles told me.

If Charles's claim was true, this was unethical and egregious.

The next example hit close to home.

Yang and I had flown to Shanxi province in late 2015 to do a story about Lüliang, a city of more than three million people that seemed to go from boom to bust overnight. It was a cautionary tale about the challenges China faced as it tried to shift from an industrial and investment-driven economy to one fueled by consumer spending. As recently as 2010, GDP growth in Lüliang had been a staggering 21 percent, but the local government continued to double down on the country's old industrial model, which emphasized investment in coal mining, infrastructure, and mile after mile of apartment buildings. Eventually, overcapacity so outstripped demand, the local economy collapsed.

Oscar had read our story and planned to visit Lüliang to do a similar one, which was fine by me. But, as Charles pointed out, the content of Oscar's story resembled ours a little too closely. We had interviewed a woman named Lei Lili, who ran a home appliance store and said business was so bad she had to offer a free refrigerator to each customer who bought a TV. In his story, Oscar quoted an appliance saleswoman with a nearly identical name, Lei Li, making the same kind of complaints.

When Yang and I drove in from the airport to Lüliang, we spotted a dormant cement factory and decided to investigate. We found a low-level factory manager named Gao sitting in his room watching a rerun of a military parade in Beijing. Gao told us the plant had been banking on producing cement for Lüliang's new $5 billion business and financial district, designed to accommodate at least three hundred thousand people. But the mayor behind the plan was fired for corruption, the government ran out of money, and the boulevard to the new district became a road to nowhere. Oscar based much of his story at the same cement factory and interviewed a man named Gao who said a lot of the same things. There was just one problem.

"That's a place we didn't visit," Charles told me. "It's fiction. He just borrowed a name from your report."

In addition to being unethical, making up information and ripping off a colleague seemed particularly reckless in the digital age. Charles's role in all of this gnawed at him. He'd helped find sources but then never sent them links to the final product because he was too embarrassed.

"They treated me well, like friends," Charles said, "but I couldn't face them. It's really a nightmare."

As his boss prepared for retirement, Charles decided to expose him.

"He cannot just walk away so proudly and arrogantly like he's a real foreign boss. He's not," said Charles, referring to Western bosses' relative prestige in China, which had been fading for years.

Charles's righteous anger reminded me of "The Swordsman," the Tang dynasty poem he'd copied and taped to the wall over his bed.

> *I have been honing this sword for a decade;*
> *Its frosty edge has never been tested.*
> *Now I am holding it and showing it to you, sir:*
> *Is there anyone suffering injustice?*

Charles wasn't just trying to right a wrong. He was also angry with his boss, who he felt had mistreated him.

"I know in this industry, many foreign journalists, unlike you," Charles said carefully, "they are very arrogant. They don't treat their Chinese colleagues as equals."

Charles said his boss didn't speak with him much and complained he didn't do enough to earn his paycheck.

"Once he claimed I was unprofessional, not diligent," Charles recalled.

I worried that going public would make Charles radioactive for any future job at an especially tough time. His father had recently passed away, he'd had to lend money to his in-laws, and a second child was on the way that Charles worried he couldn't afford.

"Maybe I will even be boycotted by the whole industry," Charles said.

I suggested Charles first reach out to Oscar's newspaper, tell them about the problems, and give them a chance to act. If they ignored him, then he could go public.

"Thanks for your valuable advice," Charles wrote back. "I will consider it seriously. I am wondering if those editors will hinder my report to protect themselves. Of course, as you said, it is a step I'd better take before taking other actions."

CHARLES TOOK MY advice and sent a message to the newspaper's general email address—he said he couldn't find one for Oscar's editor—detailing his allegations. Charles, whose English is largely self-taught, was unsparing.

"Being a news assistant who helps with pitching stories, conducting researches, conducting/arranging interviews, and translating any necessary Chinese materials but never gets to write a story or have a proper byline (not even a research byline), I dare not say I have mastered the dark art of making fake news," he began. "But I have the luck of working with one of the greatest masters of the dark art for two years and watching him fabricating, twisting and distorting stories on many occasions."

Charles sent the email, which continued in that vein, on a Sunday. When he didn't hear back, he became worried the newspaper would try to bury the allegations, so he posted them publicly on WeChat, which was like dropping a bomb. The message soon disappeared from the site, which at first seemed odd. A Chinese news assistant exposing his Western journalist boss as a fraud would be catnip to a foreign-bashing newspaper such as *Global Times*. A hint as to why his post had mysteriously disappeared could be found in WeChat's oblique online explanation.

"The content of this article damages state organs and officials' image and reputation," read a notice where Charles's article had been posted.

The problem? Charles's story repeated Oscar's claim that Xi Jinping was a golfer and, by implication, a hypocrite. Charles reposted without the golf reference and the post stayed up. Charles waited for a response. A day later, he received a text message from Oscar's wife.

"Shame on you," it read.

The foreign editor for the Dutch newspaper, *NRC,* which is a well-respected daily, wrote Charles, saying they were treating the allegations seriously and asking him to provide additional evidence. Then, separately, the newspaper's top editor, Peter Vandermeersch, responded to Charles's claims in a blog post entitled "On the Journalistic Integrity of Our Correspondent in China."

"What is going on exactly?" began Vandermeersch.

He explained that Oscar had become unhappy with Charles's work and his lack of ideas, and told him he needed to improve. Oscar said Charles didn't have a background in journalism and this had led to miscommunication and distrust "regarding his lack of openness about his contacts with state security. According to Oscar, this was one of the reasons why he often worked alone, because he was not absolutely certain that [Charles] didn't have connections with the Chinese state security."

Oscar said he had told Charles he would retire soon and couldn't guarantee his successor would keep Charles on. "'During my holidays, I decided to make a change,' says Oscar. 'Apparently, he had already decided to lash out at me.'"

"I find it remarkable," the blog post quoted Oscar as saying, "that the Chinese Party press encourages him and enthusiastically adopts his allegations. This fits in with the current climate, in which it is increasingly difficult for foreign journalists to do their work. I have been tailed, stopped and questioned on countless occasions."

Oscar was describing a fear of many foreign correspondents: that their news assistants might be working as spies for the Chinese government. When I worked in Beijing in the 1990s, one of my assistants confided in me that military intelligence had tried to recruit her to keep tabs on me because of her family ties to the People's Liberation Army. It was also common knowledge that state security agents offered gifts to some assistants for information.

In the *NRC* rebuttal, Oscar even seemed to suggest the allegations against him might be a conspiracy between a disgruntled employee and party propagandists who wanted to damage his reputation. The Dutch reporter was using the same tactic against Charles that the Chinese Communist Party uses against foreign reporters when it tries to convince its own people that we shouldn't be trusted because we are really just tools of the state. In the second half of the article, Oscar defended his work, though not terribly effectively.

Regarding Charles's claim that Oscar made up an interview with a golf caddie who implicated Xi Jinping, Oscar said he returned the next day without Charles and did the interview on his own. As to charges of ripping off my story about Lüliang, the coal boomtown gone bust, Oscar said they had visited six steel and cement factories and he couldn't understand why Charles would say otherwise.

The newspaper editor concluded the article, writing, "The editorial staff of the *NRC* regret that the former employee tried to drag the name of a well-established correspondent and the newspaper's name through the mud. To the extent that this is possible, Oscar is gathering old notes and records to refute the allegations by his former assistant in more detail."

IN THE FALL of 2017, Ashley moved to Paris to do a semester abroad as part of her MBA program in America. A few weeks after settling into school, she boarded a $17 bus, crossed beneath the English Channel, and came to London, where by that time I'd been living for more than a year. We took the tube to Borough Market, an open-air food emporium that sits beneath train tracks along the south bank of the Thames. Arriving at London Bridge, I tried to give Ashley some bearings, pointing to a sign for the Shard, the Renzo Piano–designed office tower that juts up from London's low-rise skyline like jagged fragments of glass.

"The Shard is one of the tallest skyscrapers in western Europe," I said, with a hint of pride for my newly adopted city.

"Oh, wow!" said Ashley, sounding genuinely impressed.

Then, realizing I was speaking to a Chinese person, I tried to lower expectations.

"It's only seventy-something floors," I said, "so it's really small by Shanghai standards."

At a little over one thousand feet, the Shard is about half the height of Shanghai Tower.

We weaved amid crowds and food stalls as the smell of paella and pulled pork floated through the air in Borough Market. After a quick lunch of pad thai—Ashley's choice—we walked to the embankment and sat on a bench overlooking the river. Just downstream sat the HMS *Belfast,* a naval cruiser that had bombarded the Korean coastline during the Korean War. Britain had joined the United States and other allies to beat back an invasion by North Korea, which fought with heavy Chinese support. The tide was out, leaving the piers naked and exposing the lush green moss along the brick embankment and dark sandbanks below. Ashley was at a crossroads. The job she'd hoped for in Chicago had not materialized. The firm wasn't hiring for the health-care section where she'd spent the summer working. She thought about applying for jobs at smaller funds, but felt the investing culture in the United States was comparatively risk averse.

"They're comfortable with their moderate returns," she said. "It's not like China. Everybody there is ambitious to grow."

The United States, which had once been a beacon for young, idealistic Chinese, was also continuing to lose its luster. Like many Americans, Ashley was suffering from Trump fatigue. The month before, Trump had picked fights on Twitter with NFL players, saying they should be suspended or fired for kneeling during the national anthem, and he'd threatened to "totally destroy" North Korea in a speech to the United Nations.

"He's ridiculous," Ashley said. "*Still* ridiculous. What he says has started to lose its shock value. I don't think that anybody takes what he says seriously anymore."

All this left Ashley with a question she'd thought she'd answered when she got into business school in America: Where next? Her parents wanted her to return home to western China to follow a more conventional and secure path. Ashley figured if she got a master's or PhD from Peking University—degrees that would be highly prized in provincial China—she could land a cushy government job and rise quickly. She was eyeing an investment position in Hong Kong, a city that for decades had been a comfortable mix of East and West: British rule of law and free speech with subtropical beaches and great dim sum. But Hong Kong was changing fast, and not for the better. After the city's 2014 democracy protests, the Chinese government was bent on choking off political freedom and transforming Hong Kong into just another big city in southern China. And, as the space for free speech in Hong Kong continued to shrink, the rents in the cramped city had kept rising.

"You probably work your entire life to get a not very decent flat," said Ashley, sounding a little like Charles, Sarah, and the other migrants back in Shanghai.

The more time Ashley spent with Americans and the longer Trump was in office, the more she questioned the democratic system she'd admired from a distance for so long. A few days earlier, Ashley had popped into a pub across the street from Big Ben and fallen into conversation with some American tourists. She was chatting with one from Nashville about baseball when a couple from Texas began complaining about the British, saying their personalities were too rigid. The couple then turned their ire on immigrants back in America.

"Immigrants are kind of ruining everything," the blond woman from Texas told Ashley, criticizing Latinos.

"Then they complained about Chinese grabbing all their jobs," Ashley recalled.

Ashley has a smooth American accent, honed by watching *Desperate Housewives, Grey's Anatomy,* and *The Good Wife.* "Obviously they didn't realize I'm Chinese," she said. "It was a little awkward for me to listen."

Ashley chalked it up to the couple's lack of interaction with people who weren't like them. "I think they haven't had any experience dealing with anything other than white Americans, so they don't know how to react to me," Ashley said. "They automatically assumed I was American."

In her year in the United States, she'd concluded that many Americans didn't pay a lot of attention. "In a democratic society, a lot of people think everybody is qualified to vote, but they are far from being qualified to discuss politics or policy," Ashley said. "I think people shouldn't vote at all on some federal policies. It's just not your expertise. It's not even my expertise."

This was the exact problem I had covered in Britain a year earlier. David Cameron, who was then prime minister, had put an incredibly complex question—membership in the European Union, or Brexit—to a simple in or out public vote. Everyone from Xi Jinping, to the International Monetary Fund, to five former NATO secretaries-general, to Barack Obama thought walking away from a massive market of more than half a billion people would damage the UK's economy and its global prestige. In a now-infamous exchange on Sky News, then UK justice secretary Michael Gove said, "I'm asking the public to trust themselves. I think the people of this country have had enough of experts." In the two years following the vote, British politics descended into chaos and government analyses showed the United Kingdom would be poorer after Brexit; the only question was by how much. It was a pivotal moment in what seemed like the British and American retreat from a world they had helped build.

As Ashley and I watched the river flow by, there were signs nearby of the West's past power and global reach. Our bench stood along what had once been Hay's Wharf, home to massive warehouses where clipper ships delivered tea from China during the

1850s. More than a decade earlier, Britain had broken open the China trade after easily defeating the Chinese Navy in the First Opium War. The Treaty of Nanking ceded control of Hong Kong to the British, who built it into a wildly successful colony before returning it to China in 1997.

Across the river, you could see the signs of China's resurgence amid the jumble of cranes and motley assortment of skyscrapers that make up the City of London, the capital's historic financial district. Taking advantage of the cheap pound after the Brexit vote, a Hong Kong–based firm had spent $1.7 billion to buy one of the district's most recognizable buildings, called the Walkie-Talkie. The top-heavy, thirty-seven-storey structure has a concave glass face that concentrates enough sunbeams on a bright day to fry an egg on the street. Earlier in the year, another Hong Kong company had spent $1.5 billion to buy the nearby Leadenhall Building, which looks like a cheese grater. In a case of unintended consequences, older white Britons who had voted for Brexit to limit immigration had created an opportunity for bargain-hunting Chinese companies to scoop up London landmarks.

The United States had criticized China's authoritarian system for decades, convinced its mix of state capitalism, personal freedom, and political repression wouldn't last. But the political dysfunction in the United States and the United Kingdom was making the Communist Party's management of China look more and more attractive to Ashley.

"Honestly, I'm not sure how much credit we should give to the current system of China right now, because it's just so effective and I think people should start to rethink that."

I understood Ashley's point. She was an admirer of liberal principles and a sharp critic of the Communist Party, and even she had growing doubts about the West. Ashley ticked off the advantages of the Chinese system. The government could be much more aggressive pursuing disruptive policies because it didn't have to respond immediately to domestic criticism, let alone ill-informed voters.

One reason Chinese officials had been able to muscle through new superhighways, high-speed rail lines, and real estate developments that destroyed millions of homes was that those whose properties were in their way had almost no legal recourse to stop them. And if the losers in the country's development drive tried to criticize the government publicly, that was easily taken care of.

"If somebody blames you, you can just lock them up," said Ashley. "So, you can be long-term goal driven."

If you challenged the government, you could pay a price. You could suffer like Li, the woman who was frequently detained in a secret black jail inside a Shanghai public park for protesting the destruction of her home; or her attorney, Johanna, who was abducted from her hotel room at night for supporting fellow human rights attorneys; or Gong, who had her second child taken from her womb.

Ashley pointed out, as so many have, that democracy is slow, messy, and inefficient. "Of course, it's a good thing to have opinions, but it takes time to debate and have a consensus," she said. "I think the big problem with America is that people are beginning to be unable to have any consensus on any topics anymore. In terms of being able to move the country forward versus what you see in the United States right now, it's hard to get anything done."

Ashley also noted the economic advantages of authoritarian power. Had local Chinese been able to vote, many would've blocked the polluting factories that poisoned their communities but boosted China's gross domestic product.

"Sometimes you kind of need that to drive growth," she said. "Most of the neoclassical economists believe that growth can fix pretty much everything."

"Not pollution," I said.

Ashley countered, as some Chinese do, that where we were sitting had been terribly polluted when London was still an industrial city and factories crowded the East End. Just a mile upstream from where we sat was the old Bankside Power Station, which was estimated to have spewed up to 235 tons of grit per square mile in a single month in 1950. Two years later, the Great Smog enveloped the city for four days, with clouds so thick that conductors had to walk in front of buses with lanterns to guide the way. The smog killed more than four thousand people, creating a shortage of coffins, and four years later inspired the British government to pass the Clean Air Act. There were some signs that China might be beginning to turn a corner on air pollution. In 2017, the government temporarily shut down entire industrial regions and even began jailing people in charge of polluting factories. Beijing had strings of clear, blue-sky days, something I'd never seen in my two decades in and out of the country, though pollution continued to plague Shanghai.

"I still think it's good to have a democratic system," said Ashley, in a tone that sounded not completely convinced, "but I think China's system is not all bad. It has some merits."

"Does it look better to you in some ways than it did before you left for overseas?" I asked.

"Yes," she said without hesitating. "Definitely."

CHAPTER 12

Rethinking the West
Charles and Ashley

===============

A S ASHLEY WAS losing faith in the American experiment, Charles was beginning to view Western journalism as something of a sham, at least given his experience over the past couple of years. The newspaper had responded to Charles blowing the whistle on his boss by hinting he might simply be a Chinese spy.

"It is too low to accuse me of connections with state security," Charles wrote to me in a series of exchanges. "How is this related with the fabrications he made? The enemy is cunning and stubborn and has his newspaper's support. I thought there was one rotten apple, now I found it is a basket of rotten apples."

People in the news business in China responded to the scandal in various, revealing ways. Some fellow news assistants wondered why Charles didn't raise concerns about the fabrications earlier. Others wondered why he didn't just walk away from the job.

"Why did nobody expose Oscar's serious news fabrication during his ten years' stay in China until me?" Charles responded.

Some foreign correspondents wondered if Charles was indeed a spy. Meanwhile, Chinese journalists rallied to Charles's cause on Twitter—which is blocked in China—appalled by what they saw as the editor's attempt to smear a former employee who'd been engaged in a sometimes dangerous and often thankless job.

"Ur assistant has interactiona [*sic*] with state security precisely because he works 4 u, dumbass," wrote Wang Feng, editor in chief of FTChinese.com, pointing out that most news assistants had little choice but to meet with Chinese security. "Don't know the facts in this case, don't want to judge, but the editor in chief sounds too defensive, petty & vindictive & no EIC [editor in chief] worth his salt would start by questioning the motives of the accuser."

Some mainland news websites, as well as those in Hong Kong and Singapore, covered Charles's charges against his boss. Western news organizations, on the other hand, steered clear of the allegations, a decision that some news assistants found hypocritical. The scandal seemed to divide people who worked for international media along tribal lines.

"If the foreign media choose to willfully ignore this malpractice, they hardly need any help from GT [*Global Times*] or PD [*People's Daily*] on ruining their own credibility," tweeted Luna Lin, who worked as a news assistant for the *Washington Post* in Beijing at the time.

Most in the international press didn't want to touch this story because it was a messy dispute that did not involve a global brand. In addition, Charles's claims only provided ammunition to the Chinese government's campaign to portray foreign correspondents as untrustworthy and hopelessly biased. Charles expected more from Western journalists.

"All of them are silent and choose not to take a stand," he said. "They are not stupid. Idealism is something they preach to others, pragmatism is a motto they keep to themselves. If it's as dark or as hypocritical as I feared, why should I work in this business?"

Beyond the dispute over facts and journalistic ethics, there was something deeper at work here. The willingness of Charles and other Chinese working for foreign media to press *NRC* and the international journalism community was another example of a growing confidence among Chinese to criticize and challenge the West. For years, many news assistants had operated as frustrated subordinates, providing crucial help to correspondents navigating the treacherous landscape of news gathering in China. But because the government largely forbade Chinese from working as correspondents for foreign news companies, assistants often toiled in relative anonymity, making their foreign bosses look smart while facing harassment and even police detention. Without the help of Chinese assistants, most of us couldn't do our jobs. The government restricted reporting by assistants to control them, but it was also a way to generate resentment and drive a wedge between foreign and Chinese colleagues. The Communist Party had ruled for decades by dividing its critics and sowing distrust. Its approach to the foreign media was no different.

Twenty years ago, most news assistants wouldn't have dreamed of publicly outing their bosses as Charles had. Back then, the status of a foreign correspondent was much higher in Chinese society and news assistants were far less worldly and well educated than they are today. In my first year in Beijing, we were still forced to hire through the diplomatic service bureau, essentially a Communist-era warehouse largely filled with unmotivated underachievers. Some were so bad, it seemed their job was to spy on their bosses while providing as little journalistic help as possible. Today's news assistants, like Chinese people in general, were far more sophisticated. Consider Yang, who'd spent a year as an exchange student at a historically black college in North Carolina and had earned a master's degree in journalism from Hong Kong Baptist University. Even though working as a correspondent for foreign news organizations was largely banned, over the years some Chinese had figured out a way to do so. One correspondent was Fan Wenxin, who had been a news assistant for the *New York Times,* spent a year at Harvard as a Nieman fellow, and now worked for the *Wall Street Journal* in Hong Kong. In Fan, Charles had something that wouldn't have existed in an earlier era: a prominent Chinese colleague willing to stand up for him. Fan even wrote the Dutch newspaper, questioning Oscar's description of Charles as "someone who is incapable and with dubious secret police links."

"Hope you see our perspective as well," Elske Schouten, *NRC*'s foreign editor, wrote back. "Somebody drops a super heavy accusation online, totally one-sided, without asking us for a reaction first. For our readers, we really needed to give our side of the story as well, and the relationship between Oscar and [Charles] Zhang is part of this."

She had a point, and I wished Charles had been more patient before going public.

"Why did you feel so compelled to do this?" I asked. "Most news assistants probably would not have exposed this."

"My nature is different," said Charles, who was so tortured by his own complicity that he couldn't sleep some nights. "I cannot stand these kinds of things."

Charles hated the reflexive lying that was part of the fabric of life here. When he was young, Charles said, his father often offered to buy him things but rarely followed through. For instance, when he was in high school, Charles became a big soccer fan and his father promised to buy him a jersey for the Argentine national team, but it never materialized. When Charles went to visit his dad's roast duck shop in southeastern China, he saw the jerseys hanging in a shop nearby.

"Lots of Chinese parents do things like this," said Charles. "It's just me who remembers it so well."

As Charles continued to press his case against Oscar, his family was desperate for him to drop it and move on. When he first told his wife he was quitting his job and exposing his boss, she turned pale and asked him to stop talking. Charles's family was worried he could suffer the fate of petitioners like Li, the woman who had pressed government officials for compensation for her house but instead was detained and physically abused. Charles assured his family that foreigners didn't have the power of Chinese government officials, but he took precautions. When he sent his company-issued laptop back to Shanghai, he made sure the courier did not include his family's home address. Although Charles's wife supported his decision to go public, his mother was incredulous that he would sacrifice his job for something as abstract as journalistic ethics.

"Just had an argument with my mom," Charles wrote one day. "In the evening, Mom suddenly said, 'You should stop now, and focus on job hunting. If I knew your plan, I would have stopped you. Maybe you should have just left him and found another job. Why expose it?'" She told her son he was too straightforward, too honest, "just like your father, who didn't know how to bargain when shopping."

"Many people praised my courage and honesty," Charles responded.

"They may praise you in public," his mother shot back, "but when they consider hiring you, they will worry about how you will behave in their company. Most people are not as honest as you are. Everybody has secrets. They don't want to work with an honest person."

"She is probably one hundred percent correct," said Charles, who was filled with guilt. "I put their feelings and the family's financial situation in the second place behind my pursuit of justice."

I asked Charles what he would tell his son about this episode of his life. He said he would only share the story if he won his battle with the newspaper and his life improved.

"Otherwise, he'll say, 'So this is how you end up?'"

ONE FRIDAY IN autumn, I boarded the Eurostar and headed under the English Channel to catch up with Ashley, who had just a few weeks left in her semester abroad at a business school outside of Paris. The next morning, I strolled across the Seine and came upon the bronze statue of Winston Churchill outside the Petit Palais. In ordinary times, I would have glanced at it and moved on, but this felt like a new era in both China and the West. With his right hand dug into the pocket of his double-breasted military overcoat, left hand grasping a cane, Churchill leans forward, his chin jutting out, his right foot poised in the air. On the platform below reads the words "WE SHALL NEVER SURRENDER," from Churchill's "We Shall Fight on the Beaches" speech in the House of Commons following Britain's deliverance at Dunkirk. Churchill concluded the speech by saying that, were the Nazis to invade Great Britain, the nation would continue to fight until "the New World, with all its power and might, steps forth to the rescue and the liberation of the old." More than seven decades later, the liberal world order that the United States and the United Kingdom had helped build was under threat from within and without. President Trump routinely criticized the United States' traditional European allies, while praising strongmen such as Vladimir Putin and Xi Jinping, both of whom wanted to weaken America. Staring at Churchill's flinty gaze, I could think of no current Western leader with the resolve or authority to champion liberal, global values in the face of retreat in the West and authoritarianism in the East. Within a year, UK prime minister Theresa May would be paralyzed by Brexit, her country's biggest political crisis in decades. In Germany, Chancellor Angela Merkel would step down as leader of her party, the Christian Democrats, and in France, President Emmanuel Macron would battle the violent "yellow vest" protests in Paris over income inequality.

I walked across the street to the Grand Palais, a massive exhibition center with a vaulted steel-and-glass roof, and met Ashley, who arrived fashionably dressed in a black-and-white plaid jacket, gray scarf, black pants, and a pair of raspberry-colored boots. Ashley had chosen our event for the morning, an exhibit of window displays built around the signature handbags of Hermès, the French luxury goods brand. The first display we came upon featured a small, white handbag sitting on a white beach beneath a cresting wave made of porcelain. Ashley explained that the bag was a "Kelly," named for Grace Kelly, and could cost $10,000.

"China in total buys at least one third of all luxury goods in the world," said Ashley. "It's like Japan in the eighties. Everyone has a Louis Vuitton bag."

In fact, the streets of Beijing and Shanghai were so littered with LV bags, they'd become a cliché ages ago.

"Do you own anything of Hermès?"

"I have a small wallet," said Ashley, who'd spent about $2,000 on the item.

As we strolled through the exhibit, French and Mandarin swirled around us. Around the corner, we came upon an underwater motif filled with pink fan coral and matching handbags, including one large enough to carry the shoes of a supermodel, which a guide said was an homage to Elle Macpherson. The guide asked where we were from. Ashley said China, adding that she'd worked in Beijing at the China World Trade Center, which is home to an Hermès store.

"I was in Beijing for a month," the guide said. "Can I just say—I'm sorry—but I didn't really like it. Too smoggy. I was so scared to run outside."

"You don't run outside," said Ashley, who could be blunt when someone said something that struck her as dumb.

This was a characteristic of China's industrial development and of other rising economies. As living standards rapidly rose, in some respects the quality of life fell. People now had the money to buy handbags worth thousands of dollars, to travel and study in Paris, but fresh air back home was beyond reach. Even if you were sharply critical of the party, however, you were also—like Ashley, Ray, and even Charles—already wealthier than your parents, which is not a recipe for political rebellion, especially given the costs associated with it. Suddenly, the guide leaned in, lowered her voice as if we were in the nave of Notre Dame, and—out of the blue—began pitching us her fledgling luxury travel operation. She told us she had 150 dogs and twenty horses and did hunting excursions in Burgundy. She was still trying to insure the operation, but would we be interested in signing up for a tour? I gave her my card out of respect for her chutzpah.

"She's going to be successful," said Ashley as we continued to the next exhibit.

"You know what she reminded me of?" I said. "A Chinese person. Chinese are always thinking of opportunities, always trying to figure things out, always making friends and not knowing where it's going, but always thinking."

I recalled a maître d' at my favorite courtyard restaurant back in Beijing in the 1990s. He was new to managing restaurants and always asking for tips on how to appeal to foreign customers. Navigating cultural differences proved tricky. One day he told me he was planning a Halloween party at the restaurant and showed me a poster he'd had made to try to attract foreigners, particularly Americans. The poster had a photograph of a Klansman in a white hood. As gently as I could, I explained that this wasn't a ghost, but a member of a white supremacist group that murdered black people. The maître d' stared at me expressionless, walked to the front door of the restaurant, and took down the poster.

In her time in the United States, Ashley said she had missed that sort of hustle that had been a defining feature of the China boom. She had some great contacts in Hong Kong who were eager to help her summer firm in Chicago work on some cross-border deals, but she said when she pitched her American colleagues, they were blasé.

"You don't feel they get excited about anything, and that's not very exciting for me," she said. "Their biggest dream is to make some money and buy a lake house somewhere and retire."

We moved on to the next display, the interior of a bank vault with polished metal walls riveted together and matching silver bags. A metal suitcase lay on the floor, a thick chain coiled on top. Ashley said that some Hermès products, such as the famed Birkin bags, are so ubiquitous that they're overexposed.

"For example, Victoria Beckham probably has one hundred thirty Birkin bags," she said.

"That seems like Imelda Marcos," I said.

There was not a glimmer of recognition on Ashley's face.

"You remember Imelda Marcos?"

She didn't. Ashley was born in 1989, three years after the first lady of the Philippines had become a global symbol of greed and excess.

"Imelda Marcos was the wife of the Philippine dictator Ferdinand Marcos," I began, sounding uncomfortably like a history teacher, "and when he was overthrown, the people went into Malacañang Palace and opened up her closets and she had over twelve hundred pairs of shoes. It was a symbol of the incredible corruption of the entire system."

I thought Ashley would be shocked, but my reference to Imelda Marcos was more dated than I realized.

"A thousand shoes is not so crazy," said Ashley matter-of-factly. "Think about it. I know people who own three hundred or four hundred pairs of shoes."

Now I was shocked. Over two decades, I'd seen mammoth wealth form in Beijing and then Shanghai, but I didn't know anyone with three hundred pairs of shoes.

"What are their jobs?" I asked about Ashley's friends. "What do they do?"

"I don't know," she said. "They're rich. In China, sometimes you don't know where that money comes from."

"Actually, you kind of do."

"Yeah, but you don't ask."

"Behind every great fortune lies a great crime," I said.

The line I was repeating is often attributed to French author Honoré de Balzac. He actually wrote something a bit different in his tragicomic novel *Le Père Goriot*: "The secret of a great fortune made without apparent cause is soon forgotten, if the crime is committed in a respectable way." Yet the line he's credited with seems to fit today's China. Because the Communist Party both regulates and competes in the country's economy, the route to riches for many had involved cutting some kind of deal with officials, whether it was to gain access to prime real estate or to strip state assets. The economic boom of the previous thirty years—where a significant chunk of personal gains can't be explained—had also altered the ladder of status symbols.

"Our sense of luxury was when we got an iPod Classic," said Ashley, who was in high school when the music player arrived in China. Now, she said, "real luxury stuff has started to penetrate high schools."

Most overseas Chinese students now come from moneyed families. Ashley has a friend from Peking University who teaches finance at Ohio State. The professor had managed to deal with the stratospheric wealth of many of her Chinese students, until one luxury item tipped her over the edge. Ashley recalled one of their conversations.

"I'm OK with a BMW. I'm OK with the Land Rover, the bags and shoes," the professor told Ashley, "but one day when I saw one of my kids with a gold Rolex, I thought: *What am I doing here?*"

A yellow gold Rolex starts around $33,000, according to the company website.

We strolled out of the exhibit and made our way back across the Seine along the Alexandre III bridge, a mix of beaux arts and art nouveau styles that includes half-naked nymphs draped across the central arch grasping golden miters. The bridge had been built in the heady, prosperous days of the Belle Epoque, which felt different from today's France, where GDP growth over the past decade had averaged less than 1 percent. As Ashley and I continued to walk, she told me that she'd spent many of her weekends racing around Europe, taking in as much of the culture as she could before she had to return to America. A few weeks earlier, she'd visited the Van Gogh Museum in Amsterdam, where she'd recognized a painting called *The Potato Eaters*, which she'd studied as a child. Van Gogh had painted a family of peasants sitting around a farmhouse table eating steaming potatoes and preparing tea by the glow of an oil lamp. The family members have creased faces, bulging eyes, and long, ski-slope noses, exaggerated features that seem almost cartoonish. Ashley didn't study the painting in art history class but in politics class.

"They used *The Potato Eaters* to try to tell us how badly people used to live in Europe," Ashley explained. "I think they were trying to teach us to sympathize with the peasants and tell us that all peasants in the world should unite."

"It was a message of socialism?"

"Yes, I think so."

"Did it work with you?"

"No. I was too little, but it definitely made an impression."

While Ashley's teacher was using art to urge her to sympathize with peasants across the globe, tens of millions of migrants, including Charles's father, were pouring out of the Chinese countryside looking for better-paying work in the big coastal cities. They cooked food, cleaned houses, cared for the children of local residents, and built the modern skylines that the government would show off to foreign investors and their own citizens as proof of the Communist Party's economic prowess. But the vast majority of migrants would never obtain full legal rights to basic government benefits, including education and health care. They would never be welcome in the cities they'd largely built. In fact, as we were chatting and wandering through Paris, a fire was raging in makeshift apartments five thousand miles to the east in Daxing, a southern district of Beijing filled with rural migrants, many of whom worked in nearby clothing factories. Nineteen people would die in the fire, including seven children under the age of six. Beijing officials responded by ordering a review of buildings that were potential fire hazards. Then they promptly evicted tens of thousands of migrants, leaving many homeless at a time when the temperatures at night hovered around freezing. Heavy equipment soon arrived, turning block after block of buildings into a wasteland of twisted aluminum, plywood, pipes, wires, and bricks—the latest battlefront in the long campaign to remake the ancient Chinese capital. Many people in the area thought officials used fire safety as a pretext for pushing out migrants from a city that had grown dramatically since I'd arrived two decades earlier. Back then, it was home to twelve million people. Now, the population had soared to more than twenty-one million. Officials had ordered Dang Hui'e, a migrant from the northwestern province of Shaanxi who had a nine-month-old baby, to move with just three days' notice.

"Does this country have any laws?" Dang asked Chris Buckley, my colleague with the *New York Times*.

Netizens dug up documents from Beijing district governments citing the need to clear away and regulate the *diduan renkou,* or "low-end population." More than a hundred Chinese intellectuals signed a petition urging the government to stop evicting people: "Beijing has been able to develop into what it is today not solely as a result of the hard work of Beijing citizens, but also because of the sacrifice and contribution of people from other parts of the country. Therefore, Beijing has an obligation to be grateful toward all Chinese citizens, instead of being forgetful and repaying the country people with arrogance, discrimination and humiliation."

For all the government's lip service to socialism, which it had to pay to maintain legitimacy, officials often treated migrants as ruthlessly as capitalists would. When I later contacted Charles in Shanghai, he told me he had been following the plight of his fellow migrants closely.

"Recent news in Beijing and other places made it hard for me to sleep," Charles wrote. "I'm angry and disappointed. Haven't felt like this for a long time. Maybe this eviction will only focus on Beijing, but treating our own citizens this way is so brutal and violent."

Shanghai didn't perpetrate anything quite so sudden or sweeping, but it continued to tear down old neighborhoods for new development and to drive migrants out. In the time since I'd left for London, Chen's old neighborhood near the river had been transformed. Almost all the houses across the street from his building had been demolished to make way for a high-end development. Where hundreds of homes once stood, there was now a latticework forest of yellow cranes sealed behind a white construction wall, which had already grown grimy from pollution and dirt. The wall was painted with propaganda images that recalled President Xi's Chinese Dream campaign.

"Country is home," read one sign, with an image of the character for country superimposed on a doorway of a traditional Chinese house. "Make the country your family," read another.

The message was clear: the country—and the party—were literally your family, even as they were demolishing your house. Down the street, a front-end loader scooped up piles of bricks from a migrant home that had just been leveled. Neighbors gathered around as heavy equipment drove over the remains of the house amid the sound of splitting wooden beams and the popping of roof tiles. Scavengers jumped up and down on aluminum sheets to flatten them for recycling.

"All the roads and all the subways are built by migrants," said a Shanghainese neighbor in a blue jacket and a burgundy T-shirt sitting on a chair across the street. "Now, the government doesn't need them anymore."

NRC, THE DUTCH newspaper, had pledged to investigate Charles's charges against his former boss. But it was taking time, and Charles was alone and jobless, with his reputation battered by his former employer. So we decided to try to figure out independently what had happened. I texted Yang, who tracked down the business card of Lei Lili, the appliance saleswoman in Lüliang whom we'd interviewed and whom the Dutch journalist had seemed to quote.

Yang contacted Lei on WeChat. She'd left the store and Lüliang because the economy was in tatters but still remembered us.

"After we met you, did you meet other foreign reporters?" we asked over WeChat.

"No," Lei responded. "What's up?"

"Not a single one?"

"No," she repeated.

We then set out to track down Gao, the manager from the cement plant that the Dutch reporter seemed to have quoted but whom Charles said they had never met. During our visit, the plant seemed on its last legs and was nearly abandoned. The likelihood that Gao was still there was remote. Charles, however, had stayed in touch with the cab driver who had driven him and his boss around Lüliang. So, we contacted the cabbie and asked him to go up to the plant and ask around. After a couple of days, the cabbie reported back that Gao was long gone, but he'd obtained his cell phone number. When we reached out to Gao, he confirmed on WeChat that he'd never met any foreign reporter other than me. NPR sent a letter to *NRC*, the Dutch newspaper, saying Oscar's story bore a striking resemblance to our two reports and that two crucial characters, Gao and Lei, said they'd never met him. Two hours later, we received a response from the newspaper's top editor. The tone was different from the earlier one he'd struck when writing about Charles.

"Thank you for your mail," he wrote. "I appreciate it very much. The material you submitted in your mail is very useful for this investigation."

A few days later, as I was heading into an interview on a rainy afternoon in Belfast, I received a note from Charles on my cell phone that the newspaper had issued its report on Oscar. The editor in chief wrote that Oscar had made "serious mistakes" that had damaged the trust of editors and readers, that he'd been sloppy in his reporting and had plagiarized our work, and that he would be leaving the company. Oscar, who was sixty-four, told editors that as he approached retirement he wanted to prove he could still do the job, but he had been fighting burnout and depression brought on in part by working under China's authoritarian system. *NRC* said Oscar admitted to embellishing facts, making a story "more beautiful and interesting in some parts than it was. I was so stupid and . . . I violated the standards of the newspaper and myself."

NRC said it would put a note by the offending stories, saying the newspaper could not guarantee their journalistic integrity. Elske Schouten, now the paper's deputy editor, told me Oscar made mistakes but was in no way a serial fabricator. Oscar, who took early retirement, told me he had never mistreated Charles and wished Charles had come to him first.

"Despite the mistakes that [Oscar] Garschagen has made, we will continue to carry Oscar as a person and colleague in our hearts," the editor's note concluded. "The recent mistakes must not hide the fact that he has done excellent work in recent years."

Charles and the other news assistants were disappointed.

"They didn't fire Oscar," Charles said. "They gave him a graceful exit."

Eventually, the newspaper apologized to Charles, who felt some degree of vindication.

"Oscar said I was a bad employee," Charles said, "but it turns out I'm a good fact-checker."

Although Charles won, the experience left him disillusioned with international journalism, which had always held itself out as superior to China's state-controlled model. The episode also left a bad taste in the mouths of other Chinese news assistants, including Yang.

"I know some foreign correspondents discussed this in private, but no one comes out to publicly condemn and denounce this,"

Yang told me. "This isn't right. Total silence on this issue will do nothing to help foreign media in China. I feel there is a double standard and hypocrisy."

Yang continued, "I know a Dutch reporter who was shocked by Charles's revelations, but she said this story is 'too sensitive' for her to cover. When Chinese media don't cover certain topics, they are blamed for bowing to government pressure. But this case doesn't even involve the government and she thinks it's too sensitive? If you look at Twitter, who are his [Charles's] supporters? Chinese assistants or Chinese journalists working for foreign media. I understand people's caution when facts were not clear. What about now?"

It stung to hear Yang, with whom I'd worked for five years, talk this way, but I understood why. For the record, NPR did not write about the scandal either. *NRC* was not a major media company and NPR felt it had already done its part by exposing Oscar.

Historically, China and the United States had alternated between attraction and disillusionment, and in the last two decades many Chinese seemed increasingly disappointed with America. When I'd first come to China, many young Chinese—like Charles and Ashley—admired the United States for its political freedoms and wealth, which at the time still dwarfed China's.

"Why is America so rich?" one of my news assistants had asked in wonder in the 1990s.

Back then, the United States was at peace and running budget surpluses, and the biggest political scandal was the Bill Clinton–Monica Lewinsky affair. Over time, though, young Chinese saw America less as a shining city on a hill and more as an arrogant bully. I first saw the shift in the spring of 1999, when NATO bombed the Chinese embassy in Belgrade during the war in Yugoslavia. The United States apologized and insisted it was a mistake, blaming faulty maps. The Chinese government insisted it was deliberate and encouraged thousands of protesters to descend on the American embassy in Beijing, which was right behind my office at the time.

At first, state newspapers barely mentioned that President Clinton had apologized or that NATO had said the strike was a mistake. Ordinary Chinese were, understandably, flabbergasted.

"Why hasn't Clinton apologized?" protesters asked me in disbelief at least a day after the president had already done so.

Beijing Youth Daily ran a story saying that journalists from all over the world were sending back images of the demonstrations—all except journalists from the United States. This would've been news to my colleague Rebecca MacKinnon of CNN, who was punched in the head by a protester while reporting from the scene. Young Chinese students who had been raised on Hollywood movies and who dreamed of attending US graduate schools marched past the embassy hurling chunks of concrete from the sidewalk and red, white, and blue paint bombs that splattered across the front door. One protester held up a mock American flag with the stars replaced by swastikas and drops of blood dripping from the red stripes. These were the biggest anti-Western protests since the Cultural Revolution and a reminder that China's century of humiliation was not merely history but to many people a raw nerve lying just below the surface. Protesters stalked the streets demanding Westerners reveal their nationalities; most Americans and Britons claimed to be Australians, hoping their questioners didn't have an ear for accents.

Ever since the 1989 crackdown on the Tiananmen Square democracy movement, the Chinese government had been looking for ways to hold the country together. "In the past it was Marxism, Mao's thought, and Deng Xiaoping's thought, but that's not working anymore," said Li Ming, a Beijing writer and critic, at the time of the bombing of the Chinese embassy. "I think NATO and America have done China a favor to help bring the nation together through nationalism."

Nearly two decades later, President Xi knew the party's grip was slipping even further. One way to bring people together was through the common cause of demanding global respect for the

Chinese state. Expanding Chinese territory in the South China Sea and challenging an old foe, Japan, and the world's top dog, the United States, signaled that China would play a new role on the world stage and would no longer be subservient to any nation. The party was sending a message to the Chinese people: China was no longer rising. China had risen.

CHAPTER 13

Ashley's Dilemma

Ashley

===========

ASHLEY AND I continued our stroll across Paris. We came to the Rodin museum and sat down on a wooden bench in front of *The Thinker.* The gray clouds had lifted from the Eiffel Tower, the sun had come out and shimmered on the golden dome of Les Invalides. I followed up on an earlier conversation we'd had about the Tiananmen Square crackdown. Ashley had not yet been born, and she first learned about the massacre as a high school student in the mid-2000s, when the Internet was growing rapidly in China but the Great Firewall, which the government had built to block content and protect its rule, was not fully developed. Ashley was clicking through some links at home when she came across the image of the man standing in front of the tank, then on to images of bloodied bodies lying in the streets.

"It's basically, 'Wow!'" Ashley said of her reaction when she saw the pictures. The immediate lesson, she said, was this: "There's another side to the world in which we live. The Chinese government is not always doing the right thing, which is what we'd been taught. That pretty much just opened the door for you to explore even more."

This period, when the Internet remained largely open, turned out to be a temporary window for ordinary people to examine their history and the nature of the party that ruled them. Not co-incidentally, this was roughly around the time when Charles read *Tombstone* and learned the truth about Mao's man-made famine. In the years following 1989, the government did a masterful job of erasing the history of Tiananmen Square. State-run TV had only played a video of the "Tank Man" once after the massacre. It showed the man repeatedly blocking the tank's path and the tank pivoting to try to move around him. The anchor reframed the confrontation not as David standing up to an authoritarian Goliath but as an example of the remarkable restraint of the People's Liberation Army. When I arrived in Beijing for my job as a newspaper correspondent in 1997, eight years later, memories of Tiananmen were already fading. One of my first nights in town, I went to Frank's Place, one of the first Western bars in the city. I joined several young Americans who'd just flown in from Japan and watched as they flirted with three female Chinese office workers over burgers and beers at an outdoor table. The men, in their early twenties, were earnest and enamored with these young professionals, who seemed to symbolize a new, open, and capitalist China. One of the men praised the similarities he saw between Americans and Chinese—of which, it turned out, there were not as many as he supposed.

"I remember seeing that man standing in front of the tank and I so admired him for standing up to the government," he said. "That's just what an American would do."

"Exactly!" said another.

We were sitting about four miles from the spot of the standoff. The women stared blankly at the men and then looked at each other.

"What man?" one of the women asked. "What tank?"

When I returned to China in 2011, the government had become so effective at blocking certain content on the Internet that many young people didn't know a lot about the history of Tiananmen. My then NPR colleague Louisa Lim went to Peking University—alma mater of Ashley and also of some of the protest's key leaders—and showed the Tank Man photo to one hundred students as part of research for her book *The People's Republic of Amnesia: Tiananmen Revisited.*

Only fifteen could identify it.

In a nation where life moved so fast that five years could constitute a generation, the killings seemed like ancient history.

"I'm not shocked by it anymore," Ashley said of the massacre. "It's just so natural to me. It's just what happened."

In recent years, some Chinese had argued that blood had to be spilled to keep the party united and the country's economic growth on track. In a much-talked-about opinion piece in the *New York Times* in 2012, Eric X. Li, a venture capitalist and acquaintance of mine in Shanghai, wrote that the crackdown was brutal but necessary: "The Chinese nation paid a heavy price for that violent event, but the alternatives would have been far worse. The resulting stability ushered in a generation of growth and prosperity that propelled China's economy to its position as the second largest in the world."

Ashley disagreed and thought China's rise had far more to do with economic fundamentals than political repression.

"Whether it's democracy or dictatorship, it's not very relevant," she said. China's spectacular economic growth "was basically a result of capital accumulation and open trade. East Asian people have an incredibly high savings rate. The central government was able to leverage a resource," meaning limitless cheap muscle from the countryside. "It happened everywhere: Korea, Japan, Taiwan."

One of the things I loved about talking to Chinese people was how much attention they paid to economics and their country's business model. Having spent so many decades in poverty, they didn't take prosperity for granted.

It was late November in Paris and the temperatures were in the forties. As we sat on the bench, Ashley rubbed her hands together to keep them warm. I asked her what would have happened, how the country would have been different, had the Tiananmen protesters succeeded.

"It would've probably pushed political reform," she said. "It probably would have been a more liberal party."

"But still a one-party state?"

"I think so. Perhaps it could've evolved into a multiparty system or the Communist Party could've split, but I doubt it will ever be an American-style democracy. Even if it became a multiparty system, the government would still be very powerful, much more powerful than the government in a Western system."

"I wish they had succeeded," Ashley continued, referring to the Tiananmen protesters. "At least then," she added wryly, "we wouldn't have to use VPNs"—virtual private networks, software that allows users to jump over the Great Firewall and visit websites banned by the government. In the past year, the Communist Party had increased its attacks on VPNs, an informational lifeline to the outside world and a political threat to the regime. In the summer of 2017, the party received help from a seemingly unlikely source, Apple, which removed all the major VPNs sold in its app store in China. Apple insisted it had to comply with Chinese law, which required companies that made apps to obtain government licenses. The Great Firewall was porous, but getting around it seemed to grow harder and harder. One of my colleagues had struggled so much to access websites during politically sensitive times, such as the National People's Congress, that he had had to set up a satellite transmitter in his yard in order to browse the Internet. I had had to rely on similar technology when working in the bush in Sudan and covering war in Somalia, not because of censorship but because of lack of infrastructure.

There were also signs that VPNs were not the informational magic bullets that many of us in the West had assumed. A 2017 study of more than 1,800 students at two universities in Beijing found that only one in five actually used a VPN. The numbers in the general population were even lower; no more than 8 percent of Internet users in China regularly bought tools to help them jump over the firewall. When the researchers gave a group of students free VPN access to the Internet, nearly half didn't even use it. That means, when given the opportunity at no cost to access banned sites such as Google, Facebook, Twitter, Instagram, Tumblr, Dropbox, Vimeo, the *New York Times,* the *Wall Street Journal,* and Reuters, they didn't even try.

"Censorship in China is effective not only because the regime makes it difficult to access sensitive information," wrote the researchers, economists from Peking and Harvard Universities, "but also because it fosters an environment in which citizens do not demand such information in the first place."

Why the lack of demand? The researchers thought it could be a function of the Great Firewall's effectiveness. People had been blocked from enough sites for so many years, they didn't know what they were missing and Chinese companies had built Chinese-friendly sites that fulfilled most users' basic needs. (A free Internet proved no panacea in the West. During the 2016 US presidential campaign, many Americans had trouble differentiating between reliable news and propaganda, some of which was engineered by Russia to generate confusion and conflict.)

Such low use of VPNs at the universities in Beijing meant that accurate, uncensored reporting on China and the world could not spread through the student population and have a meaningful impact. The researchers found that the students who responded to the incentives and did use VPNs knew more about current events, were more pessimistic about China's economic growth, more skeptical of the Chinese government, and more likely to take action to incite change. People who didn't *fan qiang,* or "climb over the wall," were less informed. This was what I'd found talking with my taxi passengers over the years. The people who used VPNs and had traveled overseas—Fifi the psychologist (who spent summers in Paris), Johanna the human rights lawyer (who'd studied in Sweden), Ashley, and Charles—were more critical and questioning of the government's narrative. Those most supportive of the party and optimistic about China's future under Xi Jinping were people who largely lived inside the firewall, like Sarah, whom I'd helped move apartments, and Max, who gave free haircuts to shut-ins. Venturing beyond what in some ways was a Chinese intranet could be upsetting, as it meant confronting some of the darker aspects of China's rise, an achievement that filled the vast majority of Chinese with great pride.

"Sometimes," Charles said, "it's more comfortable to live inside the wall."

The Communist Party had not only built a Great Firewall online, it was also trying to build a Great Firewall inside the minds of many of its citizens through its campaign to discredit the West, including the news media. In the first ten months of 2014, the *People's Daily* ran forty-two articles blaming China's domestic problems on hostile "Western," "foreign," or "overseas" forces, according to the *Christian Science Monitor.* In 2017, a scholar at the Shanghai Institutes for International Studies wrote that foreign reporters were part of an effort to keep China down. "When the Western media used the 'China threat' theory in its propaganda, they thought China would not rise so quickly," wrote Jiang Feng. "But now, they see an increasingly powerful China that has crossed the threshold of a superpower and is out-pacing the West on many fronts including politics, economy, technology and culture."

After Trump's election, Chinese state media embraced his criticisms, portraying the Communist Party and the US president as fellow victims of a lying, politicized American news media. A *People's Daily* op-ed seized on Trump's description of the US media as "the enemy of the American people."

"His language suggests that major US media outlets, including the *New York Times* and CNN, are hostile and subversive organizations," *People's Daily* said. "If the leader of the world's leading democratic government can't trust the Western media, why should the rest of the world?"

That did not mean that people who maintained intellectual lives outside the wall bought Western coverage of China wholesale. Not at all. Like Charles, Ashley had also grown more skeptical of the foreign press and found some reporting on China sensational and overly pessimistic. For years, some foreign reporters have been on the lookout for a closet reformer in the party leadership who might push for a liberal political opening, but so far that has proved to be just wishful thinking. Others have written articles and books predicting China's collapse, which the party has routinely proven wrong.

"I have been a subscriber to the *WSJ* and the *New York Times* for a really long time," Ashley said, "and you would find most of their projections are not true. When something bad happens in China, they would predict regime failure right away. This is a huge country, it can't fall overnight."

Ashley also thought Western reporters were too critical of Xi Jinping. A few weeks before we met in Paris, China's new Politburo Standing Committee, essentially the country's top leaders, had strode across the red carpet in Beijing's Great Hall of the People with Xi in the center and clearly in charge. Unlike in the past, there was no anointed successor in sight. On the final day of the meeting, the party congress changed the constitution to add Xi's theories—known formally as "Xi Jinping Thought on Socialism with Chinese Characteristics for a New Era"—giving him the same constitutional status as Mao. Xi's increased stature and a lack of anyone to replace him led many to wonder if he would break with tradition and try to cling to power beyond his second five-year term. If so, it would mark a momentous change.

The party had instituted term limits for top leaders to make sure no one could stay on indefinitely and devastate the country as Mao had.

"At the Communist Party Congress, Xi Jinping Plays Emperor," read a headline in the *New Yorker*, a magazine Ashley read and admired.

Ashley was wary about these developments in the party but not overly concerned.

"It's very bad if he wants to stay in power longer than allowed, but it's not like you suddenly have a tyrant ruling the country," she said. Journalists "throw out words like 'dictatorship' and make their readers feel like we are suddenly back in ancient Rome or we're looking at a [new] Stalin. It's just not true."

"I don't even read what the *WSJ* writes in China anymore, because it feels like they have a conspiracy theory that China is trying to unify the world under Communism, that everything China does serves a purpose towards reaching that goal."

"Of world domination?" I asked.

"Exactly."

There is an old expression in American newspapering that reporters should "afflict the comfortable and comfort the afflicted." In China, Ashley thought that Western reporters focused too much on those who suffer under China's authoritarian system and too little on the many who've benefited and thrived.

"You want to fairly represent the people you've met in China," she said. "You've obviously seen a lot of people who live below the poverty line, but you've also seen a lot of people in China who are like me."

She cited the French guide we'd met at the Hermès exhibit, who'd tried to sell us on her fledgling hunting vacations in Burgundy and reminded both of us of the kind of hustle that defines cities such as Shanghai and much of China.

"I think that's basically the aspiration you can feel from most Chinese at this moment. It's a more truthful representation of how China really is right now," Ashley said. "I just think that a lot of reporters have either failed or intentionally ignored that part of the story."

AFTER LUNCH, ASHLEY and I retired to the lobby of my hotel where she sat on a couch and I sipped coffee on a faux Louis XIV chair. With her final semester approaching, I asked Ashley where she might go next. She had considered a small investment bank in New York but wasn't as interested in what she feared would be financial grunt work. She was eyeing a job in Hong Kong with a different small investment firm.

"Would you go back to mainland China now?" I asked.

"Not unless I have to."

"Why?"

"China is not a place where you can reason with people," she said. "You have to show your muscle all the time. Everybody wants to become a billionaire. It's a very harsh way to live."

Even Ashley's affluence and social position couldn't shield her from the pace and Darwinian competition of daily life in China.

"I'm already a privileged person" in China, Ashley said. "The best I can do is to not piss off anybody. If you are ever the victim, there's no system to support you or help you. You just have to rely on your parents or bribe someone. It's not a very good way to live a peaceful life."

"You know there is a prominent writer in China named Lu Xun," Ashley said.

Lu was one of China's great social critics. I'd read some of his work, the best known of which is a novella, *The True Story of Ah Q*. Ah Q is a peasant with little education who focuses on his own self-interest and often makes excuses for himself. He is scared of those above him and bullies those below. He is, in essence, what Lu Xun saw as the worst of the national character. After I faced off against the taxi driver on that narrow road in Charles's village, I had thought about how the cabbie reminded me of Ah Q.

"He said something very famous," Ashley continued, referring to Lu Xun. "'You always assume the worst of the Chinese.' I think this is very true, because that's how this world works. You just have to always protect yourself and assume the worst of other people."

That is what Fifi had found when she fell on the wet street and sat in the road for twenty-five minutes, with no one stopping to help her. That was the philosophy of Li, the net man who scooped fish from the river moments after they'd been released: "The more skilled swindlers just cheat the weaker ones." For a long time, the United States—warts and all—offered an appealing alternative, providing the rule of law, freedom of religion, and civil society to mitigate and protect against people's worst instincts. It was one of the things that drew Chen and his wife, Gong, to Los Angeles, where they wouldn't have to worry about a knock on the door at night. But after the Iraq War, the global financial crisis, and now the Trump years, America's allure as an alternative has continued to dim.

"I think generally people who are born in the eighties, most people with sense, would think that democracy is a good thing," said Ashley, "but I think the younger generation doesn't think that way anymore. They don't think Western culture is that good. Look at America right now. Look at how France has fallen. They [young Chinese] don't like Paris because Paris in their eyes is falling behind."

Chinese often complained that the Paris they visited didn't seem like the city they'd seen in the movies. They thought it was dirty, the people were lazy, the merchants were rude, and the sidewalks were smeared with dog crap.

"They don't think people necessarily need liberty," Ashley continued, referring to the rising generation of college grads behind her. "They think freedom and democracy are empty notions that don't actually work."

At her school outside of Paris where she was studying business, Ashley often borrowed coins for vending machines from a
fellow Chinese student who was twenty-three, just five years her
junior. He had recently posted on WeChat that he thought the
2014 Occupy campaign for democracy in Hong Kong was crazy
and stupid and the protesters were trash. Some younger Chinese
felt the same way. There was no sense of solidarity with fellow
Chinese across the border in the former British colony trying to
resist the authoritarian leaders in Beijing. Instead, many mainland
Chinese saw the Hong Kong protesters as spoiled aspiring Brits.

"We think, OK, it's probably not very practical for Hong Kong
and Taiwan to pursue independence, but we can sympathize with
them," Ashley said of her generation. But the response of the fellow Chinese student here in France taught her that many in the
younger generation had a very different view, which would affect
her if she returned to work on the mainland.

"If I want to manage a team, I probably wouldn't understand
who they are," Ashley said. "I basically can't agree with them.
Because it contradicts my personal values, but also I don't think I
can change."

The mournful sound of a saxophone floated through the lobby
as "Summertime" played on the hotel's sound system.

"Why do you think these kids are the way they are?"

"Parents micromanage them," said Ashley, adding that when she
was young parents permitted children more time on their own,
providing space for exploration, experimentation, and mistakes.
"But right now, these kids are completely swamped by their parents and [their schoolwork]. So, they have very little freedom to do
things." Ashley didn't expect China to become more open anytime
soon and thought her parents' generation would steer the country
for another couple of decades. And then?

"To be honest, the best of my generation, they're all in America," said Ashley, who estimated that a quarter of her class from
Peking University lived in the United States. "I think if there is any

hope, it's the people who are born in the eighties, but those people are gone."

Most Chinese liked President Xi and appreciated his attack on corruption at home and assertiveness abroad, but Ashley was skeptical about his ability to steer the economy.

"Where do you see the country going?"

"Generally, I am very pessimistic," she said. For years, China had relied on manufacturing, investment, and exports to drive growth, but that had run its course long ago and the government was now trying to develop a new business model in hopes of dominating key industries of the future, including self-driving cars, artificial intelligence, and computer chips. "Since they [Chinese political leaders] are not making progress, they become more politically conservative."

Ashley is even less optimistic about America under President Trump. During her time in the United States, she had chatted up older people in restaurants, and she summarized their thoughts about the US president like this: "Personally, I don't like him. He's just a bastard, but I think he has a point. I look at these immigrants, they're making a mess of our society. They're rude and they're uneducated.

"After a short conversation, you would sense they don't know what's going on," Ashley said. "Immigrants have been economically proven to have a positive effect on a local economy. You have a lot of Mexican immigration, not because they want to be illegal, but because you have huge demand for low-wage labor in your southern states."

Ashley had moved to America at the end of the Obama administration in the hope that she could make a life there. Now, she was caught between two worlds, neither of which appealed. America was free but flawed. China offered opportunity but at a moral cost. As darkness descended on the Left Bank, I said I thought the Communist Party could probably sustain its rule for a long time, but I didn't think China could live up to its potential or develop the global influence it sought. The party craved soft power, the ability to attract and co-opt others through culture and political values rather than threats and force. But given the government's increasing assertiveness abroad and growing repression at home, building up soft power seemed a distant dream. While Xi enjoyed broad popularity at home, just 34 percent of people in Asia-Pacific countries said they had a lot or some confidence in him, according to a Pew Research Center poll in the fall of 2016.

"What if the whole world changes the criteria to judge soft power in favor of China?" Ashley said. "The value system shifts in China's direction. We see signs China is trying to work it that way."

Ashley had a point. The Chinese government was trying to bend the world to accept at least some of its authoritarian narratives with an aggressiveness it had never shown before. A few months after we chatted in Paris, a Chinese embassy official called the debating society at England's Durham University and pressed them to drop a speaker in a debate about whether China was a threat to the West. The official objected to including a woman named Anastasia Lin, a former Miss World Canada who is also a sharp human rights critic of China and a practitioner of Falun Gong, which the government has banned and branded an evil cult. Tom Harwood, the head of the debate union at the time, told me the Chinese official said that UK "trade relations with China will be damaged if we host this particular speaker."

"There were officers of the union who were a bit more shaken by it who sort of were tempted to pull the debate and felt a little bit threatened," Harwood said, "but if anything this really reinforced all the negative opinions and stories that you hear."

The debate went ahead, and Lin spoke.

During the Communist Party congress that fall, President Xi gave a three-and-a-half-hour speech in which he not only emphasized that China had entered a New Era but also said China would provide "a new option for other countries and nations who want to speed up their development while preserving their independence."

Xi even spoke of a "China solution." Bold talk of China setting a global example and beginning to take center stage would've been unthinkable just five years earlier. It was also a far cry from Deng Xiaoping's foreign-policy strategy of "hide your strength, bide your time," and from that of Xi's predecessor, Hu Jintao, who promised China's "peaceful rise." The message Xi was sending to the world and to China—known as *Zhongguo* in Mandarin, which means "middle kingdom"—was that he would restore his country to its rightful place at the center of world affairs.

Exactly what a New Era might look like was unclear, but the signs for the United States and most of China's neighbors weren't encouraging. After a UN-appointed tribunal at The Hague rejected Beijing's claims to most of the South China Sea, the Chinese government ignored the decision, just as Charles had said it would. Sensing a power shift in the Pacific, though, Philippine president Rodrigo Duterte decided not to press the issue and instead canceled joint military exercises with the United States. China responded by offering billions of dollars for infrastructure investment and a $500 million loan to the Philippine military.

Night had fallen on the French capital and Ashley needed to get back to campus. We walked toward the river where the lights had come on, bringing the twin towers of Notre Dame into relief and bouncing off the surface of the Seine. The green wooden book stalls along the river were still open but mostly empty. I hugged Ashley goodbye and she disappeared down the stairs and into the metro.

CHAPTER 14

President for Life?

Fifi, Ray, Sarah, Max, and Ashley

Y OU CAN KNOW something is coming and still not quite be prepared for its impact and implications. That's how it felt for
many in 2018 when the Communist Party's Central Committee proposed changing the constitution and scrapping term limits
for the Chinese presidency. It signaled that Xi Jinping had no intention of retiring after his second five-year term, which concludes
in 2022. In theory, he can rule until death, as Mao had done with
disastrous consequences. The government tried to bury the news
inside the state-run newspapers, but someone at the New China
News Service pushed it out in English, either by accident or design. After I read the headline, I reached out to my passengers and
Chinese friends, some of whom who were unaware of the looming
change. That I was breaking historic news to them about their
homeland from eight time zones away in London said something
about the management of information in China at this moment.

Among many of my Chinese friends, there was a shared feeling of fear.

"I was shocked!" one wrote. "There were rumors a long time ago, I didn't believe it and I'm scared, too."

"What scares you?" I asked.

"The possibility of returning to the past, to the Mao era. A person with my kind of personality can't live well in that kind of era. This really is a 'New Era.' You have to watch whatever you say, so creepy."

In fact, it seemed a throwback to the old era of centralized power but with a tighter authoritarian grip and new tools to control society, including artificial intelligence, more than 170 million surveillance cameras, and facial-recognition technology. Another friend sent me a cartoon image of a portrait of Xi partially torn away to reveal Mao beneath, then a GIF of President Trump nodding his head in agreement, Kim Jong-Un clapping, and Mao himself grinning and laughing. On Chinese social media, thousands expressed similar concerns—before censors scrubbed them away.

"Our emperor has received the Mandate of Heaven, so we have to kneel and accept," one person wrote on Weibo.

"My mom said I must get married within Daddy Xi's term in office," wrote another. "Now finally, I breathed a long sigh of relief."

Others posted memes of Winnie the Pooh, who bore some resemblance to the rotund Chinese leader and had served as his subversive Internet doppelgänger in recent years. There was an image of Pooh wearing a crown and a royal red cape and another of him hugging a giant jar of honey with a Mandarin caption that read, "Find the thing you love and stick with it." Censors wiped out comments and images, underscoring that, while Xi was making a bold power play, the party was worried about public perception. The rush to censor, as usual, signaled weakness, not strength. China's state-run media dismissed the suggestion that Xi was enthroning himself as China's new emperor. The always reliable *Global Times* tried to change the subject, taking aim at the weaknesses of Western democracy as embodied by Trump's America, Brexit Britain, and beyond.

"The most influential value system in the world now is the Western value system established by the US and Europe," the editorial read. "It has shaped and affected quite a few Chinese people's mindsets. But some key parts of the Western value system are collapsing. Democracy, which has been explored and practiced by Western societies for hundreds of years, is ulcerating."

Global Times argued that consolidating power in one leader would help China forge ahead with economic restructuring and aggressive moves overseas, which may prove true.

"China cannot stop and take a break," the newspaper said. "The country must seize the day."

When I first came to China, I developed a respect for the Communist Party. Since the death of Mao in 1976, the party had learned from its mistakes and made major changes. First, it turned its back on failed socialist policies and reimagined the economy, creating the opportunity for hundreds of millions of Chinese—including the ones I met driving my free taxi—to transform their lives. The party also recognized that it had to alter a system that had enabled tyranny. After Mao's twenty-seven years in office, politicians and legal experts enshrined term limits in the Chinese constitution. Eventually that ushered in consensus rule, in which the party general secretary was first among equals. This style of governance was slower and more ponderous but served as a check against the sort of dangerous policies that had devastated the country. Now, Xi and the party had removed that constraint.

THE ABOLITION OF term limits was the culmination not only of Xi's amassing of power but also of a growing repression that had been shrinking the space for free speech and foreign influence for years. A couple of months after the term-limit announcement, I casually mentioned in a conversation with Fifi that copies of the Bible had disappeared from China's largest online retailers, JD.com, Taobao, and Amazon.

"What?" said Fifi, who hadn't read anything about it.

The disconnect between the news I consumed and what my Chinese passengers—even those who lived outside the wall— consumed was becoming more pronounced.

"This is kind of a way of managing things," Fifi said, referring to the scant coverage inside China of the disappearing Bibles. "Something changes, but no one talks about it. Do you think it's just in China or everywhere?"

I said I thought it was a function of different systems. In America, a free press ensured that leaders had to explain themselves to the public.

"In an authoritarian system, you don't have to explain things, in detail or at all, because there's no recourse," I said.

The government provided some explanation: it was just closing a loophole that allowed Bibles, which are only legally available at church bookstores, to be sold online. In reality, this was part of a major crackdown on foreign faith and the perceived threats it posed.

"In China the atmosphere is really getting a bit weird now," Fifi continued. "If you watch TV, you will notice that the TV programs are more and more 'red,'" by which she meant more nationalistic and Communist, just like the school arts performance I'd seen. "I have some friends working in schools or as public servants, like policemen; they have to go to a lot of meetings for training. It's actually a way of controlling them by brainwashing them. It's to help them have a more 'correct' attitude. Does that sound familiar?"

It did. It sounded a little like the political indoctrination that occurred under Mao during the Cultural Revolution. Since coming to office, Xi had pushed a propaganda campaign that criticized what the party called "Western values," including genuine democracy and the rule of law, while emphasizing the centrality of the Communist Party and aspects of traditional Chinese thought and culture, such as Confucianism and Chinese medicine. Fifi and I were just half an hour into our chat and we'd already begun to resort to euphemisms because of the increasingly sensitive political environment.

"You know, recently we have a new film on screen and in the cinema just about this person," said Fifi, referring to Xi while avoiding his name.

It was called *Amazing China,* a ninety-minute, state-sponsored movie that trumpeted the accomplishments of the government under Xi's first term in office. It featured images of bridges that stretch for miles, a giant radio telescope, bullet trains, China's homegrown airliner, the Comac C919, and the world's largest off-shore exploration platform for drilling in the South China Sea. The government had organized screenings for civil servants. The New China News Service called it the country's highest-grossing "documentary" of all time.

"There's only one leader shown in this film, not the others, so you know what I mean," Fifi said, her voice growing quiet and contemplative. "It's a very strange atmosphere."

Fifi said the movie received an online audience rating of 9.6 out of 10.

"Even *Titanic* will not get a 9.6," said Fifi, laughing.

As the space for free speech continued to contract in China, Fifi's dual life, splitting her time between France and Shanghai, came into increasingly stark relief.

"For me, it's really very difficult because every time when I go to France I have a lot of chance to talk, talk, talk. Then I come back and I just can't stop then, and the first few days can be very dangerous for me."

And after the first few days?

"I shut up," she said. "I just shut up, because I can't find people to talk to me."

Fifi relies on a close circle of friends, including a colleague who grew up in Hong Kong and studied in the United States, with whom she can speak openly. And she still meets up with the Gang of Five from her teaching days, but they speak much less about politics now because government censorship has stripped them of the news and information that used to fuel their discussions. A decade ago, more independent Chinese news sources served as a bridge between China's state-run media and the rest of the world, but now, Fifi says, there is no bridge.

"I feel I've withdrawn my attention to my own small world," she said. "To focus a lot of attention on the external world makes me very tired and frustrated. I know my feeling represents many Chinese people's feelings. Sometimes I can talk with some of my clients about political things and societal things, but it always ends up with a sigh."

Fifi sounded more pessimistic than she had when I'd driven her around Shanghai to see clients two years earlier.

"I feel uncomfortable," she said. "I feel like I'm regressing back to childhood. Like, I used to be an adult and I could use a lot of information to reach my own conclusions, but now I'm waiting to be told and, hopefully, I can be told something that's true."

The Communist Party was building China into the world's largest economy. It wanted to turn the country into a global power known for innovation, a nation that could set an example for others. But in order to maintain power, it pursued policies designed to infantilize the Chinese people and monitored them much more closely. To improve behavior and combat distrust—still a big problem, as Fifi's experience on the street illustrated—local governments had begun piloting social credit-score systems that rated people based on a wide variety of factors. Citizens could earn points for doing charity work, like Max, and donating blood, or lose points for jaywalking, not paying utility bills, or walking a dog without a leash. By May 2018, people had already been blocked from boarding more than eleven million flights and making more than four million bullet-train trips based on bad behavior. Some saw the Communist Party becoming Orwell's Big Brother, while others noted China's disparate systems weren't integrated and the number of people punished so far was less than 1 percent of the population. Even some of my liberal Chinese friends supported the concept of a social credit-score system because they benefitted from their good behavior and were glad to see bad actors punished.

In theory, I'm for anything that encourages more people to abide by the law and become more trustworthy. For instance, when I was back in Shanghai in 2018, I was delighted to discover the government was now enforcing rules requiring cars to actually stop for pedestrians in crosswalks. That may seem obvious, but in all my years in China I'd never seen it. As I stepped into a crosswalk one rainy afternoon, a silver Mercedes rushed toward the intersection. I put up my hand like a traffic cop, stared him down, and he miraculously stopped. But it's also easy to see how a social credit system could create opportunities for abuse when combined with unchecked power, and the longer I lived in China, the more aware I became of just how much we were all being watched. The number of surveillance cameras exploded while I was there, and they did provide benefits. Cameras at my apartment complex captured the license plate of a taxicab in which I'd left my guitar, which made it easy to arrange its rapid return. Other potential uses worried me. In 2013, I covered a story in which an angry patient had stabbed three doctors south of Shanghai in Zhejiang province, sparking protests from medical staff who complained that hospitals were failing to keep their employees safe. Sitting in the back of a taxi, I learned that the local government was trying to track me down and detain me. I looked up and saw a video camera trained on my face and promptly threw my blue windbreaker over my head—not thinking that a passenger with a jacket over his head might arouse even more suspicion. My fears were unfounded. An analyst of the surveillance industry later told me that the facial-recognition technology was not that advanced at the time and still had a ways to go. But, like most technology, it's bound to improve.

On weekends in Shanghai, I occasionally hung out in a quiet corner of a park that hosted something you can find almost nowhere else in China: public political debate. Men in their sixties and seventies would gather in a series of scrums and say pretty much whatever they want. Standing beneath trellises, they blew off steam complaining about government corruption, what they call the "fake" system of China's village elections, and the decades of "brainwashing" that they dated back to when the Communists took over in 1949. When I visited a few years ago, one red-faced man in glasses was so passionate in his praise for the Hong Kong democracy protests, he accidentally spat on me from five feet away. On a recent visit, though, I noticed things had changed. I counted five surveillance cameras, including those with the ability to pivot and focus. Did they work? Were they just for show? I can't say, but they served as a reminder that someone could be watching.

Surveillance was far heavier in parts of the country where the government faced genuine opposition. Out in northwestern China's Xinjiang autonomous region, where Muslim extremists have staged attacks, police search the contents of cell phones at checkpoints. The government has also built a gulag of reeducation camps, where Uighurs (pronounced "we-gur")—a Turkic, mostly Muslim ethnic group—are sent for indoctrination and, according to inmates, to effectively renounce their faith. After denying the existence of the camps for months, the central government finally acknowledged what it described as vocational-training centers that carry out anti-extremist education. The government refused to say how many people it had detained, but researchers estimate numbers ranging from hundreds of thousands to more than a million. US vice president Mike Pence accused Beijing of "around-the-clock brainwashing," and the Congressional-Executive Commission on China called it "the largest mass incarceration of a minority pop-ulation in the world today." Most Chinese didn't know a lot about the camps, and the Beijing government has compared them to US efforts to combat Islamist extremists in the Middle East, such as ISIS. China's ambassador to the United States, Cui Tiankai, told Reuters that while America uses drones to kill terrorists, China was taking a more humane approach: "We are trying to re-educate most of them, trying to turn them into normal persons [who] can go back to normal life."

AS WESTERN NATIONS criticized the party's growing repression, President Xi remained popular at home. Unlike Fifi, Ray had become a big fan of the president, and with good reason. Xi had done much of what he had promised. In his first few years, he had stabilized the economy, and incomes continued to rise, though growth was now markedly slowing. On a visit to Shanghai in 2018, I noticed the Maglev train was much more crowded than it had been at the beginning of the decade. Xi was expanding China's trade ties across Asia and Europe with a $1 trillion Belt and Road infrastructure project. And, most importantly, his anti-corruption campaign had won him the gratitude of hundreds of millions of fellow Chinese.

"People had almost lost trust in the government, because there was so much corruption," said Ray. "Many officials didn't treat their jobs as public servants seriously; they just used them for profit. Now, that's changed a lot."

Ray, who was willing to criticize the party when necessary, also praised the government for breaking its addiction to GDP growth targets and putting more emphasis on the environment. And he appreciated Xi's forays into rural China to work to reduce poverty and narrow China's income gap.

"In his eyes, China is not only the big cities, like Shanghai and Beijing," said Ray. "He knows the villages. He knows the countryside."

When I asked Ray about the decision to change the constitution, he preferred not to discuss it because it touched on power at the top of the country and was simply too sensitive. It was the first time in the years that I'd known him that he had simply refused to discuss a topic. Later, when we got to talking about the US Constitution, Ray praised it as an ideal division of power, with the three branches—judicial, legislative, and executive—checking one another. Ray said he thought every American should take the sort of constitutional law class he took during his master's in Illinois.

"You will feel great to be an American, so proud of your founding fathers," Ray said. "They were great ones. The best of the best human beings. Even Washington, he did eight years and he quit. That was great."

When faced with sensitive political topics, Chinese not only speak in euphemisms but also in historical allegories, which send a message while providing plausible deniability. This wasn't the first time I'd heard George Washington's name invoked in conversations about the abolition of term limits. Another Chinese friend told me about a class he'd attended that was taught by a senior adviser to the Communist Party. The man began by praising Washington for his wisdom in relinquishing power after two terms as president.

"How can someone run a country in his eighties or nineties?" said the lecturer, clearly referring to the fear that Xi might, as Mao had, serve for life. "It's ridiculous."

Many others in Shanghai, though, were still happy with the economy, felt the government was addressing problems that mattered to people, and figured the more Xi the better. Sarah, the woman I'd helped move out of her depressing apartment, appreciated that the government had improved health care in the countryside, where her parents had lived, and given students more chances to take the English section of the college entrance exam, providing more opportunity while reducing stress. She was also thankful for the prosperity the country had enjoyed under party rule. When I'd first met Sarah, she was lost, unsure of a career path or if she could make a life in Shanghai. A few years later, she was enrolled in a master's program in psychology, which would help qualify her for full benefits in the city. Like many American kids in the 1960s and 1970s, I'd been told by my parents to eat everything on my plate because of starving children in China. Now, forty years later, Sarah, twenty-six, had known nothing but prosperity and viewed developing countries in the same way Americans had once viewed China.

"When you look around the world, you see a lot of people who can't feed themselves, who don't have drinking water, you feel grateful," she said. When I asked Sarah what she thought China's future held, she answered, *yue lai yue hao,* which means "better and better." This was the same answer I got from Rocky and Max, the hairstylist. They weren't just parroting the party line, they genuinely believed it, because that had been their own experience.

When I asked Sarah directly about the change in term limits, she began slapping her thigh nervously.

"I'm not qualified to answer this question," she said.

And then she did, sort of.

"When I heard about the term limits, I had a small concern," said Sarah. "He's a very good leader, but what if Xi leaves office and another leader who's not as good comes in, what happens then?"

Sarah seemed unaware of how much concern the change in the constitution had generated outside of China. Although she had a VPN, she was like most of the students who participated in that study of two Beijing universities and barely used it.

"There are so many things to do," she said.

Max was reluctant to talk about the removal of term limits as well. "This subject is too sensitive," he said as he poured me cups of tea in one of his new salons, which had furniture that looked like it belonged in Versailles.

Max had grown up in a mud-brick hut and now his business was growing quickly in Shanghai, so he didn't have a lot to complain about. Max dropped out of school after eighth grade, but one of his well-to-do clients who lives in America added him to a private WeChat group that included professors, authors, and intellectuals living in America. The conversations confused him.

"They said China is not good," said Max, sounding puzzled. "They say Russia and China have the same policies and are tricking their people."

Max thought these expatriate Chinese were too radical.

"They remind me of angry youth in China," said Max, referring to hypernationalistic Chinese youth who had emerged in the 1990s and were sharply critical of America and Japan.

MOST POLITICIANS IN the United States were disturbed by the party's scrapping of term limits, but one seemed to praise them publicly: the president of the United States. Soon after the move, President Trump told a gathering of donors at his Florida estate that he admired President Xi and sounded a bit envious of his seemingly limitless horizon to rule.

"He's now president for life, president for life. And he's great," Trump said, according to audio from the closed-door fundraiser. "I think it's great. Maybe we'll have to give that a shot someday," Trump concluded as his donors cheered and clapped.

The White House later said Trump was joking.

"From Trump's perspective, it's totally reasonable to say that," said Ashley. "He wants to be an emperor-ish figure. He's clearly a fan of Putin and obviously Xi's movement has been mimicking what Putin has been doing. If you look at this quote, he's not only praising [Xi], he's obviously jealous. He's saying, 'Oh my God! I want to be that, too.'"

Unlike many liberals back home in China, Ashley was not alarmed by the scrapping of term limits. "I'm not too downcast, really," she said. "He's not as young as Putin was on his second time back. I don't believe anyone can fight where the world is headed."

Ashley saw the rise of Xi, Putin, Trump, and even Duterte in the Philippines as a global shift from liberal democracy toward a more authoritarian approach and didn't see an obvious way to turn back the tide. On the bright side, she said, an extra term would give Xi more time to tackle the make-or-break challenges still facing China's economy. China's old formula, which had driven double-digit growth rates and relied on exports and heavy government investment, no longer worked. Some cities in the northeast and west, such as Lüliang, had tried to boost their GDP numbers by plowing money into useless public projects like small airports and roads to nowhere, with painful results. To create a high-income economy, the Chinese government had to make it function far more efficiently. That would mean reining in massive debt, reforming many state-owned companies, and—eventually—developing high-value products and services through innovation.

Xi "hasn't dedicated a lot of energy to economic reform," Ashley said. "He's just spent his time purging his enemies. I think he has a concern that five years is too short to basically solidify gains, and everything might just slip from his control."

Xi had made some progress overseeing the layoff of two million steel and coal workers, but the window to fix China's growth model was slowly closing and failure could trigger either a recession—in a country still accustomed to strong growth rates—or a financial crisis. Either result might lead people to reconsider their grand bargain with the party, ceding political rights and a say in how they are ruled in exchange for continued prosperity.

"Who likes it?" asked a Chinese friend over beers in Shanghai one night. "If they can fix the economy, it will be OK. But if they can't raise living standards, people will say, 'Why are you still in charge?'"

Ashley thought Xi was betting the house on his rule in a high-stakes gamble to keep China's economy on track and also save himself from the many enemies he'd accumulated in his first five years.

"I think he is afraid that his agenda will be rolled back if he steps down on schedule," Ashley said. "A lot of people are not happy with him. What he did in the past five years," meaning mass jailings for public corruption, "it could get him murdered two hundred times. He is definitely very aware of the consequences. Nobody is going to challenge him right now, but if he fails, it's going to be really ugly."

Epilogue

I BEGAN DRIVING MY free taxi on a summer night in 2014 in the heart of Shanghai. What followed was an odyssey that took me deep into central China, on to Europe and America, and into the lives of my passengers, their friends, and their families. Everyone had a goal, a dream—not a Chinese Dream as President Xi envisioned it, but a personal one. Some, like Max, wanted to build a business; others, like Crystal, Fifi, and Charles, were focused on family. In the time I've known them, some reached their dreams, while others stumbled but refused to give up. And when some found their dreams beyond reach—for now or perhaps forever—they made peace with it.

Chen and his family have now been living in suburban Los Angeles for a few years, and their old apartment near the river in Shanghai, where he had held underground church services, seems a distant memory. They had come to America to have a second child and spare their first, Jiali, from the Chinese education system, where she'd endured abuse although beatings were banned. As Jiali approached senior year of high school, the family had found the more relaxed American system a better fit than the stricter one back in China.

"If a student doesn't listen, a teacher can't hit them," said Chen, who thought that something of a revelation.

As we chatted in the living room of his apartment one spring day, Chen said he'd also come to appreciate that America was so accepting of differences—at least in greater Los Angeles—while being a less competitive environment than China. He hopes that will give Jiali, who is introverted like her father, more opportunities.

"In China, if there are ten job openings, there are one thousand applications," Chen told me. "Here, if you go to McDonald's, you see people in all shapes and sizes. You don't have to go to a famous college to get a job here."

"If Jiali had stayed in China," said Gong, "she would not be able to find a job."

Jiali, who looks like a typical American girl in jeans, a blue hoodie, and Adidas, is still reserved, but seems in better spirits than she had been as a student in Shanghai. She runs the eight hundred meters in track and plays first violin in the school orchestra. School in America was much easier than it had been in China, but her GPA had dipped to a 3.2. When we last spoke, she hoped to boost it in the first half of senior year and still apply to schools in the University of California system.

Chen and Gong lost one child to a forced abortion but were able to have Yingying. Yingying, now five, has known nothing but life in the United States. She's a budding California girl and seems as if she is from a different family, which in a way she is. While Chen and Gong eat satay and pot stickers at their favorite Asian buffet, Yingying prefers pizza and hamburgers. Yingying spends much of her time laughing, giggling, and playing on the floor of the family's apartment not far from Jiali's bed, which sits behind a curtain in the living room. The couple dotes on Yingying—during one meal out, they allowed her to climb on the table at our booth and crawl around like a puppy dog—and seems to hold out particular hope for their youngest because of her outgoing personality, her lack of emotional scar tissue, and the opportunity to grow up in a more open society.

One afternoon, I drove the family about an hour west to the Santa Monica Pier, which they had never visited. It was a bright, sunny day and the sky was an immaculate canvas of blue but for a pair of jet contrails heading up the coast. On the pier, a Chinese man in a red tunic and a floppy white beach hat sat on a stool and played an especially mournful rendition of "Scarborough Fair" on the *erhu,* a two-stringed Chinese fiddle. When Yingying, who wore black tights and a pink-and-black dress, reached the beach, she walked straight into the chilly waters of the Pacific without hesitating. I thought of the resilience and perseverance of her mother, Gong, who had lost a child, come to America with no English skills, and built a new life for her family. Chen rolled up his pant legs and waded into the ocean with his daughter, lifting her over the waves and swinging her little feet out over the water. Chen's face is usually impassive and nearly impossible to read, but as he played with Yingying in the waves, he was grinning. In all the years I'd known him, I had never seen him so content.

AFTER I MOVED to London, I met Fifi one summer in Paris when she was visiting her husband, Remi. Fifi had to visit a clinic on my first morning in town, so we met for lunch at a corner café. Fifi looked great. She wore her usual giant glasses, a blue-and-white-striped blouse, white capris, and matching sandals. Contrary to her appearance, Fifi said it had been a hard year. Remi had turned sixty-one and had become depressed, not seeing much hope or a future for himself with four years to go before retirement from his teaching job. When Fifi told me she'd visited a clinic that morning, I was hopeful she might be trying to find work in Paris as a psychologist so she and Remi could finally live together. However, it turned out not to be a psychiatric clinic but a fertility clinic.

"I want to have a baby," she said.

Fifi was an independent Shanghainese professional woman who had never talked to me before about children, but as I looked back, her choice made sense. Fifi had spent seventeen years nurturing students and another four as a psychologist, caring for the mental health of strangers. Why not put her skill and energy to even greater personal use by starting a family of her own? Remi, though, was reluctant. He already had two adult children from his earlier marriage and would turn eighty around the time the child would graduate from high school. Fifi, now forty-three, felt she was running out of time, too. In recent years, she'd experienced hot flashes, and doctors suggested she was going through early perimenopause.

A few weeks after we met in Paris, Fifi and Remi went hiking in the Pyrenees. As they climbed along a rocky trail, past lakes and groves of pine trees, families with children passed them, leaving Fifi feeling blue. Thirteen years earlier, she and Remi had hiked the same mountain with Remi's son, who was seventeen at the time. She realized now, all these years later, that Remi's son had a son of his own and Remi was a grandfather.

"And me? Fifi? Nothing happened to me," she said. "I had a feeling that I had missed everything. I have wasted my life."

Fifi and Remi sat down on a big rock and faced each other as Fifi dabbed her eyes with tissues. Fellow hikers continued to walk past as the couple discussed bringing another life into the world.

"Thirteen years from now, I would like to have a son or daughter walk in the mountains with me," Fifi said, "because I don't know what the future holds for us. I want to have a child."

Fifi continued to pursue getting pregnant and Remi was supportive. When I met up with Fifi a year later, the news, however, was not good. She had not been able to conceive, and during the gray Shanghai winter she'd slipped into depression and bought a sunlamp to try to lift her spirits.

"Last year was desperate," Fifi told me as we sat at her dining-room table amid the exotic furnishings and walls hangings she and

Remi had gathered on their travels around China and across the globe. "I'm forty-four," she said with an air of resignation. "It might not be good for the kid."

Her period had become irregular, and she was coming to terms with the fact that she might never have a child. Strong-minded and self-reliant, Fifi had rebelled against the expectations of Chinese society and married an older, foreign man who lived far away in another land. That arrangement had allowed her to continue to live life in Shanghai as she wished, but as she had grown older and her priorities had shifted, it had also made it harder for her to become a mother. She told Remi she felt his two grown children were her own. She took a small white stone Buddha and wrapped it in purple cloth with tobacco, which symbolized smoke taking her heartache away. Then she tied it with a red ribbon and placed it in her purse as a token of the sorrow she felt for having to live apart from her husband and not being able to have a child.

"This is the grief I have to face," she told me. "I carry it with me every day."

CRYSTAL CARRIED HER own grief for her sister, Winnie, whose disappearance continued to haunt her. From our travels together near the Lao border, she knew Winnie was gone. As she prepared to leave her family in China and return to America, Crystal was also looking ahead. During our drives through the mountains, she shared that she'd just become engaged to a lawyer back in Michigan named Jimmy. Having lived alone and unsettled for so many years, though, Crystal doubted herself and wasn't sure where she belonged.

Crystal had been married before. While working as a nurse in Harbin in northeast China, she'd married a security guard from the city, which she said felt like a coup for a farm girl. Relations with her in-laws, though, were fraught. Her husband's family looked down on her because she was from the countryside and blamed her for things over which she had no control. For instance, she said, the day after she married her husband, one of his friends disappeared and was later found dead from a head wound. Based on superstition, the man's relatives blamed Crystal, because her marriage had preceded the man's disappearance by a day. Crystal was labelled a *saozhouxing*, a bearer of bad luck, and was pressed to provide $500 in compensation.

Her husband's family treated her not only as a bad luck charm but also as a servant. As a daughter-in-law living with her husband's family, she said she was expected to do most of the cooking and cleaning, even as she worked five days a week.

"I didn't know I deserved better," Crystal told me. "After six years, I was going crazy. I became rebellious."

She moved out and bought her own apartment. Later, after her mother died unexpectedly, Crystal became determined not to end up trapped in northeast China. She struck out for Malta, an English-speaking archipelago east of Tunisia, because it was the easiest place for Chinese to get student visas in Europe. Crystal settled into a rambling mansion a few blocks from the Mediterranean, which she shared with twenty-nine other Chinese students and migrants. She studied English in the mornings, worked afternoons in a restaurant, and eventually found a job as an operating room nurse.

Every couple of weeks, she rode a bus along the marina past hundreds of sailboats to Valetta, a baroque fortress city of narrow streets and stone buildings with enclosed wooden balconies painted in blues, greens, and reds. Crystal sat on a bench in a garden and gazed across the harbor at the blond, limestone ramparts of a sixteenth-century fort. The vista was striking, calming, and a world away from the cold and ice of Harbin.

After three years, Crystal returned to China, then moved on to South Korea and eventually to Michigan, where she met Jimmy, her boyfriend, on the Internet. She had just enrolled in a bachelor's program—her second—in information technology. In her online profile, she said she was looking for a man with a master's degree or above.

"I set my standards really high," she said.

In leaving her first husband and working around the world, Crystal had grown more confident and overcome one of the traits she felt had led to her sister Winnie's downfall: low self-esteem.

Jimmy was a laid-back attorney eight years her senior who liked to camp and canoe. Divorced, he'd been on so many failed dates that he chose a tavern near Crystal's apartment in case the evening went poorly. Jimmy arrived wearing a yellow polo shirt and cargo shorts. Looking in his rearview mirror, he watched Crystal approach in a tan summer dress with a flowered pattern.

"Okay, wow!" he thought.

Crystal took a close look at him.

"Wow!" she thought. "He doesn't look like his profile."

"I was disappointed at first glance," she told me.

But the couple talked for two hours, and Jimmy engaged Crystal with questions about her origins, her goals, and why she was returning to school at age forty.

"I told her I was in love with her two weeks into the relationship," Jimmy said.

Soon after Crystal returned from her search for Winnie, she and Jimmy were married at the courthouse in town. One summer, I flew in to visit and see how they were doing. The couple pulled up in their Subaru Forester to the Comfort Inn where I was staying, and Crystal jumped out and greeted me with a big hug. After breakfast, we headed down a long private road, stopped to let some deer pass, and then came to a modern colonial home perched above a lake at the end of a peninsula. The house covered 5,000 square feet and had a sundeck. Jimmy and Crystal shared a master bedroom with a cathedral ceiling and water view. This was light-years from the mud-brick house where Crystal had grown up in China's far northeast and from the cinder block home where we'd interrogated Winnie's husband in Yunnan province years earlier.

The couple seemed good for one another. As Jimmy and I paddled a canoe along the marsh one day, he said he was more disciplined with Crystal in his life. He knew he couldn't drink whisky, smoke weed, or leave dirty dishes in the sink if he hoped to make the relationship work.

"I wouldn't be where I am today without her," Jimmy said.

Jimmy seemed a calming influence on Crystal, who was finally settling down in middle age. One afternoon, Jimmy offered to take us out in their pontoon boat for a spin around the lake. He brought a gray hoodie down to the dock and gently put his hand on Crystal's shoulder as he handed it to her. As Jimmy guided the boat around the shoreline we passed a flock of swans, a kid tubing off the back of a motorboat, and some boys playing on a floating dock next to a beach with a volleyball net. Crystal sat in a pair of ripped jeans, hands dug into the pockets of her hoodie, squinting in the sunlight and smiling. After rounding the lake, we returned to their house nestled amid trees on a bluff. I thought back to the photos of Winnie posing on the wooded hillside among the villas in Dalian, looking out over the ocean. Crystal now had the life Winnie had dreamed of: a good, reliable man and a home with a view of the water. Sitting on the dock, Crystal gazed out across the rippling water and the lush lawns along the lakefront.

"I never thought I would live like this," she said. "I'm the happiest I've ever been in my life."

SINCE I'D FIRST accompanied Max as he provided free haircuts to the elderly, he'd built his salon clientele from 160 paying members to 1,300, riding the wave of consumption by Shanghai's middle and upper classes. Last year, he moved to the heart of the city and was preparing to open a new salon called Maxvision on the twenty-ninth floor of a high-rise a few blocks north of People's Park. The salon was designed as a multipurpose club, covering two floors and nearly six thousand square feet, with two balconies, a kitchen, a bar, and an area for meetings and PowerPoint presentations. Max planned to bring in additional revenue by providing space for other merchants, including wine dealers and tailors. He would live on-site in a bedroom with a glassed-in shower. It was a dramatic change from a decade earlier, when he'd spent his first night in the city admiring the skyscrapers along the river and dozing on a wooden bench on the Bund.

If Max's surroundings were barely recognizable, so was Max. He'd traded in his black jacket, bright red belt, and sockless shoes for a preppy look, including a navy-blue cardigan and a white, button-down oxford shirt that made him look like a model in a Brooks Brothers catalog. Max had even changed his shaggy hairstyle to a shorter, neater one that made him look at least five years younger. The effect was so striking that when I scrolled through his photos on WeChat, I thought he was someone else. Max explained that some of his clients are entrepreneurs, and when he attends parties, he needs to dress as they do. Among Max's WeChat photos were some of him in a blue pinstripe suit and tie holding hands in a park with a woman in a bridal dress with a bouquet of roses. This turned out to be his fiancée, a woman from Anhui province whom he'd met at a photography class. When I'd last seen Max two years earlier, he was still lying to his mother, pretending to have a girlfriend.

Today Max, too, seemed like Gatsby, with his rapid transformation from provincial poverty to prosperity with an urbane facade. Looking around Max's penthouse apartment, I thought back to his recollections of childhood, walking to school barefoot with a flashlight, and his migrant journey, collecting beer bottles for recycling money. I asked him how it felt to go through so much change in just two decades.

"I've been away from home for a long time," said Max, sounding older than his thirty-eight years and unfazed by his improbable rise. "I want my business to be bigger and bigger. I want to serve more and more clients. This is going according to my original plan."

I worried about Max. He didn't have a high school education and had never studied business or economics.

"I've read books on management," he told me, "but finance is too difficult."

When we last spoke in late 2018, Max had terrible news. He had pooled his savings, membership fees, and investor funds and given them to a partner to manage. The man was a loan shark who gave Max a 20 percent return on his money. Max hoped to increase his money quickly so he could begin to invest in businesses back home in Yunnan province, to create jobs so people wouldn't have to leave as he had. But the partner stopped paying Max interest. Eventually he and the money—over $430,000—disappeared without a trace. Max was wiped out. He told me he descended into depression and his fiancée left him. He blames himself for being greedy. Max continues to cut hair to pay off his investors and has turned to Buddhism, which has helped him deal with his loss. He says he now just lives day by day. Despite his dire financial straits, Max continues to cut the hair of old folks each month at Apricot Plum Garden, including his friend who insisted that his son worked with the White House. To this day, Max said, no one has ever seen the boy.

LIKE MAX, RAY was also looking for ways to contribute and make a difference. Having grown up poor on a farm, he now owned a nice apartment, had a lucrative job at a law firm, and enjoyed trips to Europe. Ray was working with two other successful men from his and Rocky's village in Hubei to build a public plaza the size of several football fields, where the community could gather and where his mother, Guo, and her friends could practice and perform their dance routines. Most local taxes go to the central government, so the village couldn't afford it. Ray and the other native sons planned to pool their money to pay for the project, which they figured would cost between $75,000 and $150,000. The village voted in favor of the project, but some residents balked because their sheds would have to be torn down to make way for the square. The project is now on hold, but Ray hasn't given up.

One afternoon, I had lunch with Ray and Rocky on a patio at the foot of Shanghai's World Financial Center, which rises 101 stories and—from where we were sitting—resembles a knife blade pricking the sky. Over cheeseburgers and steak, Ray told me how exhausted he was from work and how fed up he was with his job.

"You have no spare time on the weekend," Ray said, sounding like so many big-city lawyers in the United States. "Your clients are so busy. You have to match everybody's rhythm. If you want to be in this society, you have to work for it. We sacrifice time with our children, maybe we sacrifice the environment," he said, pointing toward the gray sky. Ray's round-trip commute was more than two hours and, after coming home, he often worked late. "That is not sustainable," he said. "Chinese people are exhausted."

That was my sense, too, and I didn't know how they had kept up this pace for so long. I'd noticed a change since my early days in Beijing, where people rushed through the street markets in the mornings, when everyone was still scrounging for the next yuan. But in recent years, as people had become much more afflu-ent—and tired—the rat race had lost a little of its urgency. China remained dynamic but no longer drove itself at the manic pace I'd encountered two decades earlier. Unfulfilled in his work, Ray said he was interested in writing or teaching, expressing himself and giving back to society in some way. In several decades, he'd gone from a farm boy to a Shanghai lawyer to someone who now wanted to help build a more civil society in a country where that was becoming harder and harder. Listening to Ray, who had just turned forty, and thinking about the toll rapid change had taken on the people here, I wondered if in the years ahead China might face a midlife crisis of its own.

I FIRST MET Johanna, the human rights attorney, about four years ago in a Shanghai taxi, where I eavesdropped on her democracy debate with the driver. In the years that followed, Xi Jinping's government detained more than two hundred of Johanna's colleagues in an attempt to destroy China's legal-rights movement. In hindsight, that democracy conversation on the day after Christmas seemed like a relic of a more hopeful era.

Before I left Shanghai, I flew to see Johanna at her home in central China. Under pressure from local authorities, her law firm had tried to fire her, but three hundred fellow attorneys signed a petition in her defense. Johanna had recently had a son, and I thought that motherhood might make her more cautious and more risk averse, as it does with most parents. I wondered if she might switch from the thankless, dangerous work of defending people's political rights to something much safer and more lucrative, such as commercial law or intellectual property law, like Ray and Rocky.

Soon after her son was born, Johanna followed the advice of health officials and got him a series of vaccinations. A few days later, news broke that outdated or improperly stored vaccines had been given to children across the country. Eventually, the estimate would rise to about two million cases. It had taken police nearly a year to inform the public, making this just the latest in a series of government cover-ups involving the health and safety of children. Johanna embraced the vaccination scandal as a new cause. It was less politically sensitive than battling illegal detentions but no less urgent. She and a dozen other lawyers wrote a letter demanding that the government launch a national investigation. They wanted officials to find out who might have received the bad vaccines and to know who would pay for revaccinations. Instead of making Johanna more cautious, motherhood had made her bolder.

"I feel I have no ability to protect my child," said Johanna, who sat on her couch cradling her son, who was wrapped in a polka-dot blanket. "I provide clean water and good food, but that's all. I cannot promise a safe environment outside the house, safe vaccines, clean air. I can't guarantee any of these things. So, I feel really, really helpless."

Johanna was thin; she had tiny wrists and seemed to float inside her indigo dress. Her voice trembled and tears streamed down her cheeks as her son cooed in her arms.

"You seem very brave to me," I said.

"Do I have another choice?" she responded. "I don't think so. We all think we can leave some problems to our offspring's generation. Sometimes I blame my father's and other generations. Why couldn't you fight? If you fought, maybe I could live more easily and we wouldn't have to struggle like this."

Despite the risks to her career—her law firm in Shenzhen planned to let her contract lapse in 2019—Johanna was determined to protect the rights and health of ordinary people like her and her son.

"I don't plan to leave this problem for others," she said.

WHEN ASHLEY LEFT China in 2016 for school in America, she thought she was on a one-way trip to the United States and a freer life. Last summer, she graduated from business school in America, packed her two roll bags, and boarded a plane for the country she thought she had left behind: China. Ashley was returning—coming full circle really—for several reasons. Watching Donald Trump's leadership and the behavior of many of his supporters had eroded her faith in American democracy and the nation's professed values. She also thought the economic action and excitement was not in the United States but in greater China. She'd landed a job with a Hong Kong start-up working on initial public stock offerings for midsize Chinese companies. The starting salary was more than $120,000 per year plus bonus. Under Chinese law, Ashley needed a visa to work in Hong Kong, so while she waited for approval, she lived just over the mainland border in Shenzhen. Eight months earlier, as we chatted in Paris, Ashley had told me she would never go back to the mainland unless she had no other choice.

"Welcome back to China," I said, reaching out on her twenty-ninth birthday. It was a Saturday afternoon and she was alone in the office in Shenzhen, working under fluorescent lights.

"Well," Ashley said, "it's better than I thought."

In fact, it was so much better than expected, Ashley had de-cided to live in Shenzhen and commute to Hong Kong, which a new high-speed rail line had made much easier. Like many of the twists and turns in the lives of those I followed, this was one I hadn't seen coming just two years earlier. Although Hong Kong's freedoms were shrinking, it still had an open Internet and a relatively free press and permitted political demonstrations—all things that were banned on the mainland. I was struck that Ash-ley, after two years living in America's admittedly flawed democ-racy, would consider returning to a country that seemed to be growing more repressive by the day. Her thinking boiled down to cost and convenience. Hong Kong's housing prices were still high, while life in Shenzhen had improved dramatically. Just a few decades earlier, Shenzhen had been a fishing community. When I first visited in the 1990s, it had grown into a giant factory town filled with migrant workers. Now, it was in its third incarnation as a thriving metropolis with a professional class, good restau-rants, and key high-tech companies, such as Tencent, which owns WeChat, and Huawei, the telecom giant. Just around the corner from Ashley's office was a huge food emporium owned by the Chinese tech giant Alibaba that offered rows of live crabs, shrimp, prawns, scallops, lobster, and fish.

"It's a combination of Whole Foods and a seafood market," Ashley said. "You should really see it. It's amazing!"

And Shenzhen wanted people like Ashley. Even as Beijing and Shanghai were tearing down homes and pushing out some of the "low-end" migrant population, they and other major cities con-tinued to make onetime payments—in Ashley's case, $4,000—to lure in people with overseas master's degrees. For white-collar professionals like Ashley, China was more convenient, lucrative, and comfortable than it had been just two years earlier. Although Ashley was pleasantly surprised by Shenzhen, she could feel that fear and repression in mainland China had grown during her time away. In 2018, a series of sexual-harassment scandals surfaced at Chinese universities, which sparked a #MeToo movement with Chinese characteristics. In April, students at Peking University publicly demanded the school release investigative materials from a 1990s case involving a former professor accused of sexually assaulting a promising literature student, who later committed suicide. University officials tried to intimidate one of the student activists, threatening to block her graduation and forcing her to delete documents she'd collected related to the case—although one of the officials claimed such action was only taken for her safety. Ashley jumped to the woman's defense in a private WeChat group with some of her Peking University classmates. Some members of the group who worked for the government criticized the woman and backed the university. Then Ashley received a private message from one of the group's members.

"You know, you're not supposed to defend her publicly," a classmate who lived in the United States warned. The members who now work for the government "might take a screen shot of what you said and do something."

"They are really horrible people," Ashley said of her classmates who had joined the government and continued to support its repressive policies. "Sometimes, I can't believe we went to the same classes together. They were nice back then."

But China was changing. A private WeChat group was not private in Xi's New Era, and old college chums couldn't necessarily be trusted. I wondered if Ashley would continue to come to the defense of people like the crusading student at her alma mater.

"I think I would restrain myself," Ashley told me. "You just can't risk it. I know where my heart is and I don't think I deserve to be reported by some stupid people in my WeChat group. It's not worth it."

Professionally, Ashley was excited to be back in China, a land of opportunity and possibility, but she was worried about the broader economy. Amid slowing growth, China was trying to reduce harmful debt while battling a trade war launched by President Trump. Ashley thought a reckoning was ahead.

"There will be a financial crisis, I'm positive," she said. "What is the scale and how long it will last? We don't know."

AFTER CHARLES EXPOSED his boss and embarrassed his former employer, I thought the chances of him landing another job with a Western news organization were near zero. So did Charles, who was racked by worry and the constant nagging of his mother, who had opposed him going public from the beginning. After several months, Charles did land an interview with a foreign broadcaster. I asked him what he would say when they asked why he hadn't given the Dutch newspaper time to investigate his allegations before going public.

"Working here in Shanghai I didn't feel any attention from the headquarters [in Holland]; also I didn't have any communication with them," Charles said. "With this kind of level of fabrication, I also had some doubt about the integrity of the whole editorial board. So, I gave them some hours, but no reply. I was just worried I would be muffled."

Having grown up in a society marked by distrust, Charles wasn't certain the leaders of the Dutch newspaper—with whom he'd never spoken—would do the right thing, just as he didn't trust his father to buy him a soccer jersey or the Chinese government to tell the truth about Tiananmen or the Great Leap Forward. Charles interviewed for the new job and then waited for weeks for an answer. He was told that editors were still concerned about how he'd handled the case involving Oscar. Charles's mother continued to pester him about his job prospects. One morning, she called him on WeChat.

"How about your job?" she said. "What will you do after waiting so long?"

"Don't ask," Charles responded.

He returned to his computer, continued to scour a job-hunting website, then fielded a call from a headhunter suggesting a sales job with a Japanese logistics company.

"I had almost given up," he told me.

That afternoon, the broadcaster called while Charles was sitting in his room in Shanghai. Soon afterward, he sent me a message.

"They decided to hire me."

I was surprised, appreciative, and relieved. It would have been easy for a Western news organization to turn Charles down and no one would have ever questioned the decision. But I also knew that some foreign correspondents didn't think Charles should be punished for doing the right thing and should have a chance to continue to contribute. Charles's family was delighted with the news, and his mother changed her story as soon as Charles landed the job. When we last chatted, she insisted to me that she had always supported her courageous son.

When she learned her son had a new job, Charles's mother replied, "*Hao, hao zuo,*" which Charles translated as "work hard and cherish this opportunity."

Charles's response: "No more whistle-blowing."

AFTER I FINISHED driving my passengers in Shanghai and before I left for London, I had to sell my Shanghai Free Taxi, so I turned to the only used-car salesman I knew, Beer. Even though we hadn't parted on the best of terms, I was curious to see if he had changed. When I arrived at the dealership, Beer took charge, asking me for the keys so he could drive the car around back for an inspection. I hadn't seen him in more than a year, and he seemed smoother and more self-confident. The dandruff on the shoulders was gone and his hair was now swept over the top and clipper-cut short on the sides in a much more fashionable style. In other respects, he seemed the same old Beer. His name tag had someone else's name on it and falsely identified him as an intern. Yang suspected Beer portrayed himself as a trainee to tug on the heartstrings of potential buyers. I wondered if he wore the fake name tag to provide deniability.

"I like to keep a low profile," Beer said by way of explanation.

Beer said the process of finding a buyer through the dealership could take a while, so—out of earshot of his coworkers—he offered to take the car and sell it himself privately. This seemed very Beer and a very bad idea. The next week, I returned and sold my car directly to the dealership, which disappointed Beer, who handed me a few pieces of taffy and continued to insist he could get me a better price on the side.

When I first met Beer years ago, he suggested we go out drinking sometime and said he liked to down seven to eight beers in a sitting. A few days before I boarded the plane for England, Yang and I took him to a bar to shoot pool and say goodbye. Despite growing up in the countryside where outdoor pool tables are common, Beer had no experience with the game and failed to hit the rack on his first two attempts to break. For the first time, he seemed a bit vulnerable and not on a hustle. Over a few games, I tried to teach him how to shoot, pointing my finger where he needed to hit the ball, and he improved. True to his name, Beer knocked back four bottles of Tiger, one Asahi, a Brooklyn, and a shot of tequila with a lemon wedge. I asked him why he had touched me so much when he'd first tried to sell me a car. He said it was just his way—young Chinese are more and more individualistic—and he thought Americans liked it.

Last year, I looked at Beer's WeChat page and saw that he had moved to southern China, married his longtime girlfriend, and had a daughter. He was still selling used cars, but when I spoke with him, he seemed like a different person. He said he had cut down on his drinking and was focusing on his career. Over WeChat, he spent forty minutes analyzing the economy of the former manufacturing town where he was working and explaining to me why he thought leasing would be the next big thing in the Chinese auto business. I didn't know enough to evaluate his argument, but it was clear he'd done a lot of homework, and I was impressed. His dream, he said, was to open his own leasing company. At the end of our conversation, I wished him well and he offered to send me a copy of his business plan, as long as I promised not to show it to anyone else. For the first time, there was something between Beer and me: trust.

WHEN I ARRIVED in Shanghai in 2011, China was at a turning point after a decade of government inaction, corruption, and decay. It wasn't clear what path the Communist Party would take, but Xi Jinping soon changed that. As I began to shuttle passengers around town in my free taxi, President Xi tightened his grip on the nation, continued to jail corrupt officials, dispatched his rivals, built a cult of personality, and eventually amassed power in a way that hadn't been seen in decades. Instead of taking China in a more liberal direction, he recognized that one of the country's greatest achievements—an increasingly wealthy and sophisticated population—was also one of the party's greatest potential threats, especially if more and more Chinese people adopted the political values of the West. Xi did what shrewd, adaptive authoritarians do. He addressed popular concerns, inspired confidence and national pride, and tried to discredit the party's greatest ideological challenge, democracy. So far, it's working.

I was conflicted about China in Xi Jinping's New Era. After several years of driving my passengers and following their lives at home and abroad, I'd never been happier for or more optimistic about the Chinese people. My passengers were smart, driven, and

capable, and many were striving to build lives beyond their parents'
imaginations. They were living the American Dream—in China.
At the same time, I'd never been more worried about the country's
political trajectory. The United States had spent decades engaging
China in the hope that increased trade and contact with the outside
world would eventually lead to a more liberal and open system. In
fact, the opposite had happened. Trade enriched China and made
the party more powerful and outwardly confident. While Xi had
created policies that improved the lives of Chinese citizens, he had
also doubled down on repression, jailing human rights attorneys
like Johanna's colleagues; neutering the news media, which disillusioned people like Charles; and pumping up nationalism in a
way that even resonated to some degree with people like Ray. The
party knew that the better educated, better traveled, and wealthier
Chinese people became, the more likely it was that they might
someday demand more rights and protections and question the
system. The short-term strategy was to cut them off as much as
possible from critical outside voices and to frighten those who
might challenge the party's policies or rule.

Xi's crackdown at home and assertiveness abroad coincided
with the election of an American president who was much more
willing than his predecessors to confront China head-on. Wary
of a Chinese government plan to dominate key industries of the
future, President Trump launched a trade war. By fall 2018, the
world's two largest economies had imposed tariffs on more than
$360 billion in goods, and relations between the countries were the
worst they'd been in decades. The Chinese government seemed
unprepared for Trump's tough approach and had underestimated
how much goodwill it had lost among US politicians, business
leaders, and China scholars. In a speech last fall, Vice President
Pence delivered a wide-ranging indictment of Xi's government,
accusing it of everything from stealing American technology and
persecuting the religious faithful to trying to influence American

universities and movie studios and militarizing its disputes in the South China Sea.

"America had hoped that economic liberalization would bring China into a greater partnership with us and with the world," Pence said. "Instead, China has chosen economic aggression, which has in turn emboldened its growing military."

The Chinese Communist Party has defied its doubters—including most of the American foreign-policy establishment—and built a repressive form of state capitalism that has delivered extraordinary economic results. Despite some of Xi's authoritarian policies, many Chinese are happy with the president and, like Rocky and Sarah, optimistic about the future. Chinese tend to be pragmatic and patient and, it's critical to remember, they have seen far worse. If Xi can reform state-owned enterprises, manage the country's huge debt load, and build a twenty-first-century economy that creates more high-value jobs, the vast majority of Chinese—including some of the people I drove in the free taxi—will probably continue to support him.

But that is a tall order and the party faces many challenges ahead, including slowing economic growth, pollution-related health problems, an aging population, a shrinking labor force, and tortuous relations with the United States. By removing term limits, the party and Xi have taken a big gamble. If Xi fails, he will have no one else to blame at home. Although he may try to point the finger at Japan or America, that strategy can backfire, leading nationalists to turn on the government and question why it can't defend the country against foreign rivals.

These are dark days for freedom in China and liberal values in much of the West, and they could extend for years. I know my passengers will, as Chinese always have, persevere. Predicting the future of China is a fool's errand, an invitation to be proven wrong. But I hold out hope that one day the Chinese people will have a government that is more worthy of them, one that will provide them with more freedom, more protections, and more say in how they are governed. In the long run, that is what many Chinese would like, and ignoring it for decades to come carries considerable risk. I'm also reminded of what Ray said, standing on the muddy hillside in Hubei province after Rocky's wedding years ago.

"Think about it," said Ray. "If 1.4 billion people's creativity is mobilized, everyone does things they like and lives with dignity. If this comes true, it will be a blessing for the country. It will also be a remarkable thing for the world."

Acknowledgments

My journey to China began more than a quarter century ago while chatting with my father at the beach in southern New Jersey, when I was a junior reporter at the *Baltimore Sun* and dreamed of becoming a foreign correspondent. I wanted to go where history would be made but had no clue where that might be. Dad was a wise man who'd worked as a physician and a university administrator and was now running a wealth-management firm. I asked, half kidding: "Where should I go?"

"China," my father responded without pausing. His answer was swift and certain. I sat up and listened.

"China has the world's largest population, the world's fastest-growing economy, and its foreign currency reserves are up to five hundred million dollars," said Dad, who had such seemingly obscure facts at his fingertips because he was a voracious reader. "China is the future. It's going to change the world."

A few years later, when the *Baltimore Sun*'s Beijing bureau opened suddenly, I asked my wife, Julie, a veterinarian, if we should apply.

"China?" she said. "I'd go to China."

In April 1997, I boarded a flight to Beijing, sight unseen. I am forever grateful for my father's prescience and my wife's unparalleled, adventurous spirit. Covering China and getting to know the Chinese people has been one of the great privileges of my career. I owe a great debt of gratitude to my editors at the *Sun,* who took a chance assigning an untested correspondent to one of the world's most challenging postings. They include my mentor, Bill Marimow, then the *Sun's* managing editor, who had given me my first job a decade earlier, hiring me out of a taxicab to string for the *Philadelphia Inquirer.* John Carroll, the *Sun's* editor, believed in me when others did not. The *Sun's* foreign editors, Jeff Price and Robert Ruby, provided crucial guidance and support as I learned how to become a foreign correspondent.

I'm deeply indebted to my Chinese passengers and friends who informed this book. They invited me into their homes and lives for years on end and spent dozens and dozens of hours in chats and interviews. They answered every question I asked and only hesitated when doing so might put them at some risk. I consider all of them friends, including Beer.

In my decade based in Beijing and Shanghai, I relied on the wisdom and friendship of many generous colleagues, including Adam Brookes, Adam Minter, Andrea Koppel-Pollack, Andrew Browne, Anthony Kuhn, Ian Johnson, Jennifer Lin, Mary Kay Magistad, Steve Mufson, Rone Tempest, Erik Eckholm, Elisabeth Rosenthal, Michael Forsythe, Leta Hong Fincher, Stephanie Ho, Dele Olojede, Chris Buckley, John Pomfret, George Wehrfritz, Michael Laris, Peter Hessler, Scott Savitt, David Murphy, Richard McGregor, Mark Leong, Matt Forney, Bay Fang, Charles Hutzler, Melinda Liu, Michael Lev, Rob Schmitz, Robin Brant, John Sudworth, David Barboza, Brook Larmer, Hannah Beech, John Ruwitch, Russell Flannery, Lenora Chu, Margaret Conley, Bill Savadove, Tom Phillips, Paul Eckert, Chris Billing, Jaime FlorCruz,

Paul Mooney, James Palmer, Christina Larson, Paul French, Sue Anne Tay, David Bandurski, David McKenzie, Edward Gargan, Duncan Hewitt, Henry Chu, James Fallows, James Mann, Li Yuan, Mara Hvistendahl, Miro Cernetig, Peter Ford, Wang Feng, Luna Lin, Rob Gifford, Rupert Wingfield-Hayes, Susan Lawrence, Ted Anthony, Tiff Roberts, Victoria Wei, Wen Haijing, Vincent Ni, David Wertime, Fan Wenxin, Joy Ma, Mike Chinoy, David Rennie, Barbara Demick, Michael Meyer, Louisa Lim, Phil Pan, Richard Burger, Bill Bishop, Andy Xie, Qiu Xiaolong, Patrick Chovanec, Michael Pettis, Vijay Vaitheeswaran, and Curtis Rodda.

I also sought counsel from many wise China hands and writers, including Ambassador Winston Lord, David Shambaugh, Orville Schell, Bert Keidel, the late Richard Baum, the late ambassador James Lilley, Andrew Nathan, Robert Griffiths, Joseph Fewsmith, Merle Goldman, the late Roderick MacFarquhar, Elizabeth Perry, Barry Naughton, Yasheng Huang, Dali Yang, Cheng Li, Susan Naquin, Jeffrey Wasserstrom, Arthur Kroeber, Andrew Field, James Farrer, Anne Stevenson-Yang, David Zweig, Andy Rothman, Robin Bordie, Minxin Pei, Bill Dodson, Bob Kapp, Kent Kedl, Ezra Vogel, Anthony Saich, Jerome Cohen, Kenneth Jarrett, Ambassador James Sasser, Ambassador Joseph Prueher, Micah Truman, Shen Dingli, Yan Xuetong, Yanmei Xie, Zhang Xuezhong, Huang Jing, John Kamm, Suzanne Payne, Kaiser Kuo, Jeremy Goldkorn, Eric Weiner, and Louis Bayard.

At Shanghai's China Europe International Business School, I'm indebted to Charmaine Clark, Ding Yuan, Oliver Rui, Gary Liu, David Yu, and June Zhu for help decoding the Chinese economy. For help developing Chinese language skills, I'm forever grateful to my first teacher, Chuan Ouyang, and the patience and help from so many teachers at the Beijing and Shanghai campuses of the Taipei Language Institute.

Our years in Beijing and Shanghai were enriched by a wonderful group of friends including Chen Yali, Eric Hagt, Chen Yawei,

Bei Ye, Linda Zhang, Frank Wang, Christine Ching, our pastors Elyn and Peter MacInnis and Timothy Merrill, Jeanie Merrill, Ken and Brenda Erickson, Richard and Lucy Young, John and Meg Ideker, Stephen and York-Chi Harder, Stefan and Devon Whitney, and Diana Mathias.

When I first pitched the free taxi idea as a series for NPR, then international editor Edith Chapin said, "It sounds like a book." I'm grateful for her staunch support for this project from its inception and the generous book leave that she approved, along with her successor and China hand Will Dobson. Edith and Will went beyond the call of duty by providing helpful edits on later drafts. NPR Asia editor Nishant Dahiya did a wonderful job shaping the original radio series and provided crucial perspective in the late stages of the manuscript. I'm also grateful to former foreign editor Loren Jenkins for assigning me to East Africa and later Shanghai, as well as my Africa editor, Didi Schanche, and Europe and Asia editor, Kevin Beesley, and former NPR executive editor Madhulika Sikka. I'm grateful to Lauren Frayer, Joanna Kakissis, Daniella Cheslow, Debbie Elliott, and Alice Fordham, who pitched in in London during my time away, and NPR/BBC producer Sam Alwyine-Mosely, who held the bureau together in my absence and made it look easy. I'd also like to thank Soham Saxena for transcribing hours of interviews as I was just beginning the writing process, and Evan Osnos for wise advice on book writing that covered everything from software to structuring.

I first began discussing a China book with my agent, Howard Yoon, back in 2011 and appreciate his support, patience, and help in shaping the proposal, along with his business partner, Gail Ross, of the Ross Yoon Agency. At PublicAffairs, my editor Ben Adams intuitively recognized how to craft an unconventional book and how to work with an enthusiastic but anxious first-time author. I'm also grateful for the support at PublicAffairs from Peter Osnos, Clive Priddle, Jaime Leifer, Lindsay Fradkoff, Miguel Cervantes III, and Brynn Warriner, as well as Peter Garceau for his cover design and

Elizabeth Dana for her careful, thoughtful, and patient copyediting. I owe a debt of gratitude to Kuan Yang for shooting the wonderful cover photo one rainy night in Shanghai and to James McGregor for lending me a proper pair of shoes.

No one produces a book without considerable help from family and friends. My nephew, Dan Langfitt; my brother, David Langfitt; my uncle, John Payne; my aunt, Jane Payne; my NPR colleagues Anthony Kuhn and Steve Inskeep; PJ Juliano; my BBC colleagues, Vincent Ni and Feifei Feng; my Shanghai friends, Patrick Cranley and Tina Kanagaratnam; and professor Jeffrey Wasserstrom all read drafts or portions of the manuscript and provided helpful edits that identified errors and improved the writing and structure. Any errors that remain are my own. I'm especially grateful to my uncle, John Payne, who encouraged me to write this book, and my brothers, David and John, who provided valuable personal and career advice along the way. I'd also like to thank my cousin, U.S. Navy Rear Admiral (ret.) Tilghman Payne, for providing insights into the geopolitics of the South China Sea. When I was in college, my mother, Carolyn, urged me to apply to the university's premier nonfiction writing course, The Literature of Fact, taught by the legendary John McPhee. Without my mother's encouragement and John's example, I might never have become a journalist, let alone a foreign correspondent and author.

Yang Zhuo, a superb journalist with whom I worked side by side for five years in Shanghai, was a constant companion in reporting, editing, and fact-checking this book, traveling with me to central and south China and beyond. He was instrumental in the creation and execution of the free taxi concept, down to drafting the messages on the magnetic signs. Without Yang, this book would never have happened. Our many adventures in China were the journalistic highlight of my time there.

Finally, I want to thank my wife, Julie, for making all this possible. I'm grateful for her steadfast support for this project, which meant enduring long absences, late nights, missed vacations, anxious discussions, and multiple edits of chapters. I especially appreciate the encouragement of our children, Katherine and Chris, who have embraced our family life abroad with curiosity, humor, and a keen sense of adventure. Our life together is more than I ever could've hoped for. This book is for them.

FRANK LANGFITT
February 4, 2019
London

Sources

This is a work of nonfiction primarily based on reporting in Shanghai and elsewhere in China from 2011 to 2016 and subsequent reporting trips over the following two years to interview characters in Hunan province, Paris, Chicago, Kalamazoo, and Los Angeles. In some cases, I also drew from reporting and experiences from my first posting in China with the *Baltimore Sun* from 1997 to 2002. Given the increasingly repressive political climate in China, most of my subjects requested I use only their English names or Chinese surnames to protect their anonymity in case someone in the government decides to retaliate against them for speaking their minds. Only one character asked to use a pseudonym, Ashley. The vast majority of my research came through more than two hundred hours of interviews. I also relied on written sources, including books, foreign and Chinese newspapers, and analytical websites.

Chapter 1: Beginnings

Background on Maglev

"Shanghai Maglev Gets Official Approval," *China Daily,* April 4, 2006.
"Maglev Trains Stay at Front of Debate," *China Daily,* November 28, 2016.
Daniel Ren, "Shanghai's Maglev Passenger Traffic Lower Than Expected," *South China Morning Post,* December 22, 2012.
Shanghai Maglev official website, http://www.smtdc.com/en/.

Background on Xi Jinping

Chris Buckley and Didi Kirsten Tatlow, "Cultural Revolution Shaped Xi Jinping, from Schoolboy to Survivor," *New York Times,* September 24, 2013.

Nicholas Kristof, "Looking for a Jump-Start in China," *New York Times,* January 5, 2013.

John Ruwitch, "Timeline—The Rise of Chinese Leader Xi Jinping," Reuters, March 16, 2018.

Simon Denyer, "Move Over, America. China Now Presents Itself as the Model 'Blazing a New Trail' for the World," *Washington Post,* October 19, 2017.

"Xi Jinping: 'Time for China to Take Centre Stage,'" BBC, October 18, 2017.

Background on Shanghai

Rob Schmitz, *The Street of Eternal Happiness: Big City Dreams Along a Shanghai Road* (New York: Crown, 2016).

Marie-Claire Bergère, *Shanghai: China's Gateway to Modernity,* trans. Janet Lloyd (Palo Alto, CA: Stanford University Press, 2009).

Anne Warr, *Shanghai Architecture* (Sydney: Watermark Press, 2017).

James Farrer and Andrew David Field, *Shanghai Nightscapes: A Nocturnal Biography of a Global City* (Chicago: University of Chicago Press, 2015).

Tess Johnston and Deke Erh, *A Last Look: Western Architecture in Old Shanghai* (Shanghai: Old China Hand Press, 2014).

Jeffrey N. Wasserstrom, *Global Shanghai, 1850–2010* (New York: Routledge, 2009).

Chapter 2: Chinese New Year Road Trip

Background on Xi Jinping's Chinese Dream

"Potential of the Chinese Dream," *China Daily USA,* March 26, 2014.

Ian Johnson, "At China's New Museum, History Toes Party Line," *New York Times,* April 3, 2011.

Background on the Great Leap Forward

Yang Jisheng, "China's Great Shame," *New York Times,* November 13, 2012.

Yang Jisheng, *Tombstone: The Great Chinese Famine, 1958–1962* (New York: Farrar, Straus and Giroux, 2008).

Chapter 3: Two Country Weddings

Background on thinking and image of Xi Jinping

Elizabeth Economy, *The Third Revolution: Xi Jinping and the New Chinese State* (New York: Oxford University Press, 2018).

Austin Ramzy, "Musical Ode to Xi Jinping and His Wife Goes Viral," *New York Times,* November 25, 2014.

Joyce Lee, "Expressing the Chinese Dream," *Diplomat,* March 28, 2014.

Ian Johnson, "Old Dreams for a New China," *New York Review of Books,* October 15, 2013.

Javier C. Hernández and Audrey Carlsen, "Why Xi Jinping's (Airbrushed) Face Is Plastered All Over China," *New York Times,* November 9, 2017.

Kirk A. Denton, "China Dreams and the 'Road to Revival,'" *Origins* 8, no. 3 (December 2014).

"Xi Jinping: A Cult of Personality?" *ChinaFile,* March 4, 2016.

Andrew G. Walder and Yang Su, "The Cultural Revolution in the Countryside: Scope, Timing and Human Impact," *China Quarterly,* no. 173 (March 2003).

"Xi Jinping Outlines His Vision of 'Dream and Renaissance,'" *South China Morning Post,* March 18, 2013.

Chapter 4: "Morality Is Relative"

Background on Communist Party

"Without the Communist Party, There Would Be No New China," China Radio International English, August 22, 2008.

Richard McGregor, *The Party: The Secret World of China's Communist Rulers* (New York: HarperCollins, 2010).

Background on China's neighborhood committees

Dan Levin and Sue-Lin Wong, "Beijing's Retirees Keep Eye Out for Trouble During Party Congress," *New York Times,* March 15, 2013.

James L. Tyson, "The Party Patrols Neighborhoods," *Christian Science Monitor,* September 22, 1989.

Background on Chinese scams

"Police Raid Scam-Artist Teahouse," *Shanghaiist,* July 13, 2007.

Rob Schmitz, "A Chinese Woman Does a Really Bad Job Pretending to Be Hit by a Car," NPR, December 12, 2016.

Background on reluctance to help people on the street

Huang Haifeng, "What a Tragic Accident Says About Chinese Social Ethics," *Sixth Tone,* June 16, 2017.

Alex Linder, "Woman Gets Hit by Car, Dozens Pass By Without a Care Before She Gets Run Over Again," *Shanghaiist,* June 7, 2017.

Michael Wines, "Bystanders' Neglect of Injured Toddler Sets Off Soul-Searching on Web Sites in China," *New York Times,* October 18, 2011.

"'Good Samaritan' Admits He Pushed Woman," *Shanghai Daily,* January 17, 2012.

Yunxiang Yan, "The Good Samaritan's New Trouble: A Study of the Changing Moral Landscape in Contemporary China," *Social Anthropology* 17, no. 1 (February 2009).

Interview with Yunxiang Yan, 2012.

Background on freedom of religion in China

Steven Lee Myers, "China Insists on Control of Religion, Dimming Hope of Imminent Vatican Deal," *New York Times,* April 3, 2018.

Chapter 5: "A Virtuous Circle Needs to Have a Beginning"

Background on altruism in China

Caroline Reeves, "Bill and Warren's Excellent (Chinese) Adventure," *China Beat,* September 27, 2010.

"The Unkindness of Strangers," *Economist,* July 27, 2013.

William R. Jankowiak, "The Collapse of the Market and the Transformation of Moral Involvement in Urban China," *International Journal of Chinese Culture and Management* 1, no. 4 (2008): 362–374.

Jeremiah Jenne, "Charitable Past: Examples of Goodwill Throughout the Chinese Ages," *Beijinger,* February 21, 2018.

Yunxiang Yan, "The Moral Implications of Immorality: The Chinese Case for a New Anthropology of Morality," *Journal of Religious Ethics* 42, no. 3 (September 2014).

Chapter 6: A Woman Missing in the Mountains

Background on China's mistress-industrial complex

James Palmer, "Kept Women," *Aeon,* October 10, 2013.

Richard Burger, *Behind the Red Door: Sex in China* (Hong Kong: Earnshaw Books, 2012).

Christina Larson, "The Mistress-Industrial Complex. Is adultery the key to solving China's corruption problem?" *Foreign Policy,* December 4, 2012.

Clifford Coonan, "Portrait of a femme fatale who brought down China's elite," *The Independent,* February 19, 2011.

He Qinglian, "A Chinese Story for Our Time, Li Wei," *Articles by He Qinglian* (personal blog), March 1, 2011.

Chapter 7: Disillusioned with the New China

Background on government attacks on Christian churches

Ian Johnson, "Decapitated Churches in China's Christian Heartland," *New York Times,* May 21, 2016.

Frank Langfitt, "Faith, Power Collide in a Changing China," *Baltimore Sun,* August 27, 2000.

Anne Applebaum, "How the Pope 'Defeated Communism," *Washington Post,* April 6, 2005.

Background on China's rich wanting to emigrate

Frank Langfitt, "China's Rich Consider Leaving Growing Nation," NPR, January 17, 2012.

Shi Jing and Yu Ran, "Chinese Rich Are Keen to Emigrate," *China Daily,* November 3, 2011.

Robert Frank, "Chinese Millionaires Plan to Leave in Droves: Report," CNBC, September 15, 2014.

Background on excess of China's new rich

Xu Chi, "Sanya Probes Sex Party Rumors," *Shanghai Daily,* April 7, 2013.

F. Scott Fitzgerald, *The Great Gatsby* (New York: Simon & Schuster, 1925).

The Great Gatsby, directed by Jack Clayton, screenplay by Francis Ford Coppola (Hollywood, CA: Paramount Pictures, 1974).

Evan Osnos, "Reading 'Gatsby' in Beijing," *New Yorker,* May 2, 2013.

Background on home ownership in urban China

Steven Mufson, "Happy Homeowners Living the New 'Chinese Dream,'" *Washington Post,* June 2, 1998.

Background on income inequality in China

Yu Xie and Xiang Zhou, "Income Inequality in Today's China," *Proceedings of the National Academy of Sciences,* May 13, 2014.

"Income Inequality Now Greater in China Than in US," press release, University of Michigan, April 28, 2014.

Shannon Tiezzi, "Report: China's 1 Percent Owns 1/3 of Wealth," *Diplomat,* January 15, 2016.

"China's 2011 Average Salaries Revealed," *China Daily,* June 6, 2012.

Anna Lu, "Owning a Car in China Is Getting Harder and Harder," *Shanghai Daily,* June 27, 2016.

Background on Liu Xiaobo

Shen Jian, "Charter 08 Was More Than a Document for Liu Xiaobo, It Was His Whole Life," *South China Morning Post,* July 14, 2017.

"China's Charter 08," trans. Perry Link, *New York Review of Books,* January 15, 2009.

Background on things Deng Xiaoping didn't actually say

Evelyn Iritani, "Great Idea but Don't Quote Him," *Los Angeles Times,* September 9, 2004.

Background on Rebel Pepper

Frank Langfitt, "Provocative Chinese Cartoonists Find an Outlet Online," NPR, March 16, 2012.

Isaac Stone Fish, "Rebel Without a Country," *Foreign Policy,* August 31, 2015.

Chapter 9: Making China Great Again

Background on the battle of Wolf Teeth Mountain

"Five Heroes on Langya Mountain," China.org.cn, July 29, 2011.

Kiki Zhao, "Chinese Court Orders Apology over Challenge to Tale of Wartime Heroes," *New York Times,* June 28, 2016.

Zhang Yu, "Leftists and Rightists Battle over How to Interpret Stories of China's Revolutionary Past," *Global Times,* January 13, 2016.

Background on disputed islands in the South and East China Seas

"Reef Madness," Australian Broadcasting Corporation, May 21, 2014.

Manuel Mogato, "Philippines Reinforcing Rusting Ship on Spratly Reef Outpost," Reuters, July 14, 2015.

Asia Maritime Transparency Initiative, CSIS.

Zheng Wang, "The Nine-Dashed Line: 'Engraved in Our Hearts,'" *Diplomat,* August 25, 2014.

"China's Position Paper on South China Sea," Xinhua, July 12, 2014.

Michael Green, Bonnie Glaser, and Zack Cooper, "Seeing the Forest Through the SAMs on Woody Island," Asia Maritime Transparency Initiative, CSIS, February 18, 2016.

Frank Langfitt, "China Deploys Surface-to-Air Missiles on Disputed Island in South China Sea," NPR, February 17, 2016.

Zheng Wang, "The Perception Gap Between China and Its Neighbors," *Diplomat,* August 6, 2014.

"Confrontation Will Be Huge Mistake for Japan," *Global Times,* September 13, 2012.

Jane Perlez, "China Accuses Japan of Stealing After Purchase of Group of Disputed Islands," *New York Times,* September 11, 2012.

James Arredy, "Amid Protests, Shanghai Protects Japanese Consulate It Paid to Fix," *Wall Street Journal,* September 19, 2012.

Ian Johnson and Thom Shanker, "Beijing Mixes Messages over Anti-Japan Protests," *New York Times,* September 16, 2012.

Brian Spegele and Takashi Nakamichi, "Anti-Japan Protests Mount in China," *Wall Street Journal,* September 16, 2012.

Amy Qin and Edward Wong, "Smashed Skull Serves as Grim Symbol of Seething Patriotism," *New York Times,* October 11, 2012.

Chapter 10: President Donald J. Trump

Background on US-China trade and industrial espionage

Paul Mozur, "Inside a Heist of American Chip Designs, as China Bids for Tech Power," *New York Times,* June 22, 2018.

Frank Langfitt, "U.S. Security Company Tracks Hacking to Chinese Army Unit," NPR, February 19, 2013.

"U.S. and China Reach Historic Agreement on Economic Espionage," Xinhua, September 25, 2015.

Rob Schmitz, "American Business Leaders in China Concerned About Trump's Trade Actions," NPR, March 21, 2018.

Donald J. Trump, "Statement by the President Regarding Trade with China," White House, June 15, 2018.

Chapter 11: Losing Hearts and Minds

Background on the NRC plagiarism case

Fan Liya and Kevin Schoenmakers, "China Correspondent for Dutch Newspaper Accused of Fabrications," *Sixth Tone,* September 4, 2017.

Manya Koetse, "Dutch Newspaper Responds to Controversy over China Correspondent," *What's on Weibo,* September 5, 2017.

Peter Vandermeersch, "NRC Correspondent Oscar Garschagen Leaves Newspaper After Journalistic Errors," *NRC,* September 20, 2017 (Dutch).

Liu Caiyu and Shan Jie, "Shanghai-Based Dutch Journalist Leaves as Newspaper Concedes Fabrications," *Global Times,* September 20, 2017.

Frank Langfitt, "A 'Sense of Crisis' Now in a Chinese Boomtown Gone Bust," NPR, September 16, 2015.

Frank Langfitt, "China's White Elephants: Ghost Cities, Lonely Airports, Desolate Factories," NPR, October 15, 2015.

Chapter 12: Rethinking the West

Background on Paris

Kim Willsher, "Paris 1900 Exhibition Shows City of Light at Its Brightest," *Guardian*, April 3, 2014.

"Churchill Returns to Paris," BBC, November 11, 1998.

Tina Isaac-Goizé, "A New Exhibition from Hermès Salutes the Artist Behind Those Iconic Windows," *Vogue,* November 7, 2017.

"French GDP Growth Rate," *Trading Economics.*

Background on evictions in Bejiing

Stephen McDonell, "Mass Evictions as Beijing Is Spruced Up," BBC, December 1, 2017.

Chris Buckley, "Why Parts of Beijing Look Like a Devastated War Zone," *New York Times,* November 30, 2017.

Zheping Huang, "What you need to know about Beijing's crackdown on its "low-end population," *Quartz,* November 27, 2017.

Background on protests of bombing of Chinese embassy in Belgrade

Stephen Shaver, "Photo of Anti-Nato protests in Bejiing," *AFP,* May 9, 1999.

Chapter 13: Ashley's Dilemma

Background on the Tiananmen Square uprising

The Gate of Heavenly Peace, directed by Richard Gordon and Carma Hinton (Boston: Long Bow Group, 1995).

Louisa Lim, *People's Republic of Amnesia: Tiananmen Revisited* (New York: Oxford University Press, 2014).

Eric X. Li, "Why China's Political Model is Superior," *New York Times,* February 16, 2012.

Background on use and blocking of VPNs

Jon Russell, "Apple Removes VPN Apps from the App Store in China," *TechCrunch,* July 29, 2017.

"About Those 674 Apps That Apple Censored in China," Greatfire.org, November 30, 2017.

Yuyu Chen and David Y. Yang, "The Impact of Media Censorship: 1984 or Brave New World?" (Forthcoming, American Economic Review).

Jon Russell, "Apple removes VPN apps from the App Store in China," *Tech-Crunch,* July 29, 2017.

"About Those 674 Apps That Apple Censored in China," Greatfire.org, November 30, 2017.

Jiang Feng, "Western elites find new 'China threat' theory," *Global Times,* November 19, 2017.

Curtis Stone, "FAKE NEWS! Here is another example, Trump," *People's Daily Online,* March 6, 2017.

Background on Lu Xun

Lu Xun, *The True Story of Ah Q,* 1921.

Manya Koetse, "Xi Jinping Can Now Stay in Office After Second Term—Weibo Responds," What's On Weibo, February 25, 2018.

Chapter 14: President for Life?

Background on the change in Chinese presidential term limits

Richard McGregor et al., "Xi Won't Go," *ChinaFile,* February 25, 2018.

Laurent Thomet, "China Drowns Out Critics of Lifetime Xi Presidency," AFP, February 27, 2018.

Ian Johnson, "Who Killed More: Hitler, Stalin, or Mao?" *New York Review of Books,* February 2, 2018.

Background on contemporary Chinese politics

Evan Osnos, *The Age of Ambition, Chasing Fortune, Truth and Faith in the New China,* (New York: Farrar, Straus and Giroux, 2014).

Background on Xinjiang reeducation camps

James Millward, "Reeducating' Xinjiang's Muslims" *New York Review of Books,* February 7, 2019.

Background on Sino–US relations and modern Chinese history

John Pomfret, *The Beautiful Country and the Middle Kingdom: America and China, 1776 to the Present* (New York: Henry Holt and Company, 2016).

Graham Hutchings, *Modern China: A Guide to a Century of Change* (Cambridge, Massachusetts: Harvard University Press, 2001).

Epilogue

Background on sexual harassment scandal at Peking University

Jiayun Feng, "Peking University Student To School: Stop Trying To Gag Me On Rape Case!" *Supchina,* April 23, 2018.

Yue Xin, "Translation: Open Letter on PKU #MeToo Case," *China Digital Times,* April 23, 2018.

Index

abortions, 126–127, 184–186
adulterous affairs, 106
agricultural policies, 18
Ah Q (story), 231–232
air pollution, 8, 62, 158, 204
alienation, 64
Amanda (former finance worker and
 protester), 55–56, 58–61
Amazing China (movie praising Xi),
 241
America
 Chinese students in, 192
 disillusionment in, 192–193,
  200–201, 203
 values, 93, 239
America First agenda, 177, 179
American Chamber of Commerce,
 Shanghai, 179
American Dream, 13, 33, 132–133, 269
ancestor worship, 121
Anhui province, 11, 16, 46, 180, 259
anti-Communist political movement,
 123

anti-corruption campaign, 109–110,
 125
apartheid system, 131
APCO Worldwide, 178
Apple, complying with Chinese law,
 226
architecture
 British influence, 164
 in France, 214
 Intermediate People's Court, 77–78
 in Shanghai, 5, 167
 Walkie-Talkie building, London,
  202
 World Financial Center, Shanghai,
  261
arts performance, elementary school,
 157–160
Ashley (investment banker)
 on authoritarian power, 202–204,
  235, 248
 background, 139–141
 in Chicago, 189–193
 on China's rise, 225, 231–232

Ashley (investment banker) (*continued*)
  on China's change to presidential
    term-limits, 248
  on corruption, 175–176
  on democracy, 190–191, 200,
    202–204, 232
  disillusioned with America, 192,
    200–201, 203, 263
  on foreign press, 229–231
  living in Shenzhen, 264–266
  on new wealth class, 138–139
  in Paris, 210–215
  post-graduation prospects, 189,
    231
  on President Trump, 176–177, 210,
    234, 248
  on President Xi, 249
  on Tiananmen Square, 223–224,
    225–226
  on US presidential elections,
    190–191
  working in Hong Kong, 263
asylum fraud, 127, 183
asylum visa, United States, 126
authoritarian system, 2, 8–9, 33, 238,
    240

Balzac, Honoré de, 214
Baoma (BMW cars), 118
Beckham, Victoria, 213
Beer (car salesman), 46–48, 67–69,
    267–269
beggars, 51, 90–91
Beijing West Railway Station,
    11–12
Beijing Youth Daily (newspaper), 221
Belt and Road, infrastructure project,
    245
biological-weapons experiments by
    Japanese, 161
black jails, 76–77
Bo Xilai, 180
Brexit, 201–202, 210

bribes, 17
bridge collapse, Harbin, 57–58
Britain
  Brexit, 201–202, 210
  First Opium War, 164, 202
  Hong Kong investments, 202
  pollution, 204
  Walkie-Talkie building, 202
Buckley, Chris, 216
Buddhist animal release ceremony,
    50–51
Buddhist shrine, 14
The Bund (movie), 96
burial chamber, responsibility for, 23
Bush, George W., 180
business negotiations, 46–48
business relationship with US, 178
businessmen, wealthy, 124–125, 137,
    138–139
businesswomen, 106–107
butchering a pig, 35–36
BYD (Build Your Dreams), car
    company, 27, 167

cab companies, 1, 4
Caijing (business magazine), 107, 162
calligraphy, 133
Cameron, David, 201
Cao (Winnie's friend), 113–114, 144,
    146–147, 150–152
car company, BYD (Build Your
    Dreams), 27, 167
"Careless Whisper" (Michael), 16
Carpenters (pop music), 16
cars, luxury, 118, 120
censorship
  Internet crackdown, 135, 227
  self-censorship, 18, 81
  speaking freely, 56, 62–63, 89, 136,
    240–242
Center for Peace and Conflict Studies,
    168
charity work, 91–95

Charles (salesman and news assistant)
  butchering of a pig, 35–36
  calligraphy, 133
  description of, 14
  education and work, 37–39
  family, 187–188, 209
  home village, 16–19, 35, 170–171
  local cabbie on road, 39–41
  on migrants' treatment, 216–217
  on nationalism, 168–172
  New Year's road trip, 12, 14–15
  as news assistant, 135–136, 267
  post *NRC* impact, 208–209, 219,
    266–267
  self-improvement, 133
  social cultural norms, 39–42
  view of Shanghai, 131
  wedding day, 44
  wedding dowry, 34–35
  on Western journalism, 205–206,
    208, 267
"Charter 08" (Liu), 140
Chen (Christian pajama salesman)
  asylum fraud, 127, 183
  family, 7–8, 181–183
  getting family to US, 125–127
  house church, 118–121, 124
  in Los Angeles, 9, 181–186, 251–253
  meeting of, 7
  religious background, 121–122
Chen (construction worker), 11–12, 26
Chen Guangcheng (lawyer), 126–127
China
  century of humiliation, 164
  cities, ranking of, 106
  defending territory, 160–161,
    164–166
  fertility rate, 186
  income gap, 128–129, 245
  influence on British students'
    debate, 235
  "lost decade," 3
  luxury goods, purchases, 211

  as a multiparty system, 226
  new islands created by, 164–165, 172
  Ray's analysis of, 32–33
  territorial map (1948), 168
  uniting the country, 19, 221–222, 225
China National Geographic (magazine),
  168
China National Radio, 57
Chinese Dream, 9, 13, 33, 105
Chinese embassy bombing (1999),
  220–221
Chinese students in America, 191–192
Chow Yun-fat, 96
Christian faith, 7, 73, 95, 119–124
Christian Science Monitor (newspaper),
  228
Churchill, Winston, 210
cities, ranking of, 106
civil corruption, 17
civil society, 33
Clinton, Bill, 220–221
college education, 31–32
college entrance exam, 84, 173, 246
"Commiseration for the Peasants"
  (poem), 158
Communist Party
  analysis of, 239, 270–271
  Chinese Dream, 9, 13, 33
  corruption, 17–18, 175–176
  distrust of Westerners, 57
  freedom, as defined by, 72–73
  Great Firewall, 223, 226–228
  historical nihilism, 162, 163
  neighborhood committees, 57
  one-child population policy, 13, 125,
    183–185, 186
  organized faith, regulation of,
    121–123
  policies that perpetuated poverty, 31
  political indoctrination, 240
  political term limits, 230, 237–239
  rescinding membership, 86–87
  rule by fear and guilt, 56

Communist Party (*continued*)
  school system, 7, 84–85, 125,
    173–174
  secretary, at wedding, 29
  socialism, 90
  soft power, 234–235
  as taught to Fifi's students, 85,
    173–174
  see also government
Communist Youth League, 159
community-based ethics, 66–67
compassion, 91–95, 97–99
Confucian values, 93
Congressional-Executive Commission,
  244
con men, 61
  see also frauds; scammers
conviction rate, legal system, 78
corruption
  Ashley's parent's experience,
    175–176
  educational system, 17
  family-planning officials, 127
  financial institution's, 55
  golf course's, 193
  Great Famine, 17–18, 170–171
  Harbin bridge collapse, 57
  investor visas, 125
  Lüliang's economic growth,
    194
  "Tigers" (corrupt officials), 29
  see also anti-corruption campaign
court case, regarding helping people,
  64–65
court system, 76–79
Crystal (search for missing sister)
  asking for help, 101
  family history, 103–108, 257
  search for Winnie, 108–115,
    143–144, 155–156
Cui Tiankai, 244–245
cultural differences, 212

Cultural Revolution (1966), 30, 84,
  87, 92
cybersecurity, 178–179

deaths, political, 19
democracy
  Ashley on, 190–191, 200–201,
    202–204, 232
  Global Times on, 239
  Hong Kong protests, 123, 233
  Li on, 72
democratic reform, 140
Deng Xiaoping
  citizen's reverence for, 79
  on consensus rule, 239
  economic reforms, 23, 103, 118
  foreign-policy strategy, 236
  on getting rich, 120
  presidential term limits, 230, 239
  rural economy changes, 31
  Washington DC visit, 16
Denver, John, 16
Diaoyu Islands, territorial dispute, 161,
  169
DiCaprio, Leonardo, 136
divorce laws, 108
Dora (Ray's daughter), 24, 26, 28
driving conditions, 15
drug trade, 96, 114, 164
Dutch newspaper, *NRC,* 135, 188,
  193–198, 217–218
Duterte, Rodrigo, 236, 248

"eat bitter" (bear hardships), 96
EB-5 investor visas, 125
economic growth, 3, 8, 71–73, 139,
  155, 234
"edge" person, 132
embassy bombing (1999), 220–221
environment
  air pollution, 8, 62, 158, 204
  extinction of animals and plants, 174

river ecosystem, 21
  water pollution, 158
ernai (second wife), 106
ethics, community-based, 66–67
European Union, 179. *See also* Brexit
exit strategies, from China, 7–8, 89, 124–125
Ezubao, Ponzi scheme, 59

Facebook, 63, 135
fake news, 193–196
Falun Gong (spiritual meditation practice), 81, 235
family separations, 12, 26, 42–44, 131–132
family-planning officials, 127
famine (1958-1962), 18–19
Fan Wenxin, 208
farmers, 17, 18
fear, 56, 61–63
feng shui, 21
ferry rides, 6
Fifi (psychologist)
  description of, 62
  fall on sidewalk, 64–65, 67
  fear of the government, 62–66
  Gang of Five, 86, 242
  on political changes, 240–243
  political indoctrination, 240–241
  Remi, husband, 87–90, 254–255
  school system, 172–174
  teaching politics, 83–87
  wanting to start a family, 254–255
financial fraud, 55, 58–59
fireworks, 22, 26, 28
First Opium War, 164
Fitzgerald, F. Scott, 136, 138
"Five Heroes at Wolf Teeth Mountain," 159–162
Foshan hit-and-run (2011), 65
France, Chinese opinion of, 232

frauds, 53, 127. *See also* con men; scammers
freedom, 72–74

Gang of Five (Fifi's friends), 86, 242
Gao (cement plant manager), 194, 218
gaokao (college exam), 84, 173
ghost cities, 139
global inclusion, 159
Global Times (newspaper), 169, 196, 238–239
golf course corruption, 193
Gong (Chen's wife)
  asylum visa, 125–126, 182
  barber (salon) business, 183, 185, 186
  in Los Angeles, 181–183
  religious background, 121
Good Samaritan problem, 64–66
Google, 170
Gove, Michael, 201
government
  analysis of, 32–33
  fear of, 61–63
  fear of ceding power, 78, 83
  homes and property lost to, 74–75
  protesters, 53–56, 60–61
  reeducation-through-labor camps, 81, 244–245
  on trust, 56
  see also Communist Party
government employees, 128
Great Firewall, 223, 226–228. *See also* Internet crackdown
The Great Gatsby (Fitzgerald), 133–134, 136–139
Great Leap Forward (1958-1962), 18–19, 87, 170–171
Guo (Rocky's mother)
  college education for sons, 31–32
  on Cultural Revolution, 30

Guo (Rocky's mother) (*continued*)
    dinner invitation, 19
    early life, 30–31
    marriage, 31
    Rocky's visit, 22–24
    wedding performance rehearsal,
        23–24

The Hague, 177, 236
Hani, ethnic minority, 95
Harbin
    bridge collapse, 57–58
    description of, 103–104
    search for Winnie, 101, 105, 143,
        161
Harwood, Tom, 235
he cha (drink tea), 140
health care, 65–66, 128, 133, 215, 246,
        262
helping strangers, 64–66
highway system, 15–16
historical nihilism, 162, 163
history, taught in schools, 84–85
hit-and-run victims, 65
Hitler, Adolf, 19
homes lost to forced demolition,
        74–75
Hong Kong, 123, 200, 202, 233, 264
Hong Zhenkuai, 161–162
Honghong (Chen's daughter), 12, 26,
        131
hospitality, 19
housing poverty, 129–130, 132,
        216–217
Hu Jintao, 166, 236
Hubei province
    Charles's village, 34–36
    description of, 22–24, 28
    parting gift, 34
    Ray's analysis of China, 32–33
    road trip to, 12–22
    wedding, 12–24, 27–30
human rights activists, 76, 140

human rights attorneys, 73, 79–83, 123
human rights critic, 235

in vitro fertilization, 186
incivility on the streets, 64–67
income gap, 128–129, 245
independent thinkers, 86, 173
industrial espionage, 179
intellectual property rights, 179
Intermediate People's Court,
        77–78
International Monetary Fund, 201
Internet crackdown, 135, 140,
        223–224, 226–227
investment opportunities, 60
iron rice bowl (benefits to employees),
        128
Islamist extremists, 244

jails, black, 76–77
James Shoal (Chinese-claimed
        submerged territory), 168
Japan
    China invasion (1937), 161
    Chinese battle (1941), 160
    cultural invasion, 169
    island dispute, 161, 169
    protests against, 169–170
Jerusalem of China, 122
Jiali (Chen's older daughter), 7, 181,
        183, 251–252
Jiang Feng, 228
Jiang Zemin, 85
Jim (Crystal's husband), 255–256
Jinghong, Yunnan province, 102
Johanna (attorney)
    arrest, 82–83
    defending Li, 73, 75, 78–79
    as human rights lawyer, 79–81
    as a parent, 262–263
    vaccination scandal, 262
John Paul II, Pope, 123
Julie (wife), 51, 128–129

kang (bed/stove combination), 103
Kennedy Center, 16
Korean War, 199
landlords, 106–107, 128
laobaixing (common people), 46, 54
Laos, poppy cultivation, 112
Last Fantasy (Japanese cartoon), 169
law, rule of, 72, 83
Le Père Goriot (Balzac), 214
legal education center, 81
legal system
    conviction rate, 78
    court case, regarding helping people,
      64–65
    court system, 76–79
    divorce laws, 108
    rule of law, 72, 83
    see also missing persons, police
      involvement
Lei Feng, 134
Li (ex-prisoner), 72–79
Li (housemaid), 11
Li (net man), 52
Li, Eric X., 225
Li Congjun, 57
Li Ming, 221
Li Wei (businesswoman),
    106–107
Lim, Louisa, 225
Lin, Anastasia, 235
Lin, Luna, 206
Liu Xiaobo, 140, 192
"lost decade," 3
Lu Xun, 65, 231–232
Lüliang, city economy, 193–194, 218,
    249
Lund University, Sweden, 80
Luo (Winnie's husband), 107–108,
    110–112
luxury cars, 118, 120

Ma, Jack, 145
MacKinnon, Rebecca, 221

Macron, Emmanuel, 210
Maglev, magnetic levitation train, 2–3,
    245
magnetic levitation train (Maglev),
    2–3, 245
Mandarin language, 24
Mandiant (cybersecurity company),
    178–179
Mao Zedong
    Cultural Revolution, 30
    Great Leap Forward, 18–19
    landlords, as a class, 128
    prostitution eliminated, 104
    public perception of, 29, 31, 35
map of China's territory (1948), 168
Marcos, Ferdinand, 213
Marcos, Imelda, 213
market forces, economic growth and,
    90
Market-Leninism, 53–54
materialism, 119–120, 211, 213–214
Max (hairstylist)
    background, 95–99
    charity work, 9, 91–95, 98–99
    description of, 259
    fraud by a partner, 260
    new salon, Maxvision, 258
    on presidential term-limits, 247–248
May, Theresa, 210
McGregor, James, 178
McWhorter, Dan, 179
medical system. *See* health care
Meiguo (the beautiful country,
    America), 7
Merkel, Angela, 210
Michael, George, 16
microphones, fear of, 14
migrant workers
    Chen's story, 12
    conditions, 215–217
    description of, 13–14, 39
    Shenhua's story, 39
    soft apartheid system, 131

militarized islands, 166
military growth, 161
millionaires, 124–125
missing persons, police involvement,
    102, 109–110, 114–115, 143–144
mistresses, as businesswomen, 106
mistress-industrial complex, 106, 137
morality
    frauds, 53
    moral framework, 155
    scammers, 48–53
    skimming, 17
    see also values

Nanjing court case (2006), 64–65
National Museum of China, 13
National People's Congress, 13
Nationalist army, 31
NATO (North Atlantic Treaty
    Organization), 22, 179, 201
neighborhood committees, 57
net men, 51–53
netizens (citizen Internet users), 138,
    216
New China News Service, 18, 57, 59,
    163, 237, 241
New Era, 9, 172, 229, 235–236, 238
New Year celebration, 35
New York Times, 18
news assistants, 207–208
news media, 57
NRC, Dutch newspaper, 135, 188,
    193–198, 217–218

Obama, Barack, 182, 201
Occupy campaign, Hong Kong (2014),
    233
Oliver (market researcher), 125
"One World, One Dream," 89
one-child population policy, 13, 125,
    183–185, 186
online retailers in China, 240
online speech, 3

Opium War (1839–1842), 13
Oriental Pearl Tower, 97–98
Oscar (Dutch newspaper
    correspondent), 193–194,
    196–198, 219

pedestrians in crosswalks, 64–65, 67,
    243
Pence, Mike, 244, 270
Peng Liyuan, 29
pengci (bump porcelain), 65
People's Daily (newspaper), 57, 170,
    228–229
People's Liberation Army, 28, 134, 178,
    197, 224
The People's Republic of Amnesia:
    Tiananmen Revisited (Lim), 225
personal interactions, 40–42
Philippines
    Chinese island dispute, 165–166,
        171, 236
    Imelda Marcos, 213
Piao (Rocky's bride), 20, 21, 28–29
Poland, move from Communism, 123
police involvement in missing persons
    cases, 102, 109–110, 114–115,
    143–144
police terror tactics, 75, 82–83
political indoctrination
    arts performance, elementary school,
        157–160
    black jails, 76–77
    in the classroom, 83–90
    under Mao, 240
    reeducation-through-labor camps,
        81, 244–245
political openness, 134–135
pollution. See environment
Ponzi scheme, 59–60
poppy cultivation, 112
post-Tiananmen generation, 140
The Potato Eaters (Van Gogh), 215
propaganda campaigns, 134, 173, 241

property lost to forced demolition, 74–75
prostitution, 104–105
protesters
Chinese embassy bombing, Belgrade, 220–221
detention of human rights lawyers, 81–83
financial institution's fraud, 53–56, 58–61
Hong Kong democracy, 123, 233
hospital staff safety, 243
against Japan, 169–170
public bathrooms, 20–21
public political debate, 244
public services, 33
Putin, Vladimir, 210, 248

Qing dynasty (1644–1912), 65

Ray (Rocky's brother)
on America, 180
analysis of China, 32–33
birth, 13
description of, 26
Dora, daughter, 24, 26, 28
farm village visit, 26
new project for his village, 260
parent's burial chamber, 23
patriotism of, 165–168
on President Xi, 245
in Shanghai, 24, 163–164
work schedule (pace), 261
Rebel Pepper (political cartoonist), 134–135
Red Flag dealership, 55
Redford, Robert, 137
reeducation-through-labor camps, 81, 244–245
refrigerated warehouse fire, Beijing, 215–216
Reiss-Andersen, Berit, 192

religious intolerance, 52, 75, 239–240, 244–245
Remi (Fifi's husband), 87–90, 254–255
resources, battle for, 50–53
river ecosystem, 21
road conditions, 15–17, 39–40
"The Road to Rejuvenation" (museum exhibit), 13
Rocky (lawyer)
brother. *See* Ray
description of, 14
farm boy to lawyer, 8–9
farm village, 22–26
Guo, mother, 19, 22–24, 30–32
Hubei province trip, 12–22
parent's burial chamber, 23
socioeconomic climb, 21
rule of law, 72, 83

san pei xiaojie (three-accompany girls), 104
saozhouxing (bearer of bad luck), 257
Sarah (migrant with housing problems), 129–130, 246–247
scammers, 48–53, 65
school system, 7, 84–85, 125
Schouten, Elske, 208, 219
second wives, 106
self-censorship, 18, 81
self-improvement, 133–134, 145
sex industry, 104–105
sexual-harassment scandals, 265
Shaanxi province, 127
Shandong province, 126–127
Shanghai, description of, 1–10, 33
Shanghai Normal University, 84
Shanghai stock market crash (2015), 60
Shanghai Tan (movie), 96
Shanghai Tower, Lujiazui, 5, 163
Shanghai TV, 55, 80
Shen (squatter), 75
Shenhua (Charles's father), 39, 42–44, 131, 171, 187, 208

Shenzhen, China, 264
Sierra Madre transport ship, 165–166
Sina Weibo (microblog service). See
    Weibo
skimming, 17
social credit-score systems, 242–243
sociocultural norms, 39–42
social media. See WeChat; Weibo
socialism, 90, 157, 216
sociopolitical theory (Three
    Represents), 85
soft apartheid system, 131
soft interrogation, 140
South China Sea
    disputes over, 166–168, 171–173,
        236
    off-shore drilling, 241
Southern Weekend (newspaper), 86
speech
    censorship, 56, 62–63, 89
    freedom of, 200
    new freedoms, 3–4
    self-censorship, 18, 81
    speaking freely, 56, 62–63, 89, 136,
        240–242, 245–246
Stalin, Joseph, 19
state security agents, 5
state-owned apartments, 128
state-run news services, 57, 76, 157,
    169, 224
state-sanctioned churches,
    121–122
sterilizations, 127, 183
Stewart, Jon, 3
strangers, how to treat, 64–67
Sun (recipient of Max's charitable
    work), 93–94
Sun (neighborhood committee
    worker), 91–92
Sun Yat-sen, 157
surveillance cameras, 243–244
suzhi (inner quality), 32, 42, 65,
    83

"The Swordsman" (poem), 133, 195
Ta Kung Pao (newspaper), 94
"Take Me Home, Country Roads"
    (Denver), 16
Tang dynasty (618-907), 133, 158
Tank Man (video), 224–225
teahouse scam, 48
term limits, Chinese presidency
    Deng's constitutional restriction on,
        230
    proposal for changing, 237–239
    Ray on, 245–246
    Sarah on, 246
    Trump on, 248
texu fuwu anmo (special services
    massage), 49
Three Represents (sociopolitical
    theory), 85
Tiananmen Square (1989), 9, 13, 57,
    84–85, 87, 223–225
"Tigers" (corrupt officials), 29
toll taker's rules, 15, 34
Tombstone: The Great Chinese Famine,
    1958–1962 (Yang), 18, 170–171
traffic conditions, 50
trains
    Beijing West Railway Station, 11–12
    conditions on, 14
    magnetic levitation, 2–3, 245
Treaty of Nanking (1842), 202
The True Story of Ah Q (Lu), 231
Trump, Donald
    America First agenda, 177, 179
    Ashley on, 176–177, 234
    Chen's family on, 182–183
    on China's term-limit proposal,
        248–249
    Chinese media and, 228–229
    on Chinese trade, 270
    on European Union, 179
    Ray on, 177–181
    Trump's America, 9
    view of, 210

Trump fatigue, 199
Twitter, 135, 206

Uighurs (Muslim ethnic group), 244
United Nations (UN), 171, 236
United States Constitution, 180,
    245–246
United States (US)
    Chinese business policies, 178
    cyber espionage against, 179
    Internet usage, 227
    South China Sea disputes, 166–168,
        171–173
    visa program, 125–126
    as world leader, 177–178
used-car dealership, 45
used-car salesmen, 46–48, 67–69,
    267–268

vaccination scandal, 262
values
    American, 93, 239
    Confucian, 93
    wealthy Chinese, 137–138
    Western, 239, 240
    see also morality
Van Gogh, Vincent, 215
Vandermeersch, Peter, 197
VPN (virtual private networks),
    226–228

Walkie-Talkie (London building), 202
Wall Street Journal (WSJ), 230
Wang (retired accountant), 52–53
Wang, Feng, 206
Wang, Zheng, 168
Washington, George, 246
water pollution, 158
wealth-management companies, 60
wealthy businessmen, 124–125, 137,
    138–139
WeChat (social media)
    Amanda on, 56, 61

Ashley on, 265
Beer on, 268
Charles on, 188, 192, 196, 266–267
Fifi's on, 63
Max on, 98, 247, 259
on NRC story, 218
Sarah on, 129
Winnie on, 107, 109, 111, 115
Wedding
    celebration, 30
    ceremony, 29
    drive to ceremony, 27–28
    matrimonial suite, 29
    performance rehearsal, 23–24
    performances, 29
Wei (private detective), 154–155
Weibo (microblog service)
    Amanda's experience, 56
    Communist Party's tolerance of, 3,
        134
    family-planning abortion, 127
    free taxi's advertisement, 12
    The Great Gatsby readers on, 138
    Hong's account disabled, 162
    Rebel Pepper's cartoons, 134–135
    on Xi's possible term for life, 238
Wenzhou, Jerusalem of China, 122
Western journalism, 205–206, 208, 237
Western values, 239, 240
Westerners, distrust of, 57
Wham! (pop duo), 16
Winnie (Crystal's sister)
    childhood, 103–104
    divorce certificate, 112, 144–145
    last-known apartment, 144–147
    library collection, 145
    marriage to Luo, 107–108, 110–112
    as missing person, 101
    photos and videos, 147–148
    pregnancy test, 146, 149–151
    real estate ownership, 106–107, 145
    as working woman, 105–106
    see also Crystal

women, as backbone of the country, 32

work schedule (pace), 261

World Financial Center, Shanghai, 261

World Trade Organization, 177

"Xi Dada Loves Peng Mama" (song), 29–30

Xi Jinping (China's president)
  ability to steer economy, 234
  Amazing China (movie focusing on), 241
  analysis of, 269–270
  anti-corruption campaign, 109–110, 125, 176, 193
  on Brexit, 201
  China's constitution, 173, 229
  Chinese Dream, 9, 13, 33
  Communist Party culture, 162
  Communist Party support, 157–158, 162, 172
  elevation of, 9
  infrastructure project, 245
  under Mao, 30
  militarized islands, 166
  political term limits, 237–239
  song for, 29–30
  speech on China's New Era, 235–236
  Weibo crackdown, 135
  on Western values, 240

Xinjiang, autonomous region, 37, 42, 97, 140, 244

Yan, Yunxiang, 66–67

Yang Jisheng (reporter/author), 18, 170

Yang Zhuo (Frank's assistant)
  background, 207
  on Beer's behavior, 68–69
  BYD sedan, 167
  Charles's news assistant job, 135
  Chen's visa documents, 126
  on foreign media, 220
  free taxi's advertisement, 4
  Lüliang city story, 193–194, 218
  recording conversations, 9
  Winnie's story, 152–153

Yangtze River, 21

"Yesterday Once More" (The Carpenters), 16

Yingying (Chen's younger daughter), 126, 183, 268–269

Young Pioneers, 159

YouTube, 140

Yunnan province, 95, 101–102

Zengmu Ansha (Chinese submerged territory), 168

Zhang (three-accompany girl), 104–105

Zhongguo (middle kingdom), 236

Zhongjin Capital Management, 55, 58–61

Zhuo (reeducation detainee), 81